I0405578

ABOUT THIS PUBLICATION

FOR SERVICE ASSISTANCE

Customer Service
1.704.898.0770

North Carolina General Statues is published by The Muliti-Media Group of Greater Charlotte in Charlotte, North Carolina. Copyright 2015 by the Multi-Media Group of Greater Charlotte. This book or parts thereof may not be reproduced in any form, stored in a retrieval system, or transmitted in any form by any means—electronic, mechanical, photocopy, recording or otherwise—without prior written permission of the publisher, except as provided by United States of America copyright law.

The records required by U.S. Code 2257(a) through (c) and the pertinent regulations 28 C.F.R. Cli. 1, Part 75 with respect to this publication and all materials associated with such records are maintained by The Multi-Media Group of Greater Charlotte, Publisher and available for review by Attorney General.

www.visionbooks.org

TID: 5107854
ISBN (10) digit: 1503244032
ISBN (13) digit: 978-1503244030

123-4-56789-01239-Paperback
123-4-56789-01239-Hardback

First Edition

090520140547

Printed in the United States of America

2015 EDITION

North Carolina Criminal Law

And Procedure-Pamphlet # 80

Printed In conjunction with the

Administration of the Courts

North Carolina Criminal Law and Procedure
Pamphlet Reference Guide

Chapters	Pamphlet
Chapter 1 Civil Procedure	1
Chapter 1 Civil Procedure (Continue)	2
Chapter 1A Rules of Civil Procedure	2
Chapter 1B Contribution.	2
Chapter 1C Enforcement of Judgments.	2
Chapter 1D Punitive Damages.	2
Chapter 1E Eastern Band of Cherokee Indians.	2
Chapter 1F North Carolina Uniform Interstate Depositions and Discovery Act.	2
Chapter 2 - Clerk of Superior Court [Repealed and Transferred.]	3
Chapter 3 - Commissioners of Affidavits and Deeds [Repealed.]	3
Chapter 4 - Common Law	3
Chapter 5 - Contempt [Repealed.]	3
Chapter 5A - Contempt	3
Chapter 6 - Liability for Court Costs	3
Chapter 7 - Courts [Repealed and Transferred.]	3
Chapter 7A – Judicial Department	3
Chapter 7A – Continuation (Judicial Department)	4
Chapter 7A – Continuation (Judicial Department)	5
Chapter 7B - Juvenile Code	5
Chapter 8 - Evidence	6
Chapter 8A - Interpreters for Deaf Persons [Recodified.]	6
Chapter 8B - Interpreters for Deaf Persons	6
Chapter 8C - Evidence Code	6
Chapter 9 - Jurors	6
Chapter 10 - Notaries [Repealed.]	6
Chapter 10A - Notaries [Recodified.]	6
Chapter 10B - Notaries	6
Chapter 11 - Oaths	6
Chapter 12 - Statutory Construction	6
Chapter 13 - Citizenship Restored	6
Chapter 14 - Criminal Law	7
Chapter 14 –Criminal Law (Continuation)	8
Chapter 15 - Criminal Procedure	9
Chapter 15A - Criminal Procedure Act (Continuation)	10
Chapter 15A - Criminal Procedure Act (Continuation)	11
Chapter 15B - Victims Compensation	11
Chapter 15C - Address Confidentiality Program	11
Chapter 16 - Gaming Contracts and Futures	11
Chapter 17 - Habeas Corpus	11

Chapter 17A - Law-Enforcement Officers [Recodified.]   11
Chapter 17B - North Carolina Criminal Justice   11
Education and Training System [Recodified.] Chapter 17C - North Carolina
Criminal Justice Education and Training Standards Commission   11
Chapter 17D - North Carolina Justice Academy   11
Chapter 17E - North Carolina Sheriffs' Education and
Training Standards Commission   11
Chapter 18 - Regulation of Intoxicating Liquors [Repealed.]   12
Chapter 18A - Regulation of Intoxicating Liquors [Repealed.]   12
Chapter 18B - Regulation of Alcoholic Beverages   12
Chapter 18C - North Carolina State Lottery   12
Chapter 19 - Offenses against Public Morals   12
Chapter 19A - Protection of Animals   12
Chapter 20 - Motor Vehicles   13
Chapter 20 - Motor Vehicles (Continuation)   14
Chapter 20 - Motor Vehicles (Continuation)   15
Chapter 20 - Motor Vehicles (Continuation)   16
Chapter 21 - Bills of Lading   17
Chapter 22 - Contracts Requiring Writing   17
Chapter 22A - Signatures   17
Chapter 22B - Contracts Against Public Policy   17
Chapter 22C - Payments to Subcontractors   17
Chapter 23 - Debtor and Creditor   17
Chapter 24 – Interest   17
Chapter 25 – Uniform Commercial Code   18
Chapter 25 – Uniform Commercial Code (Continuation)   19
Chapter 25A – Retail Installment Sales Act   20
Chapter 25B - Credit   20
Chapter 25C - Sales of Artwork   20
Chapter 26 - Suretyship   20
Chapter 27 - Warehouse Receipts [Repealed.]   20
Chapter 28 - Administration [Repealed.]   20
Chapter 28A - Administration of Decedents' Estates   20
Chapter 28B - Estates of Absentees in Military Service   20
Chapter 28C - Estates of Missing Persons   20
Chapter 29 - Intestate Succession   21
Chapter 30 - Surviving Spouses   21
Chapter 31 - Wills   21
Chapter 31A - Acts Barring Property Rights   21
Chapter 31B - Renunciation of Property and Renunciation of
Fiduciary Powers Act   21
Chapter 31C - Uniform Disposition of Community Property
Rights at Death Act   21
Chapter 32 - Fiduciaries   21
Chapter 32A - Powers of Attorney   21
Chapter 33 - Guardian and Ward [Repealed and Recodified.]   21

5

Chapter 33A - North Carolina Uniform Transfers to Minors Act   21
Chapter 33B - North Carolina Uniform Custodial Trust Act   21
Chapter 34 - Veterans' Guardianship Act   22
Chapter 35 - Sterilization Procedures   22
Chapter 35A - Incompetency and Guardianship   22
Chapter 36 - Trusts and Trustees [Repealed.]   22
Chapter 36A - Trusts and Trustees   22
Chapter 36B - Uniform Management of Institutional Funds
Act [Repealed.]   22
Chapter 36C - North Carolina Uniform Trust Code   22
Chapter 36D - North Carolina Community Third Party Trusts,
Pooled Trusts   23
Chapter 36E - Uniform Prudent Management of Institutional Funds Act   23
Chapter 37 - Allocation of Principal and Income [Repealed.]   23
Chapter 37A - Uniform Principal and Income Act   23
Chapter 38 - Boundaries   23
Chapter 38A - Landowner Liability   23
Chapter 39 - Conveyances   23
Chapter 39A - Transfer Fee Covenants Prohibited   23
Chapter 40 - Eminent Domain [Repealed.]   23
Chapter 40A - Eminent Domain   23
Chapter 41 - Estates   23
Chapter 41A - State Fair Housing Act   23
Chapter 42 - Landlord and Tenant   23
Chapter 42A - Vacation Rental Act   23
Chapter 43 - Land Registration   23
Chapter 44 - Liens   24
Chapter 44A - Statutory Liens and Charges   24
Chapter 45 - Mortgages and Deeds of Trust   24
Chapter 45A - Good Funds Settlement Act   24
Chapter 46 - Partition   24
Chapter 47 - Probate and Registration   25
Chapter 47A - Unit Ownership   25
Chapter 47B - Real Property Marketable Title Act   25
Chapter 47C - North Carolina Condominium Act   25
Chapter 47D - Notice of Settlement Act [Expired.]   25
Chapter 47E - Residential Property Disclosure Act   25
Chapter 47F - North Carolina Planned Community Act   25
Chapter 47G - Option to Purchase Contracts   25
Chapter 47H - Contracts for Deed   25
Chapter 48 - Adoptions   26
Chapter 48A - Minors   26
Chapter 49 - Bastardy   26
Chapter 49A - Rights of Children   26
Chapter 50 - Divorce and Alimony   26
Chapter 50A - Uniform Child-Custody Jurisdiction and

Enforcement Act   26
Chapter 50B - Domestic Violence   26
Chapter 50C - Civil No-Contact Orders   26
Chapter 51 - Marriage   26
Chapter 52 - Powers and Liabilities of Married Persons   27
Chapter 52A - Uniform Reciprocal Enforcement of Support
Act [Repealed.]   27
Chapter 52B - Uniform Premarital Agreement Act   27
Chapter 52C - Uniform Interstate Family Support Act   27
Chapter 53 - Banks   27
Chapter 53A - Business Development Corporations and
North Carolina Capital Resource Corporations   28
Chapter 53B - Financial Privacy Act   28
Chapter 54 - Cooperative Organizations   28
Chapter 54A - Capital Stock Savings and Loan Associations [Repealed.] 28
Chapter 54B - Savings and Loan Associations   29
Chapter 54C - Savings Banks   29
Chapter 55 - North Carolina Business Corporation Act   30
Chapter 55A - North Carolina Nonprofit Corporation Act   31
Chapter 55B - Professional Corporation Act   31
Chapter 55C - Foreign Trade Zones   31
Chapter 55D - Filings, Names, and Registered Agents for
Corporations, Nonprofit Corporations, and Partnerships   31
Chapter 56 - Electric, Telegraph and Power Companies
[Repealed.]   31
Chapter 57 - Hospital, Medical and Dental Service
Corporations [Recodified.]   31
Chapter 57A - Health Maintenance Organization Act
[Recodified.]   31
Chapter 57B - Health Maintenance Organization Act
[Recodified.]   31
Chapter 57C - North Carolina Limited Liability Company Act.   31
Chapter 58 - Insurance.   32
Chapter 58 - Insurance (Continuation)   33
Chapter 58 - Insurance (Continuation)   34
Chapter 58 - Insurance (Continuation)   35
Chapter 58 - Insurance (Continuation)   36
Chapter 58 - Insurance (Continuation)   37
Chapter 58 - Insurance (Continuation)   38
Chapter 58A - North Carolina Health Insurance Trust
Commission [Recodified.]   38
Chapter 59 - Partnership.   39
Chapter 59B - Uniform Unincorporated Nonprofit Association Act.   39
Chapter 60 - Railroads and Other Carriers [Repealed and Transferred.] 39
Chapter 61 - Religious Societies   39
Chapter 62 - Public Utilities   39

7

Chapter 62 - Public Utilities (Continuation)   40
Chapter 62A - Public Safety Telephone Service And
Wireless Telephone Service   40
Chapter 63 - Aeronautics   40
Chapter 63A - North Carolina Global TransPark Authority   40
Chapter 64 - Aliens   40
Chapter 65 – Cemeteries   40
Chapter 66 - Commerce and Business   41
Chapter 67 - Dogs   41
Chapter 68 - Fences and Stock Law   41
Chapter 69 - Fire Protection   41
Chapter 70 - Indian Antiquities, Archaeological Resources
and Unmarked Human Skeletal Remains Protection   42
Chapter 71 - Indians [Repealed.]   42
Chapter 71A - Indians   42
Chapter 72 - Inns, Hotels and Restaurants   42
Chapter 73 - Mills   42
Chapter 74 - Mines and Quarries   42
Chapter 74A - Company Police [Repealed.]   42
Chapter 74B - Private Protective Services Act [Repealed.]   42
Chapter 74C - Private Protective Services   42
Chapter 74D - Alarm Systems   42
Chapter 74E - Company Police Act   42
Chapter 74F - Locksmith Licensing Act   42
Chapter 74G - Campus Police Act   42
Chapter 75 - Monopolies, Trusts and Consumer Protection   42
Chapter 75A - Boating and Water Safety   43
Chapter 75B - Discrimination in Business   43
Chapter 75C - Motion Picture Fair Competition Act   43
Chapter 75D - Racketeer Influenced and Corrupt Organizations   43
Chapter 75E - Unlawful Activities in Connection With
Certain Corporate Transactions   43
Chapter 76 - Navigation   43
Chapter 76A - Navigation and Pilotage Commissions   43
Chapter 77 - Rivers, Creeks, and Coastal Waters   43
Chapter 78 - Securities Law [Repealed.]   43
Chapter 78A - North Carolina Securities Act   43
Chapter 78B - Tender Offer Disclosure Act [Repealed.]   43
Chapter 78C - Investment Advisers   43
Chapter 78D - Commodities Act   43
Chapter 79 - Strays [Repealed.]   43
Chapter 80 - Trademarks, Brands, etc.   44
Chapter 81 - Weights and Measures [Recodified.]   44
Chapter 81A - Weights and Measures Act of 1975.   44
Chapter 82 - Wrecks [Repealed.]   44
Chapter 83 - Architects [Recodified.]   44

Chapter 83A - Architects   44
Chapter 84 - Attorneys-at-Law   44
Chapter 84A - Foreign Legal Consultants   44
Chapter 85 - Auctions and Auctioneers [Repealed.]   44
Chapter 85A - Bail Bondsmen and Runners [Recodified.]   44
Chapter 85B - Auctions and Auctioneers   44
Chapter 85C - Bail Bondsmen and Runners [Recodified.]   44
Chapter 86 - Barbers [Recodified.]   44
Chapter 86A - Barbers   44
Chapter 87 - Contractors   44
Chapter 88 - Cosmetic Art [Repealed.]   44
Chapter 88A - Electrolysis Practice Act   44
Chapter 88B - Cosmetic Art   45
Chapter 89 - Engineering and Land Surveying [Recodified.]   45
Chapter 89A - Landscape Architects   45
Chapter 89B - Foresters   45
Chapter 89C - Engineering and Land Surveying   45
Chapter 89D - Landscape Contractors   45
Chapter 89E - Geologists Licensing Act   45
Chapter 89F - North Carolina Soil Scientist Licensing Act   45
Chapter 89G - Irrigation Contractors   45
Chapter 90 - Medicine and Allied Occupations   45
Chapter 90 - Medicine and Allied Occupations (Continuation)   46
Chapter 90 - Medicine and Allied Occupations (Continuation)   47
Chapter 90 - Medicine and Allied Occupations (Continuation)   48
Chapter 90A - Sanitarians and Water and Wastewater
Treatment Facility Operators   48
Chapter 90B - Social Worker Certification and Licensure Act   48
Chapter 90C - North Carolina Recreational Therapy Licensure Act   48
Chapter 90D - Interpreters and Transliterators   48
Chapter 91 - Pawnbrokers [Repealed.]   48
Chapter 91A - Pawnbrokers Modernization Act of 1989   48
Chapter 92 - Photographers [Deleted.]   48
Chapter 93 - Certified Public Accountants   48
Chapter 93A - Real Estate License Law   49
Chapter 93B - Occupational Licensing Boards   49
Chapter 93C - Watchmakers [Repealed.]   49
Chapter 93D - North Carolina State Hearing Aid Dealers
and Fitters Board.   49
Chapter 93E - North Carolina Appraisers Act   49
Chapter 94 - Apprenticeship   49
Chapter 95 - Department of Labor and Labor Regulations   49
Chapter 95 - Department of Labor and Labor Regulations (Continuation)   50
Chapter 96 - Employment Security   50
Chapter 97 - Workers' Compensation Act   50
Chapter 97 - Workers' Compensation Act (Continuation)   51

Chapter 98 - Burnt and Lost Records   51
Chapter 99 - Libel and Slander   51
Chapter 99A - Civil Remedies for Criminal Actions   51
Chapter 99B - Products Liability   51
Chapter 99C - Actions Relating to Winter Sports
Safety and Accidents   51
Chapter 99D - Civil Rights   51
Chapter 99E - Special Liability Provisions   51
Chapter 100 - Monuments, Memorials and Parks   51
Chapter 101 - Names of Persons   51
Chapter 102 - Official Survey Base   51
Chapter 103 - Sundays, Holidays and Special Days   51
Chapter 104 - United States Lands   51
Chapter 104A - Degrees of Kinship   51
Chapter 104B - Hurricanes or Other Acts of Nature   51
Chapter 104C - Atomic Energy, Radioactivity and Ionizing
Radiation [Repealed and Recodified.]   51
Chapter 104D - Southern States Energy Compact   51
Chapter 104E - North Carolina Radiation Protection Act   51
Chapter 104F - Southeast Interstate Low-Level
Radioactive Waste Management Compact [Repealed]   51
Chapter 104G - North Carolina Low-Level Radioactive
Waste Management Authority Act of 1987 [Repealed]   51
Chapter 105 - Taxation   51
Chapter 105 - Taxation (Continuation)   52
Chapter 105 - Taxation (Continuation)   53
Chapter 105 - Taxation (Continuation)   54
Chapter 105A - Setoff Debt Collection Act   55
Chapter 105B - Defaulted Student Loan Recovery Act   55
Chapter 106 - Agriculture   55
Chapter 106 - Agriculture (Continue)   56
Chapter 106 - Agriculture (Continue)   57
Chapter 107 - Agricultural Development Districts
[Repealed.]   57
Chapter 108 - Social Services [Repealed and Recodified.]   57
Chapter 108A - Social Services   57
Chapter 108B - Community Action Programs   58
Chapter 108C Medicaid and Health Choice Provider Requirements.   58
Chapter 108D Medicaid Managed Care for Behavioral Health Services.   58
Chapter 109 - Bonds [Recodified.]   58
Chapter 110 - Child Welfare   58
Chapter 111 - Aid to the Blind   58
Chapter 112 - Confederate Homes and Pensions
[Repealed.]   58
Chapter 113 - Conservation and Development   58
Chapter 113 - Conservation and Development (Continuation)   59

10

Chapter 113A - Pollution Control and Environment   59
Chapter 113A - Pollution Control and Environment (Continuation)   60
Chapter 113B - North Carolina Energy Policy Act of 1975   60
Chapter 114 - Department of Justice   60
Chapter 115 - Elementary and Secondary Education
[Repealed.]   60
Chapter 115A - Community Colleges, Technical
Institutes, and Industrial Education Centers [Repealed.]   60
Chapter 115B - Tuition and Fee Waivers   60
Chapter 115C - Elementary and Secondary Education   60
Chapter 115C - Elementary and Secondary Education (Continuation)   61
Chapter 115C - Elementary and Secondary Education (Continuation)   62
Chapter 115C - Elementary and Secondary Education (Continuation)   63
Chapter 115D - Community Colleges   63
Chapter 115E - Private Educational Facilities Finance
Act [Recodified]   63
Chapter 116 - Higher Education   63
Chapter 116 - Higher Education (Continuation)   63
Chapter 116A - Escheats and Abandoned Property
[Repealed.]   64
Chapter 116B - Escheats and Abandoned Property   64
Chapter 116C - Continuum of Education Programs   64
Chapter 116D - Higher Education Bonds   64
Chapter 116E -Education Longitudinal Data System   64
Chapter 117 - Electrification   64
Chapter 118 - Firemen's and Rescue Squad
Workers' Relief and Pension Funds [Recodified.]   64
Chapter 118A - Firemen's Death Benefit Act
[Repealed.]   64
Chapter 118B - Members of a Rescue Squad
Death Benefit Act [Repealed.]   64
Chapter 119 - Gasoline and Oil Inspection and Regulation   64
Chapter 120 - General Assembly   65
Chapter 120 - General Assembly (Continuation)   66
Chapter 120 - General Assembly (Continuation)   67
Chapter 120C - Lobbying   67
Chapter 121 - Archives and History   67
Chapter 122 - Hospitals for the Mentally Disordered
[Repealed.]   67
Chapter 122A - North Carolina Housing Finance Agency   67
Chapter 122B - North Carolina Agricultural Facilities
Finance Act [Repealed.]   67
Chapter 122C - Mental Health, Developmental
Disabilities, and Substance Abuse Act of 1985   67
Chapter 122C - Mental Health, Developmental
Disabilities, and Substance Abuse Act of 1985 (Continuation)   68

11

Chapter 122D - North Carolina Agricultural Finance Act   68
Chapter 122E - North Carolina Housing Trust and Oil
Overcharge Act   68
Chapter 123 - Impeachment   69
Chapter 123A - Industrial Development [Repealed.]   69
Chapter 124 - Internal Improvements   69
Chapter 125 - Libraries   69
Chapter 126 - State Personnel System   69
Chapter 127 - Militia [Repealed.]   69
Chapter 127A - Militia   69
Chapter 127B - Military Affairs   69
Chapter 127C - Advisory Commission on Military Affairs   69
Chapter 128 - Offices and Public Officers   69
Chapter 128 - Offices and Public Officers (Continuation)   70
Chapter 129 - Public Buildings and Grounds   70
Chapter 130 - Public Health [Repealed.]   70
Chapter 130A - Public Health   70
Chapter 130A - Public Health (Continuation)   71
Chapter 130A - Public Health (Continuation)   72
Chapter 130B - Hazardous Waste Management
Commission [Repealed.]   72
Chapter 131 - Public Hospitals [Repealed.]   72
Chapter 131A - Health Care Facilities Finance Act   72
Chapter 131B - Licensing of Ambulatory Surgical
Facilities [Repealed.]   72
Chapter 131C - Charitable Solicitation Licensure Act
[Repealed.]   72
Chapter 131D - Inspection and Licensing of Facilities   72
Chapter 131E - Health Care Facilities and Services   72
Chapter 131E - Health Care Facilities and Services (Continuation)   73
Chapter 131F - Solicitation of Contributions   73
Chapter 132 - Public Records   73
Chapter 133 - Public Works   74
Chapter 134 - Youth Development [Recodified.]   74
Chapter 134A - Youth Services [Repealed.]   74
Chapter 135 - Retirement System for Teachers and
State Employees; Social Security; Health Insurance
Program for Children   74
Chapter 135 - Retirement System for Teachers and
State Employees; Social Security; Health Insurance
Program for Children   75
Chapter 136 - Transportation   75
Chapter 136 - Transportation (Continuation)   76
Chapter 137 - Rural Rehabilitation [Repealed.]   76
Chapter 138 - Salaries, Fees and Allowances   76
Chapter 138A - State Government Ethics Act   76

Chapter 139 - Soil and Water Conservation Districts 76
Chapter 140 - State Art Museum; Symphony and
Art Societies 76
Chapter 140A - State Awards System 76
Chapter 141 - State Boundaries 76
Chapter 142 - State Debt 76
Chapter 143 - State Departments, Institutions, and
Commissions 77
Chapter 143 - State Departments, Institutions, and
Commissions (Continuation) 78
Chapter 143 - State Departments, Institutions, and
Commissions (Continuation) 79
Chapter 143 - State Departments, Institutions, and
Commissions (Continuation) 80
Chapter 143A - State Government Reorganization 80
Chapter 143B - Executive Organization Act of 1973 80
Chapter 143B - Executive Organization Act of 1973 (Continuation) 81
Chapter 143B - Executive Organization Act of 1973 (Continuation) 82
Chapter 143C - State Budget Act 83
Chapter 143D - The State Governmental Accountability
and Internal Control Act 83
Chapter 144 - State Flag, Official Governmental Flags,
Motto, and Colors 83
Chapter 145 - State Symbols and Other Official
Adoptions. 83
Chapter 146 - State Lands 83
Chapter 147 - State Officers 83
Chapter 148 - State Prison System 84
Chapter 149 - State Song and Toast 84
Chapter 150 - Uniform Revocation of Licenses
[Repealed.] 84
Chapter 150A - Administrative Procedure Act
[Recodified.] 84
Chapter 150B - Administrative Procedure Act 84
Chapter 151 - Constables [Repealed.] 84
Chapter 152 - Coroners 84
Chapter 152A - County Medical Examiner [Repealed.] 84
Chapter 153 - Counties and County Commissioners
[Repealed.] 84
Chapter 153A - Counties 84
Chapter 153A - Counties (Continue) 85
Chapter 153B - Mountain Resources Planning Act 85
Chapter 153C - Uwharrie Regional Resources Act 85
Chapter 154 - County Surveyor [Repealed.] 85
Chapter 155 - County Treasurer [Repealed.] 85
Chapter 156 - Drainage 85

13

Chapter 156 – Drainage (Continuation)   86
Chapter 157 - Housing Authorities and Projects   86
Chapter 157A - Historic Properties Commissions
[Transferred.]   86
Chapter 158 - Local Development   86
Chapter 159 - Local Government Finance   86
Chapter 159 - Local Government Finance (Continuation)   87
Chapter 159A - Pollution Abatement and Industrial
Facilities Financing Act [Unconstitutional.]   87
Chapter 159B - Joint Municipal Electric Power and
Energy Act   87
Chapter 159C - Industrial and Pollution Control
Facilities Financing Act   87
Chapter 159D - The North Carolina Capital Facilities
Financing Act   87
Chapter 159E - Registered Public Obligations Act   87
Chapter 159F - North Carolina Energy Development
Authority [Repealed.]   87
Chapter 159G - Water Infrastructure   87
Chapter 159H - [Reserved.]   87
Chapter 159I - Solid Waste Management Loan Program
and Local Government Special Obligation Bonds   87
Chapter 160 - Municipal Corporations [Repealed
And Transferred.]   87
Chapter 160A - Cities and Towns   88
Chapter 160A - Cities and Towns (Continuation)   89
Chapter 160B - Consolidated City-County Act   89
Chapter 160C - Baseball Park Districts [Repealed.]   90
Chapter 161 - Register of Deeds   90
Chapter 162 - Sheriff   90
Chapter 162A - Water and Sewer Systems   90
Chapter 162B Continuity of Local Government in Emergency.   90
Chapter 163 Elections and Election Laws.   90
Chapter 163 Elections and Election Laws. (Continuation)   91
Chapter 164 Concerning the General Statutes of North Carolina.   92
Chapter 165 Veterans.   92
Chapter 166 Civil Preparedness Agencies [Repealed.]   92
Chapter 166A North Carolina Emergency Management Act.   92
Chapter 167 State Civil Air Patrol [Repealed.]   92
Chapter 168 Persons with Disabilities.   92
Chapter 168A Persons With Disabilities Protection Act.   92

§ 143-345.14. Authority to collect data; administration and enforcement; confidentiality.

(a)   The Department of Administration shall have the authority to obtain from prime suppliers of petroleum products specific petroleum supply data concerning State-level sales and projected sales by month for North Carolina that is currently reported on the federal Form EIA-782C, "Monthly Report of Petroleum Products Sold in States for Consumption" or its successor, at such time that these data requirements are not being met through any federal reporting procedure. The petroleum products subject to this reporting requirement are: finished gasoline (all grades), #1 distillate, kerosene, #2 fuel oil, #2 diesel fuel, aviation gasoline (finished), kerosene-type jet fuel, naphtha-type jet fuel, #4 fuel, residual fuel oil (less than or equal to one percent sulfur), residual fuel oil (greater than one percent sulfur), propane (consumer grade). The authority to collect energy data from suppliers of petroleum products into North Carolina, that is granted to the Department of Administration in this section, shall be limited to the petroleum volume data that is reported on the Form EIA-782C or its successor.

(b)   "Prime suppliers" shall be defined as those suppliers which make the first sale of the named product into North Carolina, excluding jobbers, distributors, and retail dealers.

(c)   The Department of Administration shall adopt rules and regulations for the administration of this data collection program and the Attorney General and the law enforcement authorities of the State and its political subdivisions shall enforce the provisions of this section and all orders, rules, and regulations promulgated thereunder. Any enforcement action may be brought upon the relation of the Department of Administration or the direction of the Attorney General.

(d)   Any person or corporation who willfully refuses to provide the petroleum supply data in accordance with the conditions described herein, or who knowingly or willfully submits false information in any reports required herein or refuses to file any reports shall be guilty of a Class 1 misdemeanor.

(e)   Any civil action brought to enforce the provisions of this section shall be brought in the Superior Court of Wake County or in the superior court of the county in which the acts or practices constituting a violation occurred or are occurring.

(f)   The Department of Administration shall keep confidential any individually identifiable energy information to the extent necessary to comply with the confidentiality requirements of the reporting agency, and any such information shall not be subject to the public disclosure requirements of G.S. 132-6. "Individually identifiable energy information" shall be defined as any individual record or portion of a record or aggregated data containing energy information about a person or persons obtained from any source, the disclosure of which could reasonably be expected to reveal information about a specific person. (2000-140, s. 76(i).)

§ 143-345.15. Reserved for future codification purposes.

Part 3. Energy Loan Fund.

§ 143-345.16: Recodified as G.S. 143B-437.14 by Session Laws 2010-96, s. 21, effective July 20, 2010.

§ 143-345.17: Recodified as G.S. 143B-437.15 by Session Laws 2010-96, s. 21, effective July 20, 2010.

§ 143-345.18: Recodified as G.S. 143B-437.16 by Session Laws 2010-96, s. 21, effective July 20, 2010.

Article 36A.

State Employee Suggestion Program (NC-Thinks).

§ 143-345.20. Definitions.

The following definitions apply in this Article:

(1)   Baseline reversion. - The two-year historical average of reversions by a State department, agency, or institution.

(1a)   NC-Thinks. - The State Employee Suggestion Program.

(2)   Repealed by Session Laws 2001-424, s. 7.2(b), effective July 1, 2001.

(2a)   Participating agency. - Any State department, agency, or institution, or any local school administrative unit that employs State employees eligible to participate in NC-Thinks. The term includes the North Carolina Community Colleges System, The University of North Carolina and its constituent institutions, and charter schools. The term does not include federal or local government agencies.

(2b)   Recodified as G.S. 143-345.20(1a).

(3)   State employee. - Any of the following:

a.   A person who is a contributing member of the Teachers' and State Employees' Retirement System of North Carolina, the Consolidated Judicial Retirement System of North Carolina, or the Optional Program.

b.   A person who receives wages from the State as a part-time or temporary worker, but is not otherwise a contributing member of one of the retirement programs listed in sub-subdivision a. of this subdivision. (1997-513, s. 2; 2001-424, s. 7.2(b); 2010-97, s. 11.)

§ 143-345.21. State employee suggestion program.

(a)   A State employee or team of State employees may receive an incentive bonus or bonuses in reward for suggestions or innovations resulting in monetary savings to the State, increased revenues to the State, or improved quality of services delivered to the public.

(b)   Repealed by Session Laws 2001-424, s. 7.2(c), effective July 1, 2001.

(b1)   The amount of savings generated by suggestions and innovations shall be determined after a 12-month period of implementation or, if applicable, no more than 90 days after the one-time savings is determined or the suggestion is approved. No suggestion payments shall be paid prior to the expiration of 12 months, or 90 days after the final one-time savings is determined or the suggestion is approved, and payment may be delayed further as reasonably required to ensure that a complete cost implementation cycle is evaluated fully.

(c)   Any savings are to be calculated using the actual expenditures for a program, activity, or service compared to the budgeted amount for the same, if

17

an amount has been budgeted for the program, activity, or service. The savings calculation shall include the amount of any reversions in excess of the baseline reversion. Any savings realized through NC-Thinks shall be weighed against continued service to the public and the assurance that there is not a negative impact on State programs.

(d)   If a suggestion or innovation affects a program, activity, or service for which no separate budgeted amount has been made, the State Coordinator, in conjunction with the agency evaluator or agency fiscal officer, or both for that suggestion or innovation, shall determine the budgetary impact of the suggestion or innovation.

(e)   No monetary award or leave can be awarded through NC-Thinks where specifically disallowed by the terms of the funding source.

(f)   The Office of State Human Resources shall establish the NC-Thinks reserve fund in which all savings for all suggestions shall be deposited as earned. Each participating agency shall be responsible for transferring savings to the NC-Thinks reserve fund. The funds may be encumbered as needed to ensure payment to the General Fund, to the suggester, and for distribution as required by G.S. 143-345.22. The Office of State Human Resources shall provide the NC-Thinks reserve fund summary at the close of each fiscal year to the Office of State Budget and Management and to the participating agencies. The Office of State Budget and Management shall have oversight responsibility for ensuring that the required reversions and transfers are made to the General Fund, and that all encumbered funds are accounted for and paid as required by law.

(g)   No distribution of suggester awards shall occur until reversion requirements to the General Fund are met and distributions as required by G.S. 143-345.22 are satisfied and verified by the Office of State Budget and Management. When all of the requirements of G.S. 143-345.22 are fulfilled, the Department of Administration shall transfer to the suggester's agency funds required to award the suggester. The suggester's agency shall make the suggestion award and ensure that all taxes and withholding requirements are met.

(h)   Implementation costs may be prorated over a maximum of three years for suggestions or innovations that are capital intensive, involve leading-edge technology, or involve unconventional processes that require longer than 12 months for implementation. The amount of the average annual savings minus

18

the average annual implementation cost shall be used as the basis for the agency to recommend a suggester award. The State Suggestion Review Committee shall consult the Office of State Budget and Management to make the final award determination in these cases.

(i)   There is established in the Office of State Human Resources a nonreverting fund to be administered by the Office of State Human Resources for the training and education of permanent State employees to address specific mission critical needs and objectives. Funds shall be credited from NC-Thinks to the fund as provided by this Article. (1997-513, s. 2; 1998-181, s. 5; 2001-424, s. 7.2(c); 2010-97, s. 11; 2011-224, s. 1; 2013-382, s. 9.1(c).)

§ 143-345.22. Allocation of suggestion program funds; nonmonetary recognition.

(a)   If a State employee's suggestion or innovation results in a monetary savings or increased revenue to the State, the funds saved or increased shall be distributed according to the following scale or subject to guidelines as set forth by the funding source:

(1)   Twenty percent (20%) of the annualized savings or increased revenues, up to a maximum of twenty thousand dollars ($20,000) for any one State employee, to constitute gainsharing. If a team of State employees is the suggester, the bonus provided in this subdivision shall be divided equally among the team members, except that no team member shall receive in excess of twenty thousand dollars ($20,000), nor shall the team receive an aggregate amount in excess of one hundred thousand dollars ($100,000). These funds shall not revert.

(2)   Thirty percent (30%) allocated as follows:

a.   Fifteen percent (15%) to the implementing agency for nonrecurring budget items to be used (i) by the implementing agency to provide equipment, supplies, training, and limited but appropriate recognition for the division, section, or group responsible for the implementation of the cost-saving measure and (ii) to meet other similar needs within the agency.

b.   Ten percent (10%) to the Office of State Human Resources for augmenting funding for the management and administration of NC-Thinks. These funds shall not revert.

c.   Five percent (5%) to the State employee education and training fund administered by the Office of State Human Resources under G.S. 143-342.21(i). These funds shall not revert when nonreversion is otherwise allowed by law or policy.

(3)   The remainder to the General Fund for nonrecurring budget items when allowed by law or policy.

(a1)   Of the pool of funds identified in subsection (a) of this section, only the General Fund appropriations shall be subject to reversion, except during declared budget emergencies. Under nonemergency budget conditions, NC-Thinks funds arising from savings at The University of North Carolina, the North Carolina Community Colleges System, the Highway Trust Fund, enterprise funds, and receipt-supported organizations shall be exempt from the General Fund reversion requirements.

(b)   The budget of a State agency shall not be reduced in the following fiscal year by an amount similar to the monetary savings or increased revenues realized by NC-Thinks. The agency budget shall be reduced in subsequent years only if structural or organizational changes are made that warrant the reductions, including the transfer of responsibility for an activity or service to another agency or the elimination of some function of State government.

(c)   If a suggestion or innovation results in improved quality of services to the public or to other State agencies, departments, and institutions, but not in monetary savings to the State, the suggester shall receive a nonmonetary award in the form of a certificate, leave with pay, or other similar recognition. (1997-513, s. 2; 1998-181, s. 6; 2001-424, s. 7.2(d); 2010-97, s. 11; 2011-224, s. 2; 2013-382, s. 9.1(c).)

§ 143-345.23. Suggestion and review process; role of agency coordinator and agency evaluator.

(a)   The process for a State employee or team of State employees to submit a cost-saving or revenue-increasing proposal shall begin with the employee or team of employees submitting the suggestion or innovation to an agency coordinator. The agency coordinator, in conjunction with an agency evaluator, shall review the suggestion or innovation for submission to the State Review Committee established in G.S. 143-345.24.

(b)   An agency coordinator shall be appointed by the head of each participating agency to serve as liaison between the agency, the suggester, the agency evaluator, and the NC-Thinks office. The duties of the agency coordinator shall include:

(1)   Serving as an information source and maintaining sufficient forms necessary to submit suggestions.

(2)   Presenting, in conjunction with the agency evaluator, the recommendation for an award to the State Suggestion Review Committee.

(3)   Working in conjunction with the agency evaluator to process a particular suggestion or innovation within 180 days, except when there are extenuating circumstances.

An agency may have more than one coordinator if required to provide sufficient services to State employees.

(c)   An agency evaluator shall be designated by the management of the implementing agency to evaluate one or more suggestions. The duties of an agency evaluator shall include:

(1)   Receiving from the agency coordinator and reviewing within 90 days, when possible, the feasibility and effectiveness of cost-saving or revenue-increasing measures suggested by State employees.

(2)   Being knowledgeable of the subject program, activity, or service.

(3)   Determining, in conjunction with the agency fiscal officer, the budgetary impact of a suggestion or innovation.

(4)   Judging impartially both the positive and negative effects of a suggestion or innovation on the current functions of the subject program, activity, or service.

(d)   The Director of the Office of State Human Resources shall be responsible for general oversight and coordination of NC-Thinks. The State coordinator shall be an employee of the Office of State Human Resources. The State coordinator shall be responsible for day-to-day NC-Thinks program management and administration of the technical aspects of the program. The State coordinator shall be an ex officio voting member of the State Suggestion Review Committee. (1997-513, s. 2; 1998-181, s. 7; 2001-424, s. 7.2(e); 2010-97, s. 11; 2011-224, s. 3; 2013-382, s. 9.1(c).)

§ 143-345.24. State Suggestion Review Committee.

(a)   The State Suggestion Review Committee shall consist of nine members, as follows:

(1)   The State Coordinator.

(2)   A representative of the Office of State Budget and Management.

(3)   A representative of the Office of State Human Resources.

(4)   A representative of The University of North Carolina.

(5)   A representative of the Department of Justice.

(6)   A representative of the Department of Labor.

(7)   One State employee appointed by the Speaker of the House of Representatives.

(8)   One State employee appointed by the President Pro Tempore of the Senate.

(9)   One State employee appointed by the Governor upon the recommendation of the State Employees Association of North Carolina, Inc.

(b)   The duties of the State Suggestion Review Committee shall include:

(1)   Receiving from the various agency coordinators recommendations on suggestions and innovations.

22

(2)   Determining the impact of a suggestion or innovation on State government services by judging the monetary savings, increased revenues, or improved quality of services generated by a suggestion or innovation.

(3)   Ensuring that the State employee incentive bonus process does not result in a negative impact on services provided to taxpayers by State government.

(c)   All administrative, management, clerical, and other functions and services required by the State Review Committee shall be supplied by the Office of State Human Resources. The Office of State Human Resources and the State Review Committee shall report annually to the Joint Legislative Commission on Governmental Operations on the administration of NC-Thinks. (1997-513, s. 2; 2000-140, s. 93.1(a); 2001-424, ss. 7.2(f), 12.2(b); 2010-97, s. 11; 2011-224, s. 4; 2013-382, s. 9.1(c).)

§ 143-345.25. Innovations deemed property of the State; effect of decisions regarding bonuses.

(a)   All suggestions or innovations submitted by State employees pursuant to this Article are the property of the State, and all related intellectual property rights shall be assigned to the State. By January 1, 2002, the Office of State Human Resources shall establish a policy regarding intellectual property rights that arise from NC-Thinks.

(b)   Decisions regarding the award of bonuses by the agency coordinator and the State Suggestion Review Committee are final and are not subject to review under the contested case procedures of Chapter 150B of the General Statutes. (1997-513, s. 2; 2001-424, s. 7.2(g); 2010-97, s. 11; 2013-382, s. 9.1(c).)

Article 37.

Salt Marsh Mosquito Control.

§ 143-346: Repealed by Session Laws 1973, c. 476, s. 183.

Article 37.

Salt Marsh Mosquito Control.

§ 143-347: Repealed by Session Laws 1995, c. 123, s. 1.

Article 37A.

Marine Science Council.

§§ 143-347.1 through 143-347.9: Repealed by Session Laws 1975, c. 879, s. 33.

Article 37B.

Marine Resources Center Administrative Board.

§§ 143-347.10 through 143-347.14: Repealed by Session Laws 1985, c. 202, s. 4.

Article 38.

Water Resources.

§§ 143-348 through 143-349. Repealed by Session Laws 1967, c. 892, s. 2.

§ 143-350. Definitions.

As used in this Article:

(1)   "Commission" means the Environmental Management Commission.

(2)   "Department" means the Department of Environment and Natural Resources.

(3)   "Essential water use" means the use of water necessary for firefighting, health, and safety; water needed to sustain human and animal life; and water necessary to satisfy federal, State, and local laws for the protection of public health, safety, welfare, the environment, and natural resources; and a minimum amount of water necessary to support and sustain the economy of the State, region, or area.

(3a)   "Gray water" means water that is discharged as waste from bathtubs, showers, wash basins, and clothes washers. "Gray water" does not include water that is discharged from toilets or kitchen sinks.

(3b)   "Gray water system" means a water reuse system that is contained within a single family residence or multiunit residential or commercial building that filters gray water or captured rain water and reuses it for nonpotable purposes such as toilet flushing and irrigation.

(4)   "Large community water system" means a community water system, as defined in G.S. 130A-313(10), that regularly serves 1,000 or more service connections or 3,000 or more individuals.

(5)   "Unit of local government" means a county, city, consolidated city-county, sanitary district, or other local political subdivision or authority or agency of local government.

(6)   "U.S. Drought Monitor" means the national drought map that designates areas of drought using the following categories D0-Abnormally Dry, D1-Moderate, D2-Severe, D3-Extreme, and D4-Exceptional. The U.S. Drought Monitor is developed and maintained by the Joint Agricultural Weather Facility, the Climate Prediction Center, the National Climatic Data Center, and the National Drought Mitigation Center with input from the United States Geological Survey, the National Water and Climate Center, the Climate Diagnostics Center, the National Weather Service, state climatologists, and state water resource agencies.

(7)   "Water shortage emergency" means a water shortage resulting from prolonged drought, contamination of the water supply, damage to water infrastructure, or other unforeseen causes that presents an imminent threat to public health, safety, and welfare or to the environment. (1959, c. 779, s. 1; 1967, c. 892, s. 12; 1973, c. 1262, s. 23; 1977, c. 771, s. 4; 1989, c. 727, s. 218(117); 1989 (Reg. Sess., 1990), c. 1004, s. 18; c. 1024, s. 34; 1991, c. 342,

s. 15(a); 1997-443, s. 11A.119(a); 2008-143, s. 3; 2010-143, s. 1; 2011-394, s. 12(a).)

§ 143-351. Repealed by Session Laws 1967, c. 892, s. 2.

§ 143-352. Purpose of Article.

The purpose of this Article is to create a State agency to coordinate the State's water resource activities; to devise plans and policies and to perform the research and administrative functions necessary for a more beneficial use of the water resources of the State, in order to insure improvements in the methods of conserving, developing and using those resources. (1959, c. 779, s. 1.)

§ 143-353. Repealed by Session Laws 1967, c. 892, s. 2.

§ 143-354. Ordinary powers and duties of the Commission.

(a)　　Powers and Duties in General. - Except as otherwise specified in this Article, the powers and duties of the Commission shall be as follows:

(1)　　The Commission shall carry out a program of planning and education concerning the most beneficial long-range conservation and use of the water resources of the State. It shall investigate the long-range needs of counties and municipalities and other local governments for water supply storage available in federal projects.

(2)　　The Commission shall advise the Governor as to how the State's present water research activities might be coordinated.

(3)　　Repealed by Session Laws 2008-143, s. 4, effective July 31, 2008.

(4)　　The Commission is authorized to call upon the Attorney General for such legal advice as is necessary to the functioning of the Commission.

(5)　　Recognizing the complexity and difficulties attendant upon the recommendation of the General Assembly of fair and beneficial legislation affecting the use and conservation of water, the Commission shall solicit from the various water interests of the State their suggestions thereon.

(6)　　The Commission may hold public hearings for the purpose of obtaining evidence and information and permitting discussion relative to water resources legislation and shall have the power to subpoena witnesses therefor.

(7)　　All recommendations for proposed legislation made by the Commission shall be available to the public.

(8)　　The Commission shall adopt such rules and regulations as may be necessary to carry out the purposes of this Article.

(9)　　Any member of the Commission or any person authorized by it, shall have the right to enter upon any private or public lands or waters for the purpose of making investigations and studies reasonably necessary in the gathering of facts concerning streams and watersheds, subject to responsibility for any damage done to property entered.

(10)　　The Commission is authorized to provide to federal agencies the required assurances, subject to availability of appropriations by the General Assembly or applicable funds or assurances from local governments, of nonfederal cooperation for water supply storage and other congressionally authorized purposes in federal projects.

(11)　　The Commission is authorized to assign or transfer to any county or municipality or other local government having a need for water supply storage in federal projects any interest held by the State in such storage, upon the assumption of repayment obligation therefor, or compensation to the State, by such local government. The Commission shall also have the authority to reassign or transfer interests in such storage held by local governments, if indicated by the investigation of needs made pursuant to subdivision (1) of subsection (a) of this section, subject to equitable adjustment of financial responsibility.

(b) through (e). Repealed by Session Laws 2008-143, s. 4, effective July 31, 2008. (1959, c. 779, s. 1; 1967, c. 1071, ss. 1, 2; 1973, c. 1262, s. 23; 1991, c. 342, s. 15(b); 1993, c. 539, s. 1033; 1994, Ex. Sess., c. 24, s. 14(c); 2008-143, s. 4.)

§ 143-355. Powers and duties of the Department.

(a)   Repealed by Session Laws 1989, c. 603, s. 1.

(b)   Functions to Be Performed. - The Department shall:

(1)   Request the North Carolina Congressional Delegation to apply to the Congress of the United States whenever deemed necessary for appropriations for protecting and improving any harbor or waterway in the State and for accomplishing needed flood control, shore-erosion prevention, and water-resources development for water supply, water quality control, and other purposes.

(2)   Initiate, plan, and execute a long-range program for the preservation, development and improvement of rivers, harbors, and inland ports, and to promote the public interest therein.

(3)   Prepare and recommend to the Governor and the General Assembly any legislation which may be deemed proper for the preservation and improvement of rivers, harbors, dredging of small inlets, provision for safe harbor facilities, and public tidewaters of the State.

(4)   Make engineering studies, hydraulic computations, hydrographic surveys, and reports regarding shore-erosion projects, dams, reservoirs, and river-channel improvements; to develop, for budget and planning purposes, estimates of the costs of proposed new projects; to prepare bidding documents, plans, and specifications for harbor, coastal, and river projects, and to inspect materials, workmanship, and practices of contractors to assure compliance with plans and specifications.

(5)   Cooperate with the United States Army Corps of Engineers in causing to be removed any wrecked, sunken or abandoned vessel or unauthorized obstructions and encroachments in public harbors, channels, waterways, and tidewaters of the State.

(6)   Cooperate with the United States Coast Guard in marking out and establishing harbor lines and in placing buoys and structures for marking navigable channels.

(7)   Cooperate with federal and interstate agencies in planning and developing water-resource projects for navigation, flood control, hurricane protection, shore-erosion prevention, and other purposes.

(8)   Provide professional advice to public and private agencies, and to citizens of the State, on matters relating to tidewater development, river works, and watershed development.

(9)   Discuss with federal, State, and municipal officials and other interested persons a program of development of rivers, harbors, and related resources.

(10)   Make investigations and render reports requested by the Governor and the General Assembly.

(11)   Participate in activity of the National Rivers and Harbors Congress, the American Shore and Beach Preservation Association, the American Watershed Council, the American Water Works Association, the American Society of Civil Engineers, the Council of State Governments, the Conservation Foundation, and other national agencies concerned with conservation and development of water resources.

(12)   Prepare and maintain climatological and water-resources records and files as a source of information easily accessible to the citizens of the State and to the public generally.

(13)   Formulate and administer a program of dune rebuilding, hurricane protection, and shore-erosion prevention.

(14)   Include in the biennial budget the cost of performing the additional functions indicated above.

(15)   Initiate, plan, study, and execute a long-range floodplain management program for the promotion of health, safety, and welfare of the public. In carrying out the purposes of this subsection, the primary responsibility of floodplain management rests with the local levels of government and it is, therefore, the policy of this State and of this Department to provide guidance, coordination, and other means of assistance, along with the other agencies of this State and with the local levels of government, to effectuate adequate floodplain management programs.

(16)   Cooperate with units of local government in the identification of water supply needs and appropriate water supply sources and water storage projects to meet those needs. By agreement with a unit of local government, the Department may do any of the following:

29

a.   Assist in the assessment of alternatives for meeting water supply needs; the conduct of engineering studies, hydraulic computations, and hydrographic surveys; and the development of a plan of study for purposes of obtaining necessary permits.

b.   For budget and planning purposes, develop estimates of the costs of the proposed new water supply project.

c.   Apply for State and federal permits for the development of regional water supplies.

(17)   Be the principal State agency to cooperate with other State agencies, the United States Army Corps of Engineers, and all other federal agencies or instrumentalities in the planning and development of water supply sources and water storage projects for the State.

(b1)   The Department is directed to pursue an active educational program of floodplain management measures, to include in each biennial report a statement of flood damages, location where floodplain management is desirable, and suggested legislation, if deemed desirable, and within its capacities to provide advice and assistance to State agencies and local levels of government.

(c)   Repealed by Session Laws 1961, c. 315.

(d)   Investigation of Coasts, Ports and Waterways of State. - The Department is designated as the official State agency to investigate and cause investigations to be made of the coasts, ports and waterways of North Carolina and to cooperate with agencies of the federal and State government and other political subdivisions in making such investigations. The provisions of this section shall not be construed as in any way interfering with the powers and duties of the Utilities Commission, relating to the acquiring of rights-of-way for the Intra-Coastal Waterway; or to authorize the Department to represent the State in connection with such duties.

(e)   Repealed by Session Laws 1998-129, s. 1, effective January 1, 2000.

(f)   Samples of Cuttings to Be Furnished the Department When Requested. - Every person, firm or corporation engaged in the business of drilling, boring, coring or constructing wells in any manner by the use of power machinery shall furnish the Department samples of cuttings from such depths as the Department may require from all wells constructed by such person, firm or corporation, when such samples are requested by the Department. The Department shall bear the expense of delivering such samples. The Department shall, after an analysis of the samples submitted, furnish a copy of such analysis to the owner of the property on which the well was constructed; the Department shall not report the results of any such analysis to any other person whatsoever until the person legally authorized to do so authorizes in writing the release of the results of the analysis.

(g)   Reports of Each Well Required. - Every person, firm or corporation engaged in the business of drilling, boring, coring, or constructing wells with power machinery within the State of North Carolina shall, within 30 days of the completion of each well, report to the Department on forms furnished by the Department the location, size, depth, number of feet of casing used, method of finishing, and formation log information of each such well. In addition such person, firm or corporation shall report any tests made of each such well including the method of testing, length of test, draw-down in feet and yield in gallons per minute. The person, firm or corporation making such report to the Department shall at the time such report is made also furnish a copy thereof to the owner of the property on which the well was constructed.

(h)   Drilling for Petroleum and Minerals Excepted. - The provisions of this Article shall not apply to drillings for petroleum and minerals.

(i)   Penalty for Violation. - Any person violating the provisions of subsections (e), (f) and (g) of G.S. 143-355 shall be guilty of a Class 3 misdemeanor and, upon conviction, shall only be punished by a fine of fifty dollars ($50.00). Each violation shall constitute a separate offense.

(j)   Miscellaneous Duties. - The Department shall make investigations of water supplies and water powers, prepare and maintain a general inventory of the water resources of the State and take such measures as it may consider necessary to promote their development; and to supervise, guide, and control the performance of the duties set forth in subsection (b) of this section and to hold hearings with regard thereto. In connection with administration of the well-drilling law the Department may prepare analyses of well cuttings for mineral and petroleum content.

(k)   Water Use Information. - Any person using, withdrawing, diverting or obtaining water from surface streams, lakes and underground water sources shall, upon the request of the Department, file a monthly report with the Department showing the amount of water used, withdrawn, diverted or obtained from such sources. Such report shall be on a form supplied by the Department and shall show the identification of the water well or other withdrawal facility, location, withdrawal rate (measured in gallons per minute), and total gallons withdrawn during the month. Reports required to be filed under this subsection shall be filed on or before the fifteenth day of the month succeeding the month during which the using, withdrawing, diverting or obtaining water required to be reported occurred. This subsection does not apply to withdrawals or uses by individuals or families for household, livestock, or gardens. All reports required under this subsection are provided solely for the purpose of the Department. Within the meaning of this subsection the term "person" means any and all persons, including individuals, firms, partnerships, associations, public or private institutions, municipalities or political subdivisions, governmental agencies, and private or public corporations organized or existing under the laws of this State or any other state or country. In the event of extreme or exceptional drought or other water shortage, the Department may require each local government water system and each large community water system in the affected area to report the amount of water used, withdrawn, diverted, or obtained on a weekly basis and may require the reporting of additional information necessary to assess and manage the drought or water shortage.

(l)   Local Water Supply Plans. - Each unit of local government that provides public water service or that plans to provide public water service and each large community water system shall, either individually or together with other units of local government and large community water systems, prepare a local water supply plan and submit it to the Department for approval. The Department shall provide technical assistance with the preparation of plans to units of local government and large community water systems upon request and to the extent that the Department has resources available to provide assistance. At a minimum, each unit of local government and large community water system shall include in local water supply plans all information that is readily available to it. Plans shall include present and projected population, industrial development, and water use within the service area; present and future water supplies; an estimate of the technical assistance that may be needed at the local level to address projected water needs; current and future water conservation and water reuse programs, including a plan for the reduction of long-term per capita demand for potable water; a description of how the local government or large community water system will respond to drought and other water shortage emergencies and continue to meet essential public water supply needs during the emergency; and any other related information as the Department may require in the preparation of a State water supply plan. A unit of local government or large community water system shall submit a revised plan that specifies how the water system intends to address foreseeable future water needs when eighty percent (80%) of the water system's available water supply based on calendar year average daily demand has been allocated to current or prospective water users or the seasonal demand exceeds ninety percent (90%). Local plans shall be revised to reflect changes in relevant data and projections at least once each five years unless the Department requests more frequent revisions. The revised plan shall include the current and anticipated reliance by the local government unit or large community water system on surface water transfers as defined by G.S. 143-215.22G. Local plans and revised plans shall be submitted to the Department once they have been approved by each unit of local government and large community water system that participated in the preparation of the plan.

(m)   In order to assure the availability of adequate supplies of good quality water to protect the public health and to support desirable economic growth, the Department shall develop a State water supply plan. The State water supply plan shall include the information and projections required to be included in local plans, a summary of water conservation and water reuse programs described in local plans, a summary of the technical assistance needs indicated by local plans, and shall indicate the extent to which the various local plans are compatible. The State plan shall identify potential conflicts among the various local plans and ways in which local water supply programs could be better coordinated.

(n)   The Department of Environment and Natural Resources shall report to the Environmental Review Commission on the implementation of this section and the development of the State water supply plan on or before 1 September of each year.

(o)   Basinwide Hydrologic Models. - The Department shall develop a basinwide hydrologic model for each of the 17 major river basins in the State as provided in this subsection.

(1)   Definitions. - As used in this subsection:

a.   "Ecological flow" means the stream flow necessary to protect ecological integrity.

b.   "Ecological integrity" means the ability of an aquatic system to support and maintain a balanced, integrated, adaptive community of organisms having a species composition, diversity, and functional organization comparable to

33

prevailing ecological conditions and, when subject to disruption, to recover and continue to provide the natural goods and services that normally accrue from the system.

c.   "Groundwater resource" means any water flowing or lying under the surface of the earth or contained within an aquifer.

d.   "Prevailing ecological conditions" means the ecological conditions determined by reference to the applicable period of record of the United States Geological Survey stream gauge data, including data reflecting the ecological conditions that exist after the construction and operation of existing flow modification devices, such as dams, but excluding data collected when stream flow is temporarily affected by in-stream construction activity.

e.   "Surface water resource" means any lake, pond, river, stream, creek, run, spring, or other water flowing or lying on the surface of the earth.

(2)   Schedule. - The Department shall develop a schedule for basinwide hydrologic model development. In developing the schedule, the Department shall give priority to developing hydrologic models for river basins or portions of river basins that are experiencing or are likely to experience water supply shortages, where the ecological integrity is threatened or likely to become threatened, or for which an existing hydrologic model has not been developed by the Department or other persons or entities.

(3)   Model. - Each basinwide hydrologic model shall:

a.   Include surface water resources within the river basin, groundwater resources within the river basin to the extent known by the Department, transfers into and out of the river basin that are required to be registered under G.S. 143-215.22H, other withdrawals, ecological flow, instream flow requirements, projections of future withdrawals, an estimate of return flows within the river basin, inflow data, local water supply plans, and other scientific and technical information the Department deems relevant.

b.   Be designed to simulate the flows of each surface water resource within the basin that is identified as a source of water for a withdrawal registered under G.S. 143-215.22H in response to different variables, conditions, and scenarios. The model shall specifically be designed to predict the places, times, frequencies, and intervals at which any of the following may occur:

1.   Yield may be inadequate to meet all needs.

2.   Yield may be inadequate to meet all essential water uses.

3.   Ecological flow may be adversely affected.

c.   Be based solely on data that is of public record and open to public review and comment.

(4)   Ecological flow. - The Department shall characterize the ecology in the different river basins and identify the flow necessary to maintain ecological integrity. The Department shall create a Science Advisory Board to assist the Department in characterizing the natural ecology and identifying the flow requirements. The Science Advisory Board shall include representatives from the Divisions of Water Resources and Water Quality of the Department, the North Carolina Wildlife Resources Commission, the North Carolina Marine Fisheries Commission, and the Natural Heritage Program. The Department shall also invite participation by the United States Fish and Wildlife Service; the National Marine Fisheries Service; representatives of organizations representing agriculture, forestry, manufacturing, electric public utilities, and local governments, with expertise in aquatic ecology and habitat; and other individuals or organizations with expertise in aquatic ecology and habitat. The Department shall ask the Science Advisory Board to review any report or study submitted to the Department for consideration that is relevant to characterizing the ecology of the different river basins and identifying flow requirements for maintenance of ecological integrity. The Department shall consider such other information, including site specific analyses, that either the Board or the Department considers relevant to determining ecological flow requirements.

(5)   Interstate cooperation. - To the extent practicable, the Department shall work with neighboring states to develop basinwide hydrologic models for each river basin shared by North Carolina and another state.

(6)   Approval and modification of hydrologic models. -

a.   Upon completion of a hydrologic model, the Department shall:

1.   Submit the model to the Commission for approval.

35

2.	Publish in the North Carolina Register notice of its recommendation that the Commission approve the model and of a 60-day period for providing comment on the model.

3.	Provide electronic notice to persons who have requested electronic notice of the notice published in the North Carolina Register.

b.	Upon receipt of a hydrologic model, the Commission shall:

1.	Receive comment on the model for the 60-day period noticed in the North Carolina Register.

2.	Act on the model following the 60-day comment period.

c.	The Department shall submit any significant modification to an approved hydrologic model to the Commission for review and approval under the process used for initial approval of the model.

d.	A hydrologic model is not a rule, and Article 2A of Chapter 150B of the General Statutes does not apply to the development of a hydrologic model.

(7)	Existing hydrologic models. - The Department shall not develop a hydrologic model for a river basin for which a hydrologic model has already been developed by a person or entity other than the Department, if the Department determines that the hydrologic model meets the requirements of this subsection. The Department may adopt a hydrologic model that has been developed by another person or entity that meets the requirements of this subsection in lieu of developing a hydrologic model as required by this subsection. The Department may make any modifications or additions to a hydrologic model developed by another person or entity that are necessary to meet the requirements of this subsection.

(8)	Construction of subsection. - Nothing in this subsection shall be construed to vary any existing, or impose any additional regulatory requirements, related to water quality or water resources.

(9)	Report. - The Department shall report to the Environmental Review Commission on the development of basinwide hydrologic models no later than November 1, of each year. (1959, c. 779, s. 3; 1961, c. 315; 1967, c. 1069, ss. 1-3; c. 1070, s. 1; c. 1071, ss. 3, 4; c. 1117, s. 1; 1973, c. 1262, ss. 23, 28, 86; 1977, c. 771, s. 4; 1981, c. 514, ss. 2, 3; 1989, c. 603, s. 1; 1993, c. 513, s. 7(a);

c. 539, s. 1034; 1994, Ex. Sess., c. 24, s. 14(c); 1995, c. 509, s. 85; 1997-358, ss. 5, 6; 1998-129, s. 1; 1998-168, s. 5; 2001-452, s. 2.7; 2002-167, ss. 1, 2; 2003-387, s. 1; 2008-143, s. 7; 2010-143, s. 2; 2010-150, s. 1; 2011-374, ss. 1.1, 3.1.)

§ 143-355.1. Drought Management Advisory Council; drought advisories.

(a)   The Department shall establish a Drought Management Advisory Council. The purposes of the Council are:

(1)   To improve coordination among local, State, and federal agencies; public water systems, as defined in G.S. 130A-313(10); and water users to improve the management and mitigation of the harmful effects of drought.

(2)   To provide consistent and accurate information on drought conditions in the State to the U.S. Drought Monitor, the Environmental Management Commission, the Secretary, the Environmental Review Commission, and the public.

(b)   The Department shall invite each of the following organizations to designate a representative to serve on the Council:

(1)   North Carolina Cooperative Extension Service.

(2)   State Climate Office at North Carolina State University.

(3)   Public Staff of the Utilities Commission.

(4)   Wildlife Resources Commission.

(5)   Department of Agriculture and Consumer Services.

(6)   Department of Commerce.

(7)   Department of Public Safety.

(8)   National Weather Service of the National Oceanic and Atmospheric Administration of the United States Department of Commerce.

(9)   United States Geological Survey of the United States Department of the Interior.

(10)   United States Army Corps of Engineers.

(11)   United States Department of Agriculture.

(12)   Federal Emergency Management Agency of the United States Department of Homeland Security.

(b1)   Representatives designated under subsection (b) of this section shall have expertise or responsibility in meteorology, groundwater and surface water hydrology, water system operation and management, reservoir management, emergency response, or another subject area related to assessment and management of drought impacts.

(c)   The Department shall also invite other agencies and organizations that represent water users, including local governments, agriculture, agribusiness, forestry, manufacturing, investor-owned water utilities regulated by the North Carolina Utilities Commission, and others as appropriate, to participate in the work of the Council with respect to particular drought related issues.

(d)   The Department shall designate an employee of the Department to serve as Chair of the Council. The Council shall meet at least once in each calendar year in order to maintain appropriate agency readiness and participation. In addition, the Council shall meet on the call of the Chair to respond to drought conditions. The provisions of Article 33C of this Chapter apply to meetings of the Council.

(e)   In order to provide accurate and consistent information to assist State agencies, local governments, and other water users in taking appropriate drought response actions, the Council may issue drought advisories that designate:

(1)   Specific areas of the State in which drought conditions are impending.

(2)   Specific areas of the State that are suffering from drought conditions.

(3)   The level of severity of drought conditions based on the drought categories used in the U.S. Drought Monitor or the drought designation approved by the Secretary under subsection (f) of this section.

38

(f)   Drought designations by the U.S. Drought Monitor shall be the default designations for drought advisories issued under subsection (e) of this section. The Council shall publish those drought designations for each county. If more than one drought designation applies to a county, the drought designation for the county shall be the highest drought designation that applies to at least twenty-five percent (25%) of the land area of the county. The Council may recommend a drought designation for a county that is different from the designation based on the U.S. Drought Monitor if the U.S. Drought Monitor does not accurately reflect localized conditions because of differences in scale or because the U.S. Drought Monitor does not consider one or more of the indicators of drought identified in this subsection. In recommending a drought designation that differs from the U.S. Drought Monitor designation, the Council shall consider stream flows, ground water levels, the amount of water stored in reservoirs, weather forecasts, the time of year, and other factors that are relevant to determining the location and severity of drought conditions.

(f1)   The Secretary shall accept the Council's recommendation to adopt a drought designation for a county that is different from the designation based on the U.S. Drought Monitor if the Secretary finds that the indicators of drought identified by the Council under subsection (f) of this section support the designation recommended by the Council.

(g)   The Council shall report on the implementation of this section to the Secretary, the Governor, and the Environmental Review Commission no later than 1 October of each year. The report shall include a review of drought advisories issued by the Council and any recommendations to improve coordination among local, State, and federal agencies; public water systems; and water users to improve the management and mitigation of the harmful effects of drought. (2003-387, s. 2; 2004-195, s. 2.5; 2008-143, s. 16; 2011-145, s. 19.1(g).)

§ 143-355.2. Water conservation measures for drought.

(a)   Each unit of local government that provides public water service and each large community water system shall develop and implement water conservation measures to respond to drought or other water shortage conditions as provided in this section. Pursuant to G.S. 143-355(l), water conservation measures to respond to drought or other water shortage conditions shall be set out in a water shortage response plan and submitted to the Department for review and approval. The Department shall approve the water shortage response plan if the plan meets all of the following criteria:

(1)   The plan includes tiered levels of water conservation measures or other response actions based on the severity of water shortage conditions.

(2)   Each tier of water conservation measures shall be based on increased severity of drought or water shortage conditions and will result in more stringent water conservation measures.

(3)   All other requirements of rules adopted by the Commission pursuant to S.L. 2002-167.

(4)   Does not contain any provision that meters or regulates private drinking water wells, as defined in G.S. 87-85.

(b)   The Department may require a unit of local government that provides public water service or a large community water system to implement the more stringent water conservation measures described in subsection (d) of this section if the Department makes written findings that any county, as determined by subsection (e) of this section, in which the source of water for the public water system operated by the unit of local government or by a large community water system is in:

(1)   Severe, extreme, or exceptional drought, and the Department finds all of the following:

a.   The unit of local government that provides water service or large community water system has not begun implementation of any level of water conservation measures set out in the water shortage response plan.

b.   Implementation of measures is necessary to minimize the harmful impacts of drought on public health, safety, and the environment, including the potential impacts of drought or other water shortage on interconnected water systems and other water systems withdrawing from the same water source, or

(2)   Extreme or exceptional drought, and the Department finds that the unit of local government that provides water service or large community water system has implemented the measures required under the water shortage response plan for the appropriate tier of water conservation measure for 30 days or more and that implementation of the measures required has not

reduced water use in an amount sufficient to minimize the harmful impacts of drought on public health, safety, and the environment, including the potential impact of drought or other water shortage on interconnected water systems and other water systems withdrawing from the same water source.

(c)   In making the findings required under subsection (b) of this section, the Department shall consider the:

(1)   Hydrological drought conditions.

(2)   Drought forecast.

(3)   Reductions in water use achieved under water conservation measures in effect.

(4)   Availability of other water supply sources and other indicators of the extent and severity of drought impacts.

(5)   Economic impacts on the community to implement more stringent water conservation measures.

(6)   Conservation measures of all registered water withdrawals within the same 8 digit hydrologic unit code established by the U.S. Geological Survey to the extent the Department is able to document those measures.

(d)   Based on the findings required under subsection (b) of this section, the Department may require the unit of local government that provides public water service or the large community water system to begin implementation of its plan or to implement the next tier of water shortage response measures. If, after consultation with the unit of local government or the large community water system, the Department makes a written finding that the next tier of measures set out in the plan, together with any other reasonable steps that may be available to reduce water use, will not reduce water use in an amount sufficient to minimize the harmful impacts of drought on public health, safety, and the environment, including the potential impact of drought or other water shortage on interconnected water systems and other water systems drawing from the same water source, then the Department may require implementation of the tier that is two levels more stringent than the tier being implemented.

(e)   For purposes of this section, the drought designation for an area shall be the U.S. Drought Monitor designation for the county in which the water source is located as published by the Drought Management Advisory Council. The Secretary may approve a county drought designation that is different from the U.S. Drought Monitor designation pursuant to G.S. 143-355.1(f1). If the water source is located in more than one county and the counties have different drought designations, the Council shall recommend to the Secretary the drought designation to be applied to water systems that withdraw water from the water source. The recommendation of the Council shall be based on the drought indicators identified in G.S. 143-355.1(f) as applied to the water source.

(f) A unit of local government that provides public water service or a large community water system that does not have a water shortage response plan shall implement the default water conservation measures for extreme and exceptional drought set out in the rules adopted by the Commission pursuant to S.L. 2002-167.

(g) A unit of local government that provides water service or a large community water system that does not have an approved water shortage response plan shall implement the default water conservation measures specified in subsection (f) of this section within 10 days following a drought designation that requires implementation of water conservation measures. A water shortage response plan is presumed to be approved until the Department notifies the unit of local government or large community water system that the plan has been disapproved. A unit of local government that provides public water service and a large community water system shall be deemed to be in compliance with this section if, within 10 days after water shortage conditions identified in the plan require implementation of water conservation measures, the water system begins implementation of the water conservation measures required by the plan.

(h) Water conservation measures imposed by a unit of local government that provides public water service or by a large community water system may be more stringent than the minimum water conservation measures required under this section.

(h1) A trade or professional organization representing commercial car washes may establish a voluntary water conservation and water use efficiency certification program to encourage and promote the use of year-round water conservation and water use efficiency measures. Implementation of a voluntary water conservation and water use efficiency program shall be considered in determining compliance with local government water shortage response plans as follows:

42

(1)   A water conservation and water use efficiency certification may only be issued to a person that demonstrates full implementation of a voluntary water conservation and water use efficiency program that is approved pursuant to subdivision (3) of this subsection. In order to receive and maintain certification, a person must have its facility inspected on an annual basis by a licensed plumbing contractor who will confirm that the applicant is in compliance with the standards of the certification program.

(2)   A unit of local government that provides public water service or a large community water system shall recognize and credit a commercial car wash that has met the standards of a certification program for at least six months prior to the most recent extreme drought designation for water conservation achieved under the program. To the extent that a tiered response stage in the water shortage response plan requires commercial or industrial users to implement a percentage reduction in use, a car wash certified under a program shall be credited with the percentage reduction achieved by measures implemented under the program. Car washes certified under a program shall not be required to reduce consumption more than any other class of commercial or industrial water users during a water shortage emergency.

(3)   To qualify as an approved water conservation and water use efficiency certification program, the Department of Environment and Natural Resources shall determine that the program achieves year-round reductions in water use and results in a reduction of twenty percent (20%) or more in average water use per vehicle. Best management practices may include, but are not limited to, recycling, reclaiming, or reusing a portion of the water in the consuming processes. If a unit of local government that provides public water service or a large community water system determines that a person certified under such a program is not complying with the terms and standards of the certification program, it may refuse to recognize and credit the conservation measures.

(i)   A unit of local government that provides public water service and a large community water system shall report that the water system has begun implementation of water conservation measures set out in the water system's water shortage response plan or the default water conservation measures to the Department within 72 hours after beginning implementation.

(j)   This section shall not be construed to authorize or require the implementation of water conservation management measures that conflict with or are superseded by the provisions of any order of a federal or State court or administrative agency, any interstate agreement governing the allocation of water to which the State is a party, or any license for a hydroelectric generating facility issued by the Federal Energy Regulatory Commission; including, without limitation, any protocol or subsidiary agreement that may be part of or incorporated in any such order, interstate agreement, or operating license. (2008-143, s. 5; 2009-480, s. 1; 2010-180, s. 8.)

§ 143-355.3. Water shortage emergency powers.

(a)   Declaration of Water Shortage Emergency. - If, after consultation with the affected water system and the unit of local government with jurisdiction over the area served by the water system, the Secretary determines that the needs of human consumption, necessary sanitation, and public safety require emergency action, the Secretary shall provide the Governor with written findings setting out the basis for declaration of a water shortage emergency. The Governor shall have the authority to declare a water shortage emergency in the area affected by the water shortage emergency, which may include both the water system experiencing a water shortage emergency and the area served by a water system required under subdivision (1) of subsection (b) of this section to provide water in response to the water shortage emergency. No emergency period shall exceed 30 days, but the Governor may declare successive emergencies based upon the written findings of the Secretary.

(b)   Water Shortage Emergency Powers and Duties. - Whenever, pursuant to this Article, the Governor declares the existence of a water shortage emergency within a particular area of the State, the Secretary shall have the powers and duties set out in subdivisions (1), (2), and (3) of this subsection. These powers may only be exercised within the designated water shortage emergency area, after the Secretary has consulted with the affected water systems and determined that the water shortage emergency cannot be effectively managed in the absence of exercising these powers, and only for the period of the water shortage emergency. Under these circumstances, the Secretary has the power and duty to:

(1)   Require any water system that has water supply in excess of that required to meet the essential water uses of its customers to provide water to a water system experiencing a water shortage emergency. The Secretary shall give preference to diversion of water from a water system within the same river basin as the water system that is experiencing a water shortage emergency. A

44

diversion of water that requires a certificate under G.S. 143-215.22L shall meet the requirements of that section. The amount required to be supplied shall be limited to the amount necessary to supply essential water uses within the receiving system. The required diversion of waters shall cease upon the termination of the water shortage emergency.

(2)   Adopt rules governing the conservation and use of water within the water shortage emergency area as shall be necessary to maintain essential water use within the water shortage emergency area. Before such rules and regulations shall become effective, they shall be published in two consecutive issues of a daily newspaper generally circulated in the emergency area.

(3)   Adopt rules governing conservation and use of water within the service area of the water system from which water is being diverted as shall be necessary to maintain essential water uses in the system while supplying water to the water shortage emergency area.

(c)   Temporary Rights-of-Way. - A water system that is affected by a water shortage emergency is authorized to lay necessary temporary waterlines for the period of a declared water shortage emergency across, under, or above any and all properties to connect the water system experiencing a water shortage emergency to an emergency intake in a new water source or to interconnect the water system to a supplying water or wastewater system without first acquiring right-of-way. The Department shall expedite the approval of temporary waterlines needed to provide emergency water supply under this section. Temporary waterlines installed under this section shall be removed within 90 days following the end of the emergency period except that the Secretary may, for good cause, authorize a 30-day extension.

(d)   Compensation for Water Allocated During Water Shortage Emergency and Temporary Rights-of-Way. - Whenever the Secretary, pursuant to this Article, has ordered any diversion of water, the receiving water or wastewater system shall reimburse the supplying water system for the cost of the water. The cost charged to the receiving system shall not exceed one hundred ten percent (110%) of the retail cost that would be charged to a customer of the supplying system for an equivalent amount of water and any additional costs incurred by the supplying system for alterations to its infrastructure or water treatment to effectuate the diversion except as provided under an interlocal agreement. Unless liability is otherwise assigned in an interlocal agreement, the receiving water system shall be liable to all persons suffering any loss or damage caused by or resulting from the laying of temporary waterlines to

45

effectuate the diversion. Within 10 days of placing the temporary waterlines, the water system that is liable shall institute a civil action in accordance with the procedures set out under Article 9 of Chapter 136 of the General Statutes to compensate the property owners for any taking caused by or resulting from the laying of temporary waterlines, with the water system that is liable having the role of the Department of Transportation and the governing board of the water system that is liable having the role of the Secretary of Transportation under Article 9 of Chapter 136 of the General Statutes. The placing of temporary waterlines pursuant to this section is not subject to the provisions of G.S. 153A-15.

(e)   This section shall not be construed to authorize or require any actions that conflict with or are superseded by the provisions of any order of a federal or State court or administrative agency, any interstate agreement governing the allocation of water to which the State is a party, or any license for a hydroelectric generating facility issued by the Federal Energy Regulatory Commission; including, without limitation, any protocol or subsidiary agreement that may be part of or incorporated in any such order, interstate agreement, or operating license.

(f)   Nothing in this section shall limit a landowner from withdrawing water for use in agricultural activities, as described in G.S. 106-581.1, when the water is withdrawn from any of the following:

(1)   Surface water sources located wholly on the landowner's property, including, but not limited to, impoundments constructed by or owned by the landowner and captured stormwater.

(2)   Groundwater sources, including, but not limited to, wells constructed on the landowner's property, springs, and artesian wells. This subsection shall not apply if the Governor determines that withdrawal of water from a groundwater source is causing negative impacts to groundwater sources not located on the landowner's property, including the diminution of water available from neighboring groundwater sources or saltwater intrusion into neighboring groundwater sources. (2008-143, s. 8; 2013-265, s. 21.)

§ 143-355.4. Water system efficiency.

(a)   Local government water systems and large community water systems shall require separate meters for new in-ground irrigation systems on lots platted and recorded in the office of the register of deeds in the county or counties in which the real property is located after July 1, 2009, that are connected to their systems.

(b)   To be eligible for State water infrastructure funds from the Drinking Water State Revolving Fund or the Drinking Water Reserve or any other grant or loan of funds allocated by the General Assembly whether the allocation of funds is to a State agency or to a nonprofit organization for the purpose of extending waterlines or expanding water treatment capacity, a local government or large community water system must demonstrate that the system:

(1)   Has established a water rate structure that is adequate to pay the cost of maintaining, repairing, and operating the system, including reserves for payment of principal and interest on indebtedness incurred for maintenance or improvement of the water system during periods of normal use and periods of reduced water use due to implementation of water conservation measures. The funding agency shall apply guidelines developed by the State Water Infrastructure Authority in determining the adequacy of the water rate structure to support operation and maintenance of the system.

(2)   Has implemented a leak detection and repair program.

(3)   Has an approved water supply plan pursuant to G.S. 143-355.

(4)   Meters all water use except for water use that is impractical to meter, including, but not limited to, use of water for firefighting and to flush waterlines.

(5)   Does not use a rate structure that gives residential water customers a lower per-unit water rate as water use increases.

(6)   Has evaluated the extent to which the future water needs of the water system can be met by reclaimed water.

(7)   Has implemented a consumer education program that emphasizes the importance of water conservation and that includes information on measures that residential customers may implement to reduce water consumption. (2008-143, s. 9; 2010-142, s. 13; 2010-180, s. 16; 2011-374, s. 3.2; 2013-360, s. 14.21(l).)

§ 143-355.5. Water reuse; policy; rule making.

(a)   Water Reuse Policy. - It is the public policy of the State that the reuse of treated wastewater or reclaimed water and the use of gray water or captured rain water is critical to meeting the existing and future water supply needs of the State. The General Assembly finds that reclaimed water systems permitted and operated under G.S. 143-215.1(d2) in an approved wastewater reuse program can provide water for many beneficial purposes in a way that is both environmentally acceptable and protective of public health. This finding includes and applies to conjunctive facilities that require the relocation of a discharge from one receiving stream to another under all of the following conditions:

(1)   The relocation is necessary to create an approved comprehensive wastewater reuse program.

(2)   The reuse program provides significant reuse benefits.

(3)   The relocated discharge will comply with all applicable water quality standards; will not result in degradation of water quality in the receiving waters; will not contribute to water quality impairment in the receiving watershed; and will result in net benefits to water quality, such as the elimination of a wastewater discharge in a nutrient sensitive river basin.

(b)   Water Reuse Rule Making. - The Commission shall encourage and promote safe and beneficial reuse of treated wastewater as an alternative to surface water discharge. The Commission shall adopt rules to:

(1)   Identify acceptable uses of reclaimed water, including toilet flushing, fire protection, decorative water features, and landscape irrigation.

(2)   Facilitate the permitting of reclaimed water systems.

(3)   Establish standards for reclaimed water systems that are adequate to prevent the direct distribution of reclaimed water as potable water.

(c)   Gray Water Rule Making. - The Commission shall encourage and promote the safe and beneficial use of gray water. The Commission shall adopt rules to:

(1)   Identify acceptable uses of gray water, including toilet flushing, fire protection, decorative water features, and landscape irrigation.

(2)   Facilitate the permitting of gray water systems.

(3)   Establish standards, in coordination with the Commission for Public Health, for gray water systems that protect public health and safety and the environment and reduce the use of potable water within individual structures.

(d)   The Department shall develop policies and procedures to promote the voluntary adoption and installation of gray water systems. (2008-143, s. 10; 2010-155, s. 6; 2011-394, s. 12(b).)

§ 143-355.6. Enforcement.

(a)   The Secretary may assess a civil penalty of not less than one hundred dollars ($100.00) nor more than five hundred dollars ($500.00) against any person who:

(1)   Fails to report water use or other information required under G.S. 143-355(k).

(2)   Fails to act in accordance with the terms, conditions, or requirements of an order issued by the Secretary under G.S. 143-355.3.

(3)   Violates any provision of this Article or any rule adopted by the Commission, the Department, or the Secretary implementing this Article.

(b)   For each willful action or failure to act for which a penalty may be assessed under this section, the Secretary may consider each day the action or inaction continues after notice is given of the violation as a separate violation. A separate penalty may be assessed for each separate violation.

(c)   The Secretary may assess a civil penalty of not more than ten thousand dollars ($10,000) per month against a unit of local government that provides public water service or a large community water system that fails to implement the water conservation measures set out in the water shortage response plan approved by the Department under G.S. 143-355.2, measures required by the Department under subsections (b) and (d) of G.S. 143-355.2, or the default measures required under rules adopted by the Commission under S.L. 2002-167.

(c1)   The amount of the civil penalty shall be based on the factors set out in G.S. 143B-282.1(b). The procedures set out in G.S. 143B-282.1 shall apply to civil penalty assessments that are presented to the Commission for final agency decision.

(c2)   Requests for remission of civil penalties shall be filed with the Secretary. Remission requests shall not be considered unless made within 30 days of receipt of the notice of assessment. Remission requests must be accompanied by a waiver of the right to a contested case hearing pursuant to Chapter 150B of the General Statutes and a stipulation of the facts on which the assessment was based. Consistent with the limitations in G.S. 143B-282.1(c) and (d), remission requests may be resolved by the Secretary and the violator. If the Secretary and the violator are unable to resolve the request, the Secretary shall deliver remission requests and the Secretary's recommended action to the Committee on Civil Penalty Remissions of the Commission appointed pursuant to G.S. 143B-282.1(c).

(c3)   If any civil penalty has not been paid within 30 days after the notice of assessment has been served on the violator, the Secretary shall request the Attorney General to institute a civil action in the superior court of any county in which the violator resides or in which the violator's principal place of business is located to recover the amount of the assessment, unless the violator contests the assessment as provided in subsection (e) of this section, or requests remission of the assessment in whole or in part as provided in subsection (c2) of this section. If any civil penalty has not been paid within 30 days after the final agency decision or court order has been served on the violator, the Secretary shall request the Attorney General to institute a civil action in the superior court of any county in which the violator resides or in which the violator's principal place of business is located to recover the amount of the assessment.

(d)   The violation of emergency water conservation rules adopted by the Secretary pursuant to G.S. 143-355.3(b) is a Class 1 misdemeanor.

(e)   The Secretary shall notify any person assessed a civil penalty of the assessment and the specific reasons for the assessment by registered or certified mail or by any means authorized by G.S. 1A-1, Rule 4. Contested case petitions shall be filed within 30 days of receipt of the notice of assessment.

(f)   The clear proceeds of civil penalties assessed pursuant to this section shall be remitted to the Civil Penalty and Forfeiture Fund in accordance with G.S. 115C-457.2. (2008-143, s. 11; 2010-180, s. 9.)

§ 143-355.7. Water supply development; State-local cooperation.

(a)   At the request of one or more units of local government, the Department may assist the local government in identifying the preferred water supply alternative that alone or in combination with other water sources will provide for the long-term water supply needs documented in the local water supply plan and meet all of the following criteria:

(1)   Are economically and practically feasible.

(2)   Make maximum, practical beneficial use of reclaimed wastewater and stormwater.

(3)   Comply with water quality classifications and standards.

(4)   Avoid or mitigate impacts to threatened or endangered species to the extent such species are protected by State or federal law.

(5)   Maintain downstream flows necessary to protect downstream users.

(6)   Do not have significant adverse impacts on other water withdrawals or wastewater discharges.

(7)   Avoid or mitigate water quality impacts consistent with the requirements of rules adopted by the Environmental Management Commission to implement 33 U.S.C. § 1341.

(b)   During the alternatives analysis, the Department shall request relevant information regarding the potential alternatives, including the establishment or expansion of the water supply reservoir or other water supply resources, from other State agencies with jurisdiction over any natural resources that will be impacted under the alternatives identified by the Department. Unless the local government agrees to an extension of time, the Department shall determine the preferred alternative within two years of the execution of a contract with the requesting local government for the costs of the analysis. The determination of the preferred alternative shall be binding on all State agencies unless the Department determines from its further evaluation during its review of any State or federal permit applications for the project that another preferred alternative should be selected in light of additional information brought forward during the permit reviews.

(c)   If the Department provides an analysis of practicable alternatives for meeting a water supply need under this section, the analysis shall be accepted by the Department and the Department of Administration for purposes of satisfying the requirements of the North Carolina Environmental Policy Act and any State permit or authorization that requires identification and assessment of alternatives, including, but not limited to, a request for an interbasin transfer pursuant to G.S. 143-215.22L.

(d)   The Department may provide technical assistance to a unit of local government in obtaining federal permits for the preferred water supply alternative identified pursuant to subsection (a) of this section. For purposes of providing technical assistance and conducting studies in support of a proposed water supply project under this section, the Department may enter into an agreement with one or more units of local government to conduct studies or modeling. The agreement shall specify the allocation of costs for any studies or modeling prepared by the Department in support of the project.

(e)   When the Department has identified the most practicable alternative, a regional water supply system may request that the Department become a co-applicant for all required federal approvals for the alternative identified by the Department. The Department may become a co-applicant when all of the following conditions are met:

(1)   The regional water supply system has acquired or will acquire the property necessary for construction of the water supply reservoir or other water supply resource.

(2)   The local water supply plan shows that the regional water supply system has implemented appropriate conservation measures similar in effect to the measures in comparably sized North Carolina regional water supply systems.

(3)   The regional water supply system has developed and is implementing measures to replace existing leaking infrastructure that is similar in effect to the measures being implemented by comparably sized North Carolina regional water systems.

(4)   The regional water supply system has entered into a contractual agreement to pay the expenses incurred by the Department as a co-applicant for the project approval.

(f)   Nothing in this section shall be construed to limit the authority of the Department to require environmental permits or to apply and enforce environmental standards pursuant to State law. (2011-374, s. 1.2.)

§ 143-355.8. Regional water supply planning organizations.

(a)   One or more water systems may establish a water supply planning organization to plan for and coordinate water resource supply and demand on a regional basis. A water supply planning organization may include representatives of local government water systems, water authorities, nongovernmental water systems, and registered water withdrawers.

(b)   A regional water supply planning organization may do any of the following:

(1)   Identify sources of raw water supply for regional systems.

(2)   Identify areas suitable for the development of new regional water sources.

(3)   Identify opportunities for purchase and sale of water between water systems to meet regional water supply needs.

(4)   Prepare joint water supply plans.

(5)   Enter into agreements with the Department for technical assistance in identifying practical alternatives to meet regional water supply needs pursuant to G.S. 143-355.7 or to provide studies in support of a proposed regional water supply project.

(6)   Support cooperative arrangements between water systems for purchase and sale of water by providing technical assistance and voluntary mediation of disputes concerning water supply.

(c)   Nothing in this section shall be construed to alter the requirements for obtaining a certificate for an interbasin transfer. (2011-374, s. 1.2.)

§§ 143-356 through 143-357: Repealed by Session Laws 1983, c. 222, ss. 1, 2.

§ 143-358. Cooperation of State officials and agencies.

All State agencies and officials shall cooperate with and assist the Commission in enforcing and carrying out the provisions of this Article and rules adopted by the Commission under this Article. (1959, c. 779, s. 6; 1973, c. 1262, s. 23; 1991, c. 342, s. 15(b); 1991 (Reg. Sess., 1992), c. 890, s. 19.)

§ 143-359: Repealed by Session Laws 2001-452, s. 1.1.

Article 39.

U.S.S. North Carolina Battleship Commission.

§§ 143-360 through 143-362: Repealed by Session Laws 1977, c. 741, s. 5.

§§ 143-363 through 143-365. Repealed by Session Laws 1973, c. 476, s. 59.

§ 143-366. Recodified as § 143B-73.1 by Session Laws 1977, c. 741, s. 8.

§§ 143-367 through 143-369. Recodified as §§ 143B-74.1 to 143B-74.3 by Session Laws 1977, c. 741, s. 8.

Article 39A.

Frying Pan Lightship Marine Museum Commission.

§§ 143-369.1 through 143-369.3: Repealed by Session Laws 1973, c. 476, s. 116.

Article 40.

Advisory Commission for State Museum of Natural History.

§§ 143-370 through 143-373: Recodified as §§ 143B-344.18 through 143B-344.21 by Session Laws 1993, c. 561, s. 116.

Article 41.

Science and Technology Research Center.

§§ 143-374 through 143-377: Recodified as §§ 143B-442 through 143B-445 by Session Laws 1977, c. 198, s. 26.

Article 42.

Board of Science and Technology.

§§ 143-378 through 143-383: Repealed by Session Laws 1973, c. 1262, s. 79.

Article 43.

North Carolina Seashore Commission.

§§ 143-384 through 143-391: Repealed by Session Laws 1969, c. 1143, s. 1.

Article 44.

North Carolina Traffic Safety Authority.

§§ 143-392 through 143-395: Repealed by Session Laws 1981, c. 90, s. 1.

Article 45.

North Carolina American Revolution Bicentennial Commission.

§§ 143-396 through 143-399: Repealed by Session Laws 1973, c. 476, s. 70.

Article 46.

Governor's Committee on Law and Order.

§§ 143-400 through 143-402.2: Repealed by Session Laws 1969, c. 1145, s. 4.

Article 47.

Promotion of Arts.

§ 143-403. "Arts" defined.

The term "arts" includes, but is not limited to: music, dance, drama, creative writing, architecture and allied fields, painting, sculpture, photography, crafts, television, radio, and the execution and exhibition of such major art forms. (1967, c. 164, s. 1; 1973, c. 476, s. 79.)

§§ 143-404 through 143-405. Repealed by Session Laws 1973, c. 476, s. 79.

§ 143-406. Duties of Department of Cultural Resources.

The Department of Cultural Resources shall take action to carry out the following purposes as funds and staff permit:

(1)   Study, collect, maintain, and otherwise disseminate factual data and pertinent information relative to the arts;

(2)   Assist local organizations and the community at large with needs, resources and opportunities in the arts;

(3)   Serve as an agency through which various public and nonpublic organizations concerned with the arts can exchange information, coordinate programs and stimulate joint endeavors;

(4)   Identify research needs, encourage research and assist in obtaining funds for research;

(5)   Assist in bringing the highest obtainable quality in the arts to the State; promote the maximum opportunity for the people to experience, enjoy, and profit from those arts.

The Department of Cultural Resources shall, in addition to such other recommendations, studies and plans as it may submit from time to time, submit a biennial report of progress to the Governor, and thus, to the General Assembly. (1967, c. 164, s. 4; 1973, c. 476, s. 79.)

§ 143-407. Appropriations; funds.

In addition to the appropriations out of the general fund of the State, the Department may accept gifts, devises, matching funds, or other considerations for use in promoting the arts. (1967, c. 164, s. 5; 1973, c. 476, s. 79; 2011-284, s. 93.)

§ 143-407.1. Composer laureate.

(a)   The Governor of North Carolina may appoint a distinguished living composer as "Composer-Laureate for the State of North Carolina."

(b)   Any person appointed "Composer-Laureate for the State of North Carolina" shall be appointed for life but may voluntarily resign at any time. (1991, c. 56, ss. 1, 2.)

§ 143-408: Repealed by Session Laws 1973, c. 476, s. 79.

Article 47A.

Art Works in State Buildings.

§§ 143-408.1 through 143-408.7: Repealed by Session Laws 1995, c. 324, s. 12.2.

Article 48.

Executive Mansion.

§ 143-409: Repealed by Session Laws 1973, c. 476, s. 67.

§ 143-410. Purpose.

The purpose of the Department of Cultural Resources shall be:

(1)   To preserve and maintain the Executive Mansion, located at 200 North Blount Street, Raleigh, North Carolina, as a structure having historical significance and value to the State of North Carolina;

(2)   To improve the furnishing of the Executive Mansion by encouraging gifts and objects of art, furniture and articles which may have historical value, and to approve major changes in the furnishings of the Mansion;

(3)   To recommend to the Department of Administration any major renovations to the Executive Mansion which the Department of Cultural Resources deems necessary to preserve and maintain the structure;

(4)   To keep a complete list of all gifts and articles received, together with their history and value; and

(5)   To publicize work of the Executive Mansion Fine Arts Committee. (1967, c. 273, s. 2; 1973, c. 476, s. 67.)

§ 143-411. Powers of Department of Cultural Resources.

The Department of Cultural Resources is hereby empowered on behalf of the State of North Carolina to receive gifts, contributions of money and objects of art consistent with the purpose for which the Department is created. Title to all gifts, articles and moneys received by the Department shall be vested in the State of North Carolina and shall remain in the custody and control of the Department. The Department is authorized to accept loans of furniture and other objects as, in its discretion, it deems suitable. The Department is empowered to employ clerical assistance on such basis as it may deem reasonable. Provided, however, that the salary of such person shall be paid out of funds the Department has received in the conduct of its work, and it is specifically provided that no other funds belonging to the State of North Carolina shall be used for this purpose. (1967, c. 273, s. 3; 1973, c. 476, s. 67.)

§§ 143-412 through 143-414. Repealed by Session Laws 1973, c. 476, s. 67.

§ 143-415. Authority, etc., of Department of Administration not affected.

This Article shall not be construed as divesting the Department of Administration of any powers, duties and authority relating to the budget or the operation and maintenance of the Executive Mansion. (1967, c. 273, s. 7.)

Article 49.

North Carolina Human Relations Commission.

§§ 143-416 through 143-422. Repealed by Session Laws 1975, c. 879, s. 36.

Article 49A.

Equal Employment Practices.

§ 143-422.1. Short title.

This Article shall be known and may be cited as the Equal Employment Practices Act. (1977, c. 726, s. 1.)

§ 143-422.2. Legislative declaration.

It is the public policy of this State to protect and safeguard the right and opportunity of all persons to seek, obtain and hold employment without discrimination or abridgement on account of race, religion, color, national origin, age, sex or handicap by employers which regularly employ 15 or more employees.

It is recognized that the practice of denying employment opportunity and discriminating in the terms of employment foments domestic strife and unrest, deprives the State of the fullest utilization of its capacities for advancement and development, and substantially and adversely affects the interests of employees, employers, and the public in general. (1977, c. 726, s. 1.)

§ 143-422.3. Investigations; conciliations.

The Human Relations Commission in the Department of Administration shall have the authority to receive charges of discrimination from the Equal Employment Opportunity Commission pursuant to an agreement under Section 709(b) of Public Law 88-352, as amended by Public Law 92-261, and investigate and conciliate charges of discrimination. Throughout this process, the agency shall use its good offices to effect an amicable resolution of the charges of discrimination. (1977, c. 726, s. 1; 1989 (Reg. Sess., 1990), c. 979, ss. 1(5), 2.)

Article 50.

Commission on the Status of Women.

§§ 143-423 through 143-428. Repealed by Session Laws 1975, c. 879, s. 39.

Article 51.

Tobacco Museums.

§§ 143-429 through 143-430. Repealed by Session Laws 1973, c. 476, s. 116.

§ 143-431. Tobacco museums.

It shall be the duty of the Department of Cultural Resources to establish, supervise, manage and maintain the tobacco museums. The Department of Cultural Resources may establish a reasonable fee for viewing the museums which fees shall be used to defray the expenses of the museums. To accomplish these purposes, the Department of Cultural Resources shall have authority to buy and sell real and personal property and to accept donations of real or personal property from any source. The Department of Cultural Resources shall not contract any debt in its purchase of real or personal property. (1969, c. 840, s. 3; 1973, c. 476, s. 116.)

§ 143-432. Location of museums.

One of the tobacco museums shall be located within Rockingham County at a site to be determined by the Department of Cultural Resources, and shall emphasize the history and development of tobacco manufacturing. One of the tobacco museums shall be located in Nash or Edgecombe Counties at a site to be determined by the Department of Cultural Resources and shall emphasize the history and development of growing and marketing of tobacco. (1969, c. 840, s. 4; 1973, c. 476, s. 116.)

Article 51A.

Tax Study Commission.

§§ 143-433 through 143-433.5: Repealed by Session Laws 1979, c. 14, s. 1.

Article 51B.

North Carolina Federal Tax Reform Allocation Committee.

§ 143-433.6. Legislative findings.

(a)   The General Assembly finds and determines that the Tax Reform Act of 1984 established a federal volume limitation upon the aggregate amount of "private activity bonds" that may be issued by each state; that, pursuant to Section 103(n) of the Internal Revenue Code of 1954, as amended, a previous Governor of North Carolina issued Executive Order 113 proclaiming a formula for allocating the federal volume limitation for North Carolina; that on October 22, 1986, the Tax Reform Act of 1986, hereinafter referred to as the "Tax Reform Act", was enacted; that the Tax Reform Act (i) establishes a new unified limitation for private activity bonds on a state by state basis, (ii) establishes a new definition of the types of private activity bonds to be included under those new limitations, (iii) establishes a new low-income housing credit to induce the construction of and the improvement of housing for low-income people, and (iv) limits the aggregate use of this low-income housing credit on a state by state basis; that the Tax Reform Act provides for federal formulas for the allocation of these "state by state" resources, and also provides for states which cannot use the federal formula for allocation to set allocation procedures and formulas which are more appropriate for the individual states; that the Tax Reform Act gives authority for the legislature of each state to formulate and execute plans for allocation; and that Section 146 of the Internal Revenue Code of 1986, as amended, and Section 42 of the Internal Revenue Code of 1986, as amended, will require continued inquiry and study in the ways in which North Carolina can best and most fairly manage and utilize resources provided therein.

(b)   The General Assembly further finds and determines that the Economic Growth and Tax Relief Reconciliation Act of 2001 added new subsections (a)(13) and (k) to section 142 of the Internal Revenue Code of 1986, as amended, which (i) establish a new type of private activity bond that can be issued to finance "qualified public educational facilities," (ii) establish an annual aggregate limitation on the face amount of qualified public educational facility bonds that may be issued on a state-by-state basis, (iii) provide that each state may allocate the annual aggregate limitation for any calendar year in such manner as each state determines appropriate, and (iv) provide for an elective carryforward by each state of the unused annual aggregate limitation; and that subsections (a)(13) and (k) will require continued inquiry and study in the ways

62

in which North Carolina can best and most fairly manage and utilize the resource provided therein.

(c)   The General Assembly further finds and determines that section 1400U-3 of the American Recovery and Reinvestment Tax Act of 2009 (ARRTA) added a new type of exempt facility bond called "recovery zone facility bonds" to be used to finance construction, renovation, and equipping of recovery zone property for use in any trade or business in a recovery zone, all as defined in ARRTA, and a new type of governmental bond called "recovery zone economic development bonds." The ARRTA provides a formula for allocation of authority to issue recovery zone facility bonds and recovery zone economic development bonds to the states and by which the authority is to be reallocated by the State to counties and large municipalities within the State.

(d)   The General Assembly further finds and determines that section 54D of the Internal Revenue Code of 1986, as amended, permits the issuance of tax credit bonds called "qualified energy conservation bonds" (QECBs), the proceeds of which must be used for certain energy conservation purposes enumerated in section 54D. Section 54D and ARRTA provide a national bond limitation for the issuance of QECBs, and the Treasury Department has allocated that authority among the states. Under section 54D, the United States is required to reallocate the authority to issue QECBs to the counties and large local governments within the states based on population, in accordance with the guidelines provided by the Treasury Department, and to assure that not more than thirty percent (30%) of the QECBs issued in a state are used for private activity bonds, as defined in section 54D. (1987, c. 588, s. 1; 2008-204, s. 6.1; 2009-140, s. 2.)

§ 143-433.7. North Carolina Federal Tax Reform Allocation Committee.

The North Carolina Federal Tax Reform Allocation Committee, hereinafter referred to as the "Committee", is hereby established. The Committee is a continuation of the Interim Private Activity Bond Allocation Committee established under Executive Order 28 and amended under Executive Order 31 and the North Carolina Federal Tax Reform Allocation Committee established under Executive Order 37. The Secretary of the Department of Commerce, the Executive Assistant to the Governor for Budget Management, and the Treasurer of the State of North Carolina shall constitute the membership of this Committee. The Secretary of the Department of Commerce shall serve as Chairman of the Committee. (1987, c. 588, s. 2.)

§ 143-433.8. Duties.

The Committee shall perform the following duties:

(1)   Manage the allocation of private activity bonds, low-income housing credits, qualified public educational facility bonds, recovery zone facility bonds, recovery zone economic development bonds, and qualified energy conservation bonds and receive advice from bond issuers, elected officials, and the General Assembly.

(2)   Continue to monitor bond markets, economic development financing trends, school financing trends, housing markets, and tax incentives available to induce events and programs favorable to North Carolina, its cities and counties, and individual citizens.

(3)   Continue to study the ways in which North Carolina can best and most fairly manage and utilize the allocation of private activity bonds, low-income housing credits, qualified public educational facility bonds, recovery zone facility bonds, recovery zone economic development bonds, and qualified energy conservation bonds.

(4)   Report to the Governor, Lieutenant Governor, the Speaker of the House of Representatives, the President Pro Tempore of the Senate, and the Revenue Laws Study Committee as requested and on not less than an annual basis. The annual report is due by November 1 of each year. (1987, c. 588, s. 3; 2008-204, s. 6.2; 2009-140, s. 3.)

§ 143-433.9. Allocation.

(a)   To provide for the orderly and prompt issuance of bonds the allocation of which is managed under this Article, the Committee must follow formulas for allocating the following: (i) the unified volume limitation, (ii) the state housing credit ceiling, (iii) the annual aggregate limitation on the face amount of qualified public educational facility bonds, (iv) the limitation on issuance of recovery zone facility bonds, (v) the limitation on issuance of recovery zone economic development bonds, and (vi) the limitation on issuance of qualified energy conservation bonds. The unified volume limitation for all issues of private activity bonds, other than qualified public educational facility bonds and recovery zone facility bonds, in North Carolina shall be considered as a single resource to be allocated under this Article. The annual aggregate limitation on the face amount of qualified public educational facility bonds for all issues in North Carolina shall be considered as a single resource to be allocated under this Article. The Committee shall issue the following: (i) allocations of the unified volume limitation, (ii) allocations of the state housing credit ceiling, (iii) allocations and reallocations of the aggregate limitation on the face amount of qualified public educational facility bonds, (iv) allocation and reallocation of the authority for issuance of recovery zone facility bonds allocated to the State, (v) allocation and reallocation of the authority for issuance of recovery zone economic development bonds allocated to the State, (vi) allocation and reallocation of authority for issuance of qualified energy conservation bonds allocated to the State, and (vii) allocation of other limitations on authority to issue bonds as may be directed by the Governor. The Committee shall set forth procedures for making such allocations and in the making of such allocations shall take into consideration the best interest of the State of North Carolina with regard to the economic development, school facility needs, energy conservation, green initiatives, and general prosperity of the people of North Carolina. In making the initial allocations for recovery zone facility bonds and recovery zone economic development bonds, the Committee shall follow the formula provided in section 1400U-1(a)(3) of ARRTA. In making the initial allocation for qualified energy conservation bonds, the Committee shall follow the guidelines provided in section 54D of the Internal Revenue Code of 1986. The Committee shall make all elective carryforwards of the unused unified volume limitation, the annual aggregate limitation on the face amount of qualified public educational facility bonds, recovery zone facility bonds, qualified energy conservation bonds, and any other bonds or tax credits over which it has allocation authority on behalf of the State. The Committee shall monitor the issuance of qualified energy conservation bonds to ensure that not more than thirty percent (30%) of such bonds are used for purposes that would be treated as private activity bonds under the Internal Revenue Code of 1986, as amended. The Committee is authorized to establish a procedure to monitor whether the initial allocations of recovery zone facility bonds or recovery zone economic development bonds to counties and large municipalities pursuant to ARRTA will be utilized, for an allocation that will not be utilized to be waived by notice to the Committee, and

65

for the reallocation of the waived allocation to other projects that qualify pursuant to ARRTA.

(b)   In administering the low-income housing credit program, the Committee shall adopt a Qualified Allocation Plan (the Plan) as required by 26 U.S.C. § 42(m) annually. Solely with respect to the adoption of the Plan, the Committee is exempt from the requirements of Article 2A of Chapter 150B of the General Statutes. Prior to adoption or amendment of the Plan, the Committee shall:

(1)   Publish the proposed Plan in the North Carolina Register at least 30 days prior to the adoption of the final Plan;

(2)   Notify any person who has applied for the low-income housing credit in the previous year and any other interested parties of its intent to adopt the Plan;

(3)   Accept oral and written comments on the proposed Plan; and

(4)   Hold at least one public hearing on the proposed Plan. (1987, c. 588, s. 4; 2001-299, s. 1.1; 2008-204, s. 6.3; 2009-140, s. 4.)

Article 52.

Pesticide Board.

Part 1. Pesticide Control Program: Organization and Functions.

§ 143-434. Short title.

This Article may be cited as the North Carolina Pesticide Law of 1971. (1971, c. 832, s. 1.)

§ 143-435. Preamble.

(a)   The Legislative Research Commission was directed by House Resolution 1392 of the 1969 General Assembly "to study agricultural and other pesticides," and to report its findings and recommendations to the 1971 General Assembly. Pursuant to said Resolution a report was prepared and adopted by the Legislative Research Commission in 1970 concerning pesticides. In this report the Legislative Research Commission made the following findings concerning the use and effects of pesticides and the need for legislation concerning control of pesticide use, of which the General Assembly hereby takes cognizance:

(1)   The use of chemical pesticides has developed since the 1940's into a major, new billion-dollar industry. Pesticides have bettered the lot of mankind in many ways and especially have assisted the farmer by their contribution to a stable and inexpensive supply of high quality food, fiber and forest products. The control of insects, fungi and other pests is essential to the public health and welfare and specifically to the prevention of disease, to the production and preservation of food, fiber, and forests and to the protection of other aspects of modern civilization.

(2)   The use of pesticides for these important purposes is currently a matter of serious public concern and their use in some instances presents risks to man and the environment which must be weighed against the benefits of those uses in the overall public interest. Evidence is accumulating that extensive use of persistent pesticides poses hazards to health and the environment. Environmental problems resulting from the use, overuse and misapplication of some chemicals, and the disposal of unused chemicals and containers, have grown to the point where contamination of the environment is approaching significant proportions. There is concern among scientists and public health personnel about the long-term chronic effects of pesticide pollution on human health. Contamination by DDT has been shown to be global in extent. Moreover, recent experience in North Carolina and elsewhere has shown that the more toxic but less persistent pesticides cannot safely be substituted for the persistent "hard" pesticides without stringent safeguards.

(3)   More extensive observation, study and monitoring of the effectiveness and the use of pesticides and of undesirable side effects on man and on the environment and of their relative importance for the overall public health and welfare are desirable in the public interest.

(4)   Continued and strengthened control of the quality of pesticides and the control of labeling claims, direction for use and warnings are necessary for the protection of the purchasing public, including the household consumer, the farmer and other users.

(5)   No existing legislation in North Carolina effectively limits or controls the use of pesticides. Misuse and misapplication of pesticides, while effectively controlled by law with respect to structural pest control operators, is not adequately controlled with respect to some other major groups of pesticide applicators. Careless disposal of unused pesticides and contaminated containers is not controlled by law, and no North Carolina legislation requires that pesticide dealers, who are the principal source of advice for many pesticide users, be qualified to give advice or be held responsible for their advice. These gaps in legal control of pesticides are important and should be remedied.

(b)   The purpose of this Article is to regulate in the public interest the use, application, sale, disposal and registration of insecticides, fungicides, herbicides, defoliants, desiccants, plant growth regulators, nematicides, rodenticides, and any other pesticides designated by the North Carolina Pesticide Board. New pesticides are continually being discovered or synthesized which are valuable for the control of insects, fungi, weeds, nematodes, rodents, and for use as defoliants, desiccants, plant regulators and related purposes. However, such pesticides may be ineffective or may seriously injure health, property, or wildlife if not properly used. Pesticides may injure man or animals, either by direct poisoning or by gradual accumulation of poisons in the tissues. Crops or other plants may also be injured by their improper use. The drifting or washing of pesticides into streams or lakes can cause appreciable danger to aquatic life. A pesticide applied for the purpose of killing pests in a crop, which is not itself injured by the pesticide, may drift and injure other crops or nontarget organisms with which it comes in contact. In furtherance of the findings and recommendations of the Legislative Research Commission, it is hereby declared to be the policy of the State of North Carolina that for the protection of the health, safety, and welfare of the people of this State, and for the promotion of a more secure, healthy and safe environment for all the people of the State, the future sale, use and application of pesticides shall be regulated, supervised and controlled by the State in the manner herein provided. (1971, c. 832, s. 1.)

§ 143-436. North Carolina Pesticide Board; creation and organization.

(a)   There is hereby established the North Carolina Pesticide Board which, together with the Commissioner of Agriculture, shall be responsible for carrying out the provisions of this Article.

(b)   The Pesticide Board shall consist of seven members, to be appointed by the Governor, as follows:

(1)   One member each representing the North Carolina Department of Agriculture and Consumer Services, the State Health Director or his designee, and one member from an environmental protection agency in the Department of Environment and Natural Resources. The persons so selected may be either members of a policy board or departmental officials or employees.

(2)   A representative of the agricultural chemical industry.

(3)   A person directly engaged in agricultural production.

(4)   Two at-large members, from fields of endeavor other than those enumerated in subdivisions (2) and (3) of this subsection, one of whom shall be a nongovernmental conservationist.

(c)   The members of the Pesticide Board shall serve staggered four-year terms. Of the persons originally appointed, the members representing State agencies shall serve two-year terms, and the four at-large members shall serve four-year terms. All members shall hold their offices until their successors are appointed and qualified. Any vacancy occurring in the membership of the Board prior to the expiration of the term shall be filled by appointment by the Governor for the remainder of the unexpired term. The Governor may at any time remove any member from the Board for gross inefficiency, neglect of duty, malfeasance, misfeasance, or nonfeasance in office. Each appointment to fill a vacancy in the membership of the Board shall be of a person having the same credentials as his predecessor.

(d)   The Board shall select its chair from its own membership, to serve for a term of two years. The chair shall have a full vote. Any vacancy occurring in the chair's position shall be filled by the Board for the remainder of the term. The Board may select such other officers as it deems necessary.

(e)   Any action of the Board shall require at least four concurring votes.

(f)   The members of the Board who are not officers or employees of the State shall receive for their services the per diem and compensation prescribed in G.S. 138-5. (1971, c. 832, s. 1; 1973, c. 476, s. 128; 1989, c. 727, s. 170; 1997-261, s. 90; 1997-443, s. 11A.97.)

§ 143-437. Pesticide Board; functions.

The Pesticide Board shall be the governing board for the programs of pesticide management and control set forth in this Article. The Pesticide Board shall have the following powers and duties under this Article:

(1)   To adopt rules and regulations and make policies for the programs set forth in this Article.

(2)   To carry out a program of planning, environmental and biological monitoring, and of investigation into long-range needs and problems concerning pesticides. In order to encourage the cooperation of private property owners needed to implement the provisions of this subdivision, the Board may enter into agreements with private property owners to conduct sampling, testing, monitoring, and related activities on their property. Information obtained pursuant to these agreements shall not be disclosed in a manner that would permit the identification of an individual property owner unless the property owner has given permission to disclose the information.

(3)   To collect, analyze and disseminate information necessary for the effective operation of the programs set forth in this Article.

(4)   To provide professional advice to public and private agencies and citizens of the State on matters relating to pesticides, in cooperation with other State agencies, with professional groups, and with North Carolina State University and other educational institutions.

(5)   To accept gifts and devises, and with the approval of the Governor to apply for and accept grants from the federal government and its agencies and from any foundation, corporation, association or individual, and may comply with the terms, conditions and limitations of the grant, in order to accomplish any of the purposes of the Board, such grant funds to be expended pursuant to the Executive Budget Act.

(6)   To inform and advise the Governor on matters involving pesticides, and to prepare and recommend to the Governor and the General Assembly any legislation which may be deemed proper for the management and control of pesticides in North Carolina.

(7)　　To make annual reports to the Governor and to make such other investigations and reports as may be requested by the Governor or the General Assembly.

(8)　　To exempt any federal or State agency from any provision of this Article if it is determined by the Board that emergency conditions exist which require exemption. (1971, c. 832, s. 1; 1977, c. 199; 1979, c. 448, s. 14; 1995, c. 445, s. 1; 2011-284, s. 94.)

§ 143-438. Commissioner of Agriculture to administer and enforce Article.

The Commissioner of Agriculture shall have the following powers and duties under this Article:

(1)　　To administer and enforce the provisions of this Article.

(2)　　To attend all meetings of the Pesticide Board, but without power to vote (unless he be designated as the ex officio member of the Board from the Department of Agriculture and Consumer Services).

(3)　　To keep an accurate and complete record of all Board meetings and hearings, and to have legal custody of all books, papers, documents and other records of the Board.

(4)　　To assign and reassign the administrative and enforcement duties and functions assigned to him in this Article to one or more of the divisions and other units within the Department of Agriculture and Consumer Services.

(5)　　To direct the work of the personnel employed by the Board and of the personnel of the Department of Agriculture and Consumer Services who have responsibilities concerning the programs set forth in this Article.

(6)　　To delegate to any division head or other officer or employee of the Department of Agriculture and Consumer Services any of the powers and duties given to the Department by statute or by the rules, regulations and procedures established pursuant to this Article.

(7)　　To perform such other duties as the Board may from time to time direct. (1971, c. 832, s. 1; 1997-261, s. 91.)

71

§ 143-439. Pesticide Advisory Committee; creation and functions.

(a)   There is hereby authorized the establishment of the Pesticide Advisory Committee, which shall assist the Board and the Commissioner in an advisory capacity on matters which may be submitted to it by the Board or the Commissioner, including technical questions and the development of rules and regulations.

(b)   The Pesticide Advisory Committee shall consist of: three practicing farmers; one conservationist (at large); one ecologist (at large); one representative of the pesticide industry; one representative of agribusiness (at large); one local health director; three members of the North Carolina State University School of Agriculture and Life Sciences, at least one of which shall be from the area of wildlife or biology; one member representing the North Carolina Department of Agriculture and Consumer Services; one member representing the Department of Environment and Natural Resources; the State Health Director or his designee; one representative of a public utility or railroad company which uses pesticides; one representative of the Board of Transportation; one member of the North Carolina Agricultural Aviation Association; one member of the general public (at large); one member actively engaged in forest pest management; and one member representing the Division of Waste Management of the Department of Environment and Natural Resources. Each State agency represented [representative] on the Committee shall be appointed by the head of the agency. Other members of the Committee shall be appointed by the Board.

(c)   Members of the Pesticide Advisory Committee shall serve at the pleasure of the Board. The members who are not officers or employees of the State shall receive regular State subsistence and travel expenses. (1971, c. 832, s. 1; 1973, c. 476, s. 128; c. 507, s. 5; 1975, c. 824; 1987, c. 559, s. 1; 1989, c. 727, s. 171; 1989 (Reg. Sess., 1990), c. 1004, s. 14; 1995 (Reg. Sess., 1996), c. 743, s. 19; 1997-261, s. 109; 1997-443, s. 11A.119(a).)

Part 2. Regulation of the Use of Pesticides.

§ 143-440. Restricted use pesticides regulated.

(a)   The Board may, by regulation after a public hearing, adopt and from time to time revise a list of restricted use pesticides for the State or for designated areas within the State. The Board may designate any pesticide or device as a "restricted use pesticide" upon the grounds that, in the judgment of the Board (either because of its persistence, its toxicity, or otherwise) it is so hazardous or injurious to persons, pollinating insects, animals, crops, wildlife, lands, or the environment, other than the pests it is intended to prevent, destroy, control, or mitigate that additional restriction on its sale, purpose, use or possession are required.

(b)   The Board may include in any such restricted use regulation the time and conditions of sale, distribution, or use of such restricted use pesticides, may prohibit the use of any restricted use pesticide for designated purposes or at designated times; may require the purchaser or user to certify that restricted use pesticides will be used only as labeled or as further restricted by regulation; may require the certification and recertification of private applicators, and charge a fee of up to ten dollars ($10.00), with the fee set at a level to make the certification/recertification program self-supporting, and, after opportunity for a hearing, may suspend, revoke or modify the certification for violation of any provision of this Article, or any rule or regulation adopted thereunder; and may, if it deems it necessary to carry out the provisions of this Part, require that any or all restricted use pesticides shall be purchased, possessed, or used only under permit of the Board and under its direct supervision in certain areas and/or under certain conditions or in certain quantities or concentrations except that any person licensed to sell such pesticides may purchase and possess such pesticides without a permit. The Board may require all persons issued such permits to maintain records as to the use of the restricted use pesticides. The Board may authorize the use of restricted use pesticides by persons licensed under the North Carolina Structural Pest Control Act without a permit. A nonrefundable fee of ten dollars ($10.00) shall be charged for each examination required by this section. This examination fee is in addition to the certification or recertification fee, and any other fee authorized pursuant to any other provision of Article 4C of Chapter 106 of the General Statutes.

(c)   A fee of fifty dollars ($50.00) shall be charged for examination of individuals seeking to be designated as Worker Protection Designated Trainers, in accordance with provisions of the Federal Worker Protection Standard set forth in 40 C.F.R. Part 170, and subsequent amendments to those regulations. (1971, c. 832, s. 1; 1979, c. 448, s. 1; 1981, c. 592, s. 1; 1987, c. 559, s. 2; c. 846; 2010-31, s. 11.1(a).)

§ 143-441. Handling, storage and disposal of pesticides.

(a)   The Board may adopt regulations:

(1)   Concerning the handling, transport, storage (which may include security precautions), display or distribution of pesticides, and concerning the disposal of pesticides and pesticide containers.

(2)   Restricting or prohibiting the use of certain types of containers or packages for specific pesticides. These restrictions may apply to type of construction, strength, and/ or size to alleviate danger of spillage, breakage, or misuse.

(b)   No person shall handle, transport, store, display, or distribute pesticides in such a manner as to endanger man and his environment or to endanger food, feed, or any other products that may be transported, stored, displayed, or distributed with pesticides, or in any manner contrary to the regulations of the Board.

(c)   No person shall dispose of, discard, or store any pesticides or pesticide containers in such a manner as may cause injury to humans, vegetation, crops, livestock, wildlife, or to pollute any water supply or waterway, or in any manner contrary to the regulations of the Board. (1971, c. 832, s. 1.)

§ 143-442. Registration.

(a)   Every pesticide prior to being distributed, sold, or offered for sale within this State or delivered for transportation or transported in intrastate commerce or between points within this State through any point outside this State shall be registered in the office of the Board, and such registration shall be renewed annually before January 1 for the ensuing calendar year. Beginning in 1988, the Board may by rule adopt a system of staggered three-year registrations. The applicant for registration shall file with the Board a statement that includes all of the following:

(1)   The name and address of the applicant and the name and address of the person whose name will appear on the label, if other than the applicant.

(2)   The name of the pesticide.

(3)   A complete copy of the labeling accompanying the pesticide and a statement of all claims to be made for it including directions for use.

(4)   If requested by the Board, a full description of the tests made and the results thereof upon which the claims are based.

(5)   In the case of renewal of registration, a statement with respect to information which is different from that furnished when the pesticide was last registered.

(6)   Repealed by Session Laws 2011-239, s. 1, effective June 23, 2011, and applicable to applications for registration or renewals of registration filed on or after that date.

(7)   Any other information needed by the Board to determine the amount of annual assessment payable by the applicant.

(b)   The applicant shall pay an annual registration fee of one hundred fifty dollars ($150.00) plus an additional annual assessment for each brand or grade of pesticide registered. The annual assessment shall be fifty dollars ($50.00) if the applicant's gross sales of the pesticide in this State for the preceding 12 months for the period ending September 30th were more than five thousand dollars ($5,000.00) and twenty-five dollars ($25.00) if gross sales were less than five thousand dollars ($5,000.00). An additional two hundred dollars ($200.00) delinquent registration penalty shall be assessed against the registrant for each brand or grade of pesticide which is marketed in North Carolina prior to registration as required by this Article. In the case of multi-year registration, the annual fee and additional assessment for each year shall be paid at the time of the initial registration. The Board shall give a pro rata refund of the registration fee and additional assessment to the registrant in the event that registration is canceled by the Board or by the United States Environmental Protection Agency.

(c)   The Board, when it deems necessary in the administration of this Article, may require the submission of the complete formula of any pesticide.

(d)   If the pesticide is properly registered with the United States Environmental Protection Agency and is in compliance with the requirements of G.S. 143-443, the Board shall register the pesticide. Provided, however, that if it does not appear to the Board that the article is such as to warrant the proposed claims for it or if the article and its labeling and other material required to be submitted do not comply with the provisions of this Part, it shall not register the article and in turn shall notify the applicant of the manner in which the article, labeling, or other material required to be submitted fail to comply. The Board may suspend or cancel the registration of a pesticide when the pesticide or its labeling does not comply with this Part.

(e)   The Board is authorized and empowered to refuse to register, or to cancel the registration of any brands and grades of pesticides as herein provided, if the registrant fails or refuses to comply with the provisions of this Part, or any rules and regulations promulgated thereunder, or, upon satisfactory proof that the registrant or applicant has been guilty of fraudulent and deceptive practices in the evasions or attempted evasions of the provisions of this Part, or any rules and regulations promulgated thereunder. The Board may require the manufacturer or distributor of any pesticide, for which registration has been refused, cancelled, suspended or voluntarily discontinued or which has been found adulterated or deficient in its active ingredient, to remove such pesticide from the marketplace.

(f)   Notwithstanding any other provisions of this Part, registration is not required in the case of a pesticide shipped from one plant within this State to another plant within this State operated by the same person.

(g)   Any pesticide declared to be discontinued by the registrant must be registered by the registrant for one full year after distribution is discontinued. Any pesticide in channels of distribution after the aforesaid registration period may be confiscated and disposed of by the Board, unless the pesticide is acceptable for registration and is continued to be registered by the manufacturer or the person offering the pesticide for wholesale or retail sale. Provided, however, this subsection shall not apply to any brand or grade of pesticide which the Board determines does not remain in channels of distribution due to method of sale by registrant directly to users thereof.

(h)   A pesticide may be registered by the Board for experimental use, including use to control wild animal or bird populations, even though the Wildlife Resources Commission may not have concurred in the declaration of the animal or bird populations as pests under the terms of Article 22A of Chapter 113 of the General Statutes.

(i)   The Board shall be empowered to set forth criteria for determining when a given product constitutes a different or separate brand or grade of pesticide.

(j)   Each manufacturer, distributor or registrant of a pesticide shall supervise the activities of any employee or agent to prevent the making of deceptive or misleading statements about the pesticide. (1971, c. 832, s. 1; 1973, c. 389, ss. 1, 7; 1975, c. 425, ss. 1, 2; 1979, c. 448, ss. 2, 3; c. 830, s. 10; 1981, c. 592, s. 2; 1987, c. 559, ss. 3-7; c. 827, s. 39; 1989, c. 544, s. 13; 1993, c. 481, ss. 1.1, 2; 1995, c. 445, s. 2; 2003-284, s. 35.4(e); 2009-451, s. 11.2; 2011-239, s. 1.)

§ 143-443. Miscellaneous prohibited acts.

(a)   It shall be unlawful for any person to distribute, sell, or offer for sale within this State or deliver for transportation or transport in intrastate commerce or between points within this State through any point outside this State any of the following:

(1)   Any pesticide which has not been registered pursuant to the provisions of G.S. 143-442, or any pesticide if any of the claims made for it or any of the directions for its use differ in substance from the representations made in connection with the registration, or if the composition of a pesticide differs from its composition as represented in connection with its registration: Except that, in the discretion of the Board, a change in the labeling or formula of a pesticide may be made within a registration period without requiring reregistration of the product.

(2)   Any pesticide unless it is in the registrant's or the manufacturer's unbroken immediate container, and there is affixed to such container, and to the outside container or wrapper of the retail package, if there be one through which the required information on the immediate container cannot be clearly read, a label bearing:

a.   The name and address of the manufacturer, registrant, or person for whom manufactured;

b.   The name, brand, or trademark under which said article is sold; and

c.   The net weight or measure of the content subject, however, to such reasonable variations as the Board may permit.

(3)   Any pesticide which contains any substance or substances in quantities highly toxic to man, determined as provided in G.S. 143-444, unless the label shall bear, in addition to any other matter required by this Part:

a.   The skull and crossbones;

b.   The word "poison" prominently, in red, on a background of distinctly contrasting color; and

c.   A statement of an antidote for the pesticide.

(4)   The pesticides commonly known as standard lead arsenate, basic lead arsenate, calcium arsenate, magnesium arsenate, zinc arsenate, zinc arsenite, sodium fluoride, sodium fluosilicate, and barium fluosilicate unless they have been distinctly colored or discolored as provided by regulations issued in accordance with this Part, or any other white or lightly colored pesticide which the Board, after investigation of and after public hearing on the necessity for such action for the protection of the public health and the feasibility of such coloration or discoloration, shall, by regulation, require to be distinctly colored or discolored; unless it has been so colored or discolored, provided, that the Board may exempt any pesticide to the extent that it is intended for a particular use or uses from the coloring or discoloring required or authorized by this section if the Board determines that such coloring or discoloring for such use or uses is not necessary for the protection of the public health.

(5)   Any pesticide which is adulterated or misbranded, (or any device which is misbranded).

(6)   Any pesticide in containers violating regulations adopted pursuant to G.S. 143-441. Pesticides found in containers which are unsafe due to damage or defective construction may be seized and impounded.

(b)   It shall be unlawful:

(1)   For any person to detach, alter, deface, or destroy, in whole or in part, any label or labeling provided for in this Part or regulations promulgated hereunder, or to add any substance to, or take any substance from a pesticide in a manner that may defeat the purpose of this Part;

(2)   For any person to use for his own advantage or to reveal, other than to the Board or proper officials or employees of the State or federal government or

to the courts of this State in response to a subpoena, or to physicians, or in emergencies to pharmacists and other qualified persons, for use in the preparation of antidotes, any information relative to formulas of products acquired by authority of G.S. 143-442.

(2a)   Repealed by Session Laws 1981, c. 592, s. 3.

(3)   For any person to use any pesticide in a manner inconsistent with its labeling.

(4)   For any person who contracts for the aerial application of a pesticide to permit the application of any pesticide that is designated on its labeling as toxic to bees without first notifying, based on available listings, the owner or operator of any apiary registered under the North Carolina Bee and Honey Act of 1977 that is within a distance designated by the Pesticide Board as necessary and appropriate to prevent damage or injury.

(5)   For any person to distribute, sell or offer for sale any restricted use pesticide to any dealer who does not hold a valid North Carolina Pesticide Dealer License.

(6)   For any person to assault, resist, impede, intimidate, or interfere with any State employee while that employee is engaged in the performance of his or her duties under this Article.

(7)   For any person to apply, for compensation, a pesticide that has not been registered pursuant to G.S. 143-442. (1971, c. 832, s. 1; 1975, c. 425, s. 3; 1979, c. 448, ss. 4, 5; 1981, c. 547; c. 592, ss. 3, 4; 1987, c. 559, s. 8; 1995, c. 445, s. 3.)

§ 143-444. Determinations.

The Board is authorized:

(1)   To declare as a pest any form of plant or animal life or virus which is injurious to plants, man, domestic animals, articles, or substances;

(2)   To determine whether pesticides are highly toxic to man; and

(3)   To determine standards of coloring or discoloring for pesticides, and to subject pesticides to the requirements of G.S. 143-443(a)(4). (1971, c. 832, s. 1.)

§ 143-445. Exemptions.

(a)   The penalties provided for violations of G.S. 143-443(a) shall not apply to:

(1)   Any carrier while lawfully engaged in transporting pesticides within this State, if such carrier shall, upon request, permit the Board or its designated agent to copy all records showing the transactions in and movement of the articles;

(2)   Public officials of this State or local subdivisions thereof and the federal government engaged in the performance of their official duties;

(3)   The manufacturer or shipper of a pesticide for experimental use only,

a.   By or under the supervision of an agency of this State or of the federal government authorized by law to conduct research in the field of pesticides, or

b.   By others if the pesticide is not sold and if the container thereof is plainly and conspicuously marked "For experimental use only -Not to be sold," together with the manufacturer's name and address; (except that if a written permit has been obtained from the Board, pesticides may be sold for experimental purposes subject to such restrictions and conditions as may be set forth in the permit).

(b)   No article shall be deemed in violation of this Part when intended solely for export to a foreign country, and when prepared or packed according to the specifications or directions of the purchaser. If not so exported, all the provisions of this Part shall apply. (1971, c. 832, s. 1.)

§ 143-446. Samples; submissions.

(a)   The Board, or its agent, is authorized and directed to sample, test, inspect and make analyses of pesticides sold or offered for sale or distributed within this State, at time and place and to such an extent as it may deem necessary to determine whether such pesticides are in compliance with the provisions of this Article. The Board is authorized to adopt regulations concerning the collection and examination of samples (or devices), and to adopt regulations establishing tolerances providing for reasonable deviations from the guaranteed analysis.

(b)   The official analysis shall be made from the official sample. Official samples shall be collected from material that has been packaged, labeled and released for shipment. A sealed and identified sample, herein called "official check sample" shall be kept until the analysis is completed on the official sample, except that the registrant may obtain upon request a portion of said official sample. If the official analysis conforms with the provisions of this Part, the official check sample may be destroyed. If the official analysis does not conform with the provisions of this Part, then the official check sample shall be retained for a period of 90 days from the date of the certificate of analysis of the official sample.

(c)   The Board, of its own motion or upon complaint, may cause an examination to be made for the purpose of determining whether any pesticide complies with the requirements of this Part. If it shall appear from such examination that a pesticide fails to comply with the provisions of this Part, the Board may cause notice to be given to the offending person in the manner provided in G.S. 143-464, and the proceedings thereupon shall be as provided in such section; provided that pesticides may be seized and confiscated as provided in G.S. 143-447.

(d)   The Board shall, by publication in such manner as it may prescribe, give notice of all judgments entered in actions instituted under the authority of this Article. (1971, c. 832, s. 1; 1987, c. 559, s. 9.)

§ 143-447. Emergency suspensions; seizures.

(a)   The Board may order the summary suspension of the registration of a pesticide if it finds the suspension necessary to prevent an imminent hazard to the public, a nontarget organism, or a segment of the environment. In no event shall registration of a pesticide be construed as a defense to any charge of an offense prohibited under this Article.

(b)   It shall be the duty of the Board to issue and enforce a written or printed "stop sale, stop use, or removal" order to the owner or custodian of any lot of pesticide and for the owner or custodian to hold said lot at a designated place when the Board finds said pesticide is being offered or exposed for sale in violation of any of the provisions of this Article until the law has been complied with and said pesticide is released in writing by the Board or said violation has been otherwise legally disposed of by written authority. The Board shall release the pesticide so withdrawn when the requirements of the provisions of this Article have been complied with and upon payment of all costs and expenses incurred in connection with the withdrawal.

The Board may issue a "stop sale, use or removal order" to prevent or stop the use of a pesticide in a manner inconsistent with its labeling or to prevent or stop the disposal of a pesticide or a pesticide container in violation of this Article or the rules of the Board adopted thereunder.

(c)   Any pesticide (or device) that is distributed, sold, or offered for sale within this State or delivered for transportation or transported in intrastate commerce between points within this State through any point outside this State shall be liable to be proceeded against in superior court in any county of the State where it may be found and seized for confiscation by process or libel for condemnation:

(1)   In the case of a pesticide,

a.   If it is adulterated or misbranded,

b.   If it has not been registered under the provisions of G.S. 143-442, or has had its registration suspended or revoked or is the subject of a stop sale, stop use, or removal order,

c.   If it fails to bear on its label the information required by this Part,

d.   If it is a white or lightly colored pesticide and is not colored as required under this Part.

(2)   In the case of a device, if it is misbranded.

(d)   If the article is condemned, it shall, after entry of decree, be disposed of by destruction or sale as the court may direct and the proceeds, if such article is sold, less legal costs, shall be paid to the State Treasurer; provided that the article shall not be sold contrary to the provisions of this Part; and provided further that upon payment of costs and execution and delivery of a good and sufficient bond conditioned that the article shall not be disposed of unlawfully, the court may direct that said article be delivered to the owner thereof for relabeling or reprocessing or disposal, as the case may be.

(e)   When a decree of condemnation is entered against the article, court costs and fees and storage and other proper expenses shall be awarded against the person, if any, intervening as claimant of the article. (1971, c. 832, s. 1; 1979, c. 448, s. 6; 1981, c. 592, s. 5; 1987, c. 559, s. 10, c. 827, s. 41.)

Part 3. Pesticide Dealers.

§ 143-448. Licensing of pesticide dealers; fees.

(a)   No person shall act in the capacity of a pesticide dealer, or shall engage or offer to engage in the business of, advertise as, or assume to act as a pesticide dealer unless he is licensed annually as provided in this Part. A separate license and fee shall be obtained for each location or outlet from which restricted use pesticides are distributed, sold, held for sale, or offered for sale.

(b)   Applications for a pesticide dealer license shall be in the form and shall contain the information prescribed by the Board. Each application shall be accompanied by a non-refundable fee of seventy-five dollars ($75.00). All licenses issued under this Part shall expire on December 31 of the year for which they are issued.

(c)   The license for a pesticide dealer may be renewed annually upon application to the Board, accompanied by a fee of seventy-five dollars ($75.00) for each license, on or before the first day of January of the calendar year for which the license is issued.

(d)   Repealed by Session Laws 1981, c. 592, s. 6.

(e)   Every licensed pesticide dealer who changes his address or place of business shall immediately notify the Board.

(f)   The Board shall issue to each applicant that satisfies the requirements of this Part a license which entitles the applicant to conduct the business described in the application for the calendar year for which the license is issued, unless the license is sooner revoked or suspended. (1971, c. 832, s. 1; 1981, c. 592, s. 6; 1987, c. 559, ss. 2, 11; 1989, c. 544, s. 11; 1995, c. 445, s. 4; 2003-284, ss. 35.4(b), 35.4(c); 2010-31, s. 11.1(b); 2011-145, s. 31.8(c).)

§ 143-449. Qualifications for pesticide dealer license; examinations.

(a)   An applicant for a license must present evidence satisfactory to the Board concerning his qualifications for such license.

(b)   Each applicant shall satisfy the Board as to his responsibility in carrying on the business of a pesticide dealer. Each applicant for an original license must demonstrate upon written, or written and oral, examination to be prescribed by the Board his knowledge of pesticides, their usefulness and their hazards; his competence as a pesticide dealer; and his knowledge of the laws and regulations governing the use and sale of pesticides. A nonrefundable fee of fifty dollars ($50.00) shall be charged for each examination required by this section. This examination fee is in addition to any fee authorized pursuant to any other provision of Article 4C of Chapter 106 of the General Statutes.

(c)   The Board shall by regulation:

(1)   Designate what persons or class of persons shall be required to pass the examination in the case of a pesticide dealer operating more than one location, and in the case of an applicant that is a corporation, governmental unit or agency, or other organized group;

(2)   Provide for renewal license examinations at intervals not more frequent than four years. (1971, c. 832, s. 1; 1975, c. 425, s. 4; 2010-31, s. 11.1(c).)

§ 143-450. Employees of pesticide dealers; dealer's responsibility.

(a)   Every licensed pesticide dealer shall submit to the Board, at such times as the Board or the Commissioner may prescribe, the names of all persons employed by him who sell or recommend "restricted use pesticides."

(b)   Each pesticide dealer shall be responsible for the actions of every person who acts as his employee or agent in the solicitation or sale of pesticides, and in all claims and recommendations for use or application of pesticides. (1971, c. 832, s. 1; 1979, c. 448, s. 7; 1987, c. 559, s. 2.)

§ 143-451. Denial, suspension and revocation of license.

(a)   The Board may deny, suspend, modify, or revoke a license issued under this Part if it finds that the applicant or licensee or his employee has committed any of the following acts, each of which is declared to be a violation of this Part:

(1)   Made false or fraudulent claims through any media, misrepresenting the effect of materials or methods to be utilized or sold;

(2)   Made a pesticide recommendation not in accordance with the label registered pursuant to this Article;

(3)   Violated any provision of this Article or of any rule or regulation adopted by the Board or of any lawful order of the Board;

(4)   Failed to pay the original or renewal license fee when due, and continued to sell restricted use pesticides without paying the license fee, or sold restricted use pesticides without a license;

(5)   Was guilty of gross negligence, incompetency or misconduct in acting as a pesticide dealer;

(6)   Refused or neglected to keep and maintain the records required by this Article, or to make reports when and as required, or refusing to make these records available for audit or inspection;

(7)   Made false or fraudulent records, invoices, or reports;

(8)   Used fraud or misrepresentation, or presented false information, in making an application for a license or renewal of a license, or in selling or offering to sell restricted use pesticides;

(9)   Refused or neglected to comply with any limitations or restrictions on or in a duly issued license or permit;

(10)   Aided or abetted a licensed or an unlicensed person to evade the provisions of this Article, combined or conspired with such a licensed or unlicensed person to evade the provisions of this Article, or allowed one's license to be used by an unlicensed person;

(11)   Impersonated any state, county, or city inspector or official;

(12)   Stored or disposed of containers or pesticides by means other than those prescribed on the label or adopted regulations.

(13)   Provided or made available any restricted use pesticide to any person other than a certified private applicator, licensed pesticide applicator, certified structural pest control applicator, structural pest control licensee or an employee under the direct supervision of one of the aforementioned certified or licensed applicators.

(b)   Any licensee whose license is revoked under the provisions of this Article shall not be eligible to apply for a new license hereunder until such time has elapsed from the date of the order revoking said license as established by the Board (not to exceed two years), or if an appeal is taken from said order or revocation, not to exceed two years from the date of the order or final judgment sustaining said revocation. (1971, c. 832, s. 1; 1975, c. 425, ss. 6, 7; 1987, c. 559, ss. 2, 13, c. 827, s. 40.)

Part 4. Pesticide Applicators and Consultants.

§ 143-452. Licensing of pesticide applicators; fees.

(a)   No person shall engage in the business of pesticide applicator within this State at any time unless he is licensed annually as a pesticide applicator by the Board.

(b)   Applications for pesticide applicator license shall be in the form and shall contain the information prescribed by the Board. Each application shall be accompanied by a non-refundable fee of seventy-five dollars ($75.00) for each pesticide applicator's license. In addition, an annual inspection fee of twenty-five dollars ($25.00) shall be submitted for each aircraft to be licensed. Should any aircraft fail to pass inspection, making it necessary for a second inspection to be made, the Board shall require an additional twenty-five-dollar ($25.00) inspection fee. In addition to the required inspection, unannounced inspections may be made without charge to determine if equipment is properly calibrated and maintained in conformance with the laws and regulations. All aircraft licensed to apply pesticides shall be identified by a license plate or decal furnished by the Board at no cost to the licensee, which plate or decal shall be affixed on the aircraft in a location and manner prescribed by the Board. No applicator inspection or license fee, original or renewal, shall be charged to State agencies or local governments or their employees. Inspections of ground pesticide application equipment may be made. Any such equipment determined to be faulty or unsafe shall not be used for the purpose of applying a pesticide(s) until such time as proper repairs and/or alterations are made.

(c)   Repealed by Session Laws 1981, c. 592, s. 6.

(d)   The Board shall classify licenses to be issued under this Part. Separate classifications or subclassifications shall be specified for (i) ground and aerial methods of application, and (ii) State and local government units engaged in the control of rodents and insects of public health significance. The Board may include such further classifications and subclassifications as the Board considers appropriate, including provisions for licensing of apprentice pesticide applicators. For aerial applicators, a license shall be required for both the contractor and the pilot. Each classification and subclassification may be subject to separate testing procedures and requirements.

(e)   Every licensed pesticide applicator who changes his address shall immediately notify the Board.

(f)   If the Board finds the applicant qualified to apply pesticides in the classifications he has applied for and, if the applicant files the bond or insurance required under G.S. 143-467, and if the applicant applying for a license to engage in aerial application of pesticides has met all of the requirements of the Federal Aviation Agency to operate the equipment described in the application, the Board shall issue a pesticide applicator's license limited to the classifications for which he is qualified. Every such license shall expire at the end of the

87

calendar year of issue unless it has been revoked or suspended prior thereto by the Board for cause, or unless such financial security required under G.S. 143-467 is dated to expire at an earlier date, in which case said license shall be dated to expire upon expiration date of said financial security. The license may restrict the applicant to the use of a certain type or types of equipment or pesticides or to certain areas if the Board finds that the applicant is qualified to use only such type or types. If a license is not issued as applied for, the Board shall inform the applicant in writing of the reasons therefor.

(g)   A pesticide applicator's license shall not be transferable. When there is a transfer of ownership, management, or operation of a business of a licensee hereunder, the new owner, manager, or operator (as the case may be) whether it be an individual, firm, partnership, corporation, or other entity, must have available a licensed pesticide applicator to supervise the pesticide application business prior to continuance of such business.

(h)   Repealed by Session Laws 1987, c. 559, s. 15. (1971, c. 832, s. 1; 1973, c. 389, ss. 2, 5; 1977, c. 100; 1981, c. 592, ss. 6, 7; 1987, c. 559, ss. 14, 15; 1989, c. 544, s. 10; 2003-284, s. 35.4(a); 2010-31, s. 11.1(d).)

§ 143-453. Qualifications for pesticide applicator's license; examinations.

(a)   An applicant for a license must present satisfactory evidence to the Board concerning his qualifications for a pesticide applicator license. The contractor and each pilot involved in aerial application of pesticides shall be licensed.

Those qualifications, in the case of a pilot, shall include at least 125 hours and one year's flying experience as a pilot in the field of aerial pesticide application. A pilot lacking 125 hours and one year's experience as a pilot in the field of aerial pesticide application shall be licensed as an apprentice aerial pesticide applicator pilot. All aerial applications of pesticides by a licensed apprentice shall be conducted under the direct supervision of a licensed pesticide applicator pilot. The supervising pilot, while directly supervising an apprentice, shall operate out of the same airstrip as the apprentice and shall be available periodically throughout each day to provide advice and assistance to the apprentice. A nonrefundable fee of fifty dollars ($50.00) shall be charged for the examination required by this subsection. Such examination fee shall be charged

88

in addition to the fees authorized pursuant to subsection (b) of this section or any other provision of Article 4C of Chapter 106 of the General Statutes.

(b)   Each applicant shall satisfy the Board as to his knowledge of the laws and regulations governing the use and application of pesticides in the classifications he has applied for (manually or with various equipment that he may have applied for a license to operate), and as to his responsibility in carrying on the business of a pesticide applicator. Each applicant for an original license must demonstrate upon written, or written and oral, examination to be prescribed by the Board his knowledge of pesticides, their usefulness and their hazards; his competence as a pesticide applicator; and his knowledge of the laws and regulations governing the use and application of pesticides in the classification for which he has applied. A nonrefundable fee of fifty dollars ($50.00) shall be charged for the core examination, and an additional twenty dollars ($20.00) shall be charged for each additional specific classification licensure. Such examination fees shall be charged in addition to the fees authorized pursuant to subsection (a) of this section or any other provision of Article 4C of Chapter 106 of the General Statutes.

(c)   The Board shall by regulation:

(1)   Designate what persons or class of persons shall be required to pass the examination in the case of an applicant that is a corporation or governmental unit or agency;

(2)   Provide for license renewal examinations at intervals not more frequent than four years, or more frequently if found by the Board to be required to be necessary in order to qualify North Carolina's State pesticide control plan for federal approval. (1971, c. 832, s. 1; 1973, c. 389, s. 4; 1975, c. 425, ss. 5, 9; 1977, c. 1125; 1985, c. 163; 2010-31, s. 11.1(e).)

§ 143-454. Solicitors, salesmen and operators; applicator's responsibility.

(a)   Every licensed pesticide applicator shall submit to the Board, at such times as the Board or the Commissioner may prescribe, the names of all solicitors, salesmen, and operators employed by him.

(b)   Each licensed pesticide applicator shall be responsible for solicitors, salesmen, and operators in his employment to assure that pesticides are used in a manner consistent with the intent of this Article. (1971, c. 832, s. 1; 1979, c. 448, s. 8.)

§ 143-455. Pest control consultant license.

(a)   No person shall perform services as a pest control consultant without first procuring from the Board a license. Applications for a consultant license shall be in the form and shall contain the information prescribed by the Board. The application for a license shall be accompanied by a non-refundable annual fee of seventy-five dollars ($75.00).

(b)   An applicant for a consultant license must present satisfactory evidence to the Board concerning his qualifications for such license. The Board may classify consultant licenses into one or more classifications or subclassifications based upon types of consulting services performed or to be performed. Such classifications and subclassifications may reflect the crops involved in the consulting service, the discipline or training of consultant, the discretion or lack of discretion involved in the consulting service, and the site or location of the service. Each classification and subclassification may be subject to separate testing procedures and requirements, and may be subject to its own minimum standards of training in specialized subject matter from a recognized college or university, or equivalent specialized consulting experience or training. A nonrefundable fee of fifty dollars ($50.00) shall be charged for the consultant examination, and an additional twenty dollars ($20.00) shall be charged for each additional specific classification licensure permitted by this subsection. Such examination fee shall be charged in addition to the fees authorized pursuant to subsection (a) of this section or any other provision of Article 4C of Chapter 106 of the General Statutes. Qualifications for licensing may be less stringent if the licensee is restricted to making recommendations contained in publications recognized by the Board as appropriate for a specific consulting classification or subclassification.

(c)   Each applicant shall satisfy the Board as to his responsibility in carrying on the business of a pesticide consultant. Each applicant for an original license must demonstrate upon written, or written and oral, examination to be prescribed by the Board his knowledge of pesticides, their usefulness and their hazards; his competence as a pesticide consultant; and his knowledge of the laws and regulations governing the use and sale of pesticides.

90

(d)   Pest control consultants shall be subject to the same provisions as pesticide applicators concerning penalties for late applications for license, changes of address, transferability of licenses, periodic reexamination, and examinations for corporate applicants. (1971, c. 832, s. 1; 1975, c. 425, s. 10; 1987, c. 559, s. 16; 1989, c. 544, s. 12; 2003-284, s. 35.4(d); 2010-31, s. 11.1(f).)

§ 143-456. Denial, suspension and revocation of license.

(a)   The Board may deny, suspend, modify, or revoke a license issued under this Part if it finds that the applicant or licensee or his employee has committed any of the following acts, each of which is declared to be a violation of this Part:

(1)   Made false or fraudulent claims through any media, misrepresenting the effect of materials or methods to be utilized;

(2)   Made a pesticide recommendation or application not in accordance with the label registered pursuant to this Article;

(3)   Operated faulty or unsafe equipment;

(4)   Operated in a faulty, careless, or negligent manner;

(5)   Violated any provision of this Article or of any rule or regulation adopted by the Board or any lawful order of the Board;

(6)   Refused or neglected to keep and maintain the records required by this Article, or to make reports when and as required;

(7)   Made false or fraudulent records, invoices, or reports;

(8)   Operated unlicensed equipment;

(9)   Used fraud or misrepresentation, or presented false information, in making an application for a license or renewal of a license;

(10)   Refused or neglected to comply with any limitations or restrictions on or in a duly issued license or permit;

91

(11)   Aided or abetted a licensed or an unlicensed person to evade the provisions of this Article, combined or conspired with such a licensed or unlicensed person to evade the provisions of this Article, or allowed one's license to be used by an unlicensed person;

(12)   Made false or misleading statements during or after an inspection concerning any infestation or infection of pests found on land;

(13)   Impersonated any state, county, or city inspector or official;

(14)   Stored or disposed of containers or pesticides by means other than those prescribed on the labeling or by rule;

(15)   Failed to pay the original or renewal license fee when due and continued to operate as an applicator, or applied pesticides without a license.

(16)   Failed to pay a civil penalty assessed under this Article within 30 days after the date it is assessed.

(b)   Any licensee whose license is revoked under the provisions of this Article shall not be eligible to apply for a new license hereunder until such time has elapsed from the date of the order revoking said license as established by the Board (not to exceed two years), or if an appeal is taken from said order or revocation, not to exceed two years from the date of the order or final judgment sustaining said revocation. (1971, c. 832, s. 1; 1975, c. 425, ss. 6, 8; 1987, c. 559, s. 17; c. 827, s. 42; 1995, c. 445, s. 5.)

§ 143-457: Repealed by Session Laws 1981, c. 592, s. 8.

§ 143-458. Rules and regulations concerning methods of application.

(a)   The Board may adopt rules prescribing the method to be used in the application of pesticides and the times and places pesticides may be applied. The Board may adopt rules restricting or prohibiting the sale and use of pesticides in designated areas during specified time periods. In adopting rules under this subsection, the Board shall consider factors required to prevent damage or injury to the following by the drift or misapplication of pesticides:

92

(1)   Plants, including forage plants, on adjacent or nearby land;

(2)   Wildlife in the adjoining or nearby areas;

(3)   Fish and other aquatic life in waters in reasonable proximity to the area to be treated; or

(4)   Other animals, persons or beneficial insects.

In issuing such regulations, the Board shall give consideration to pertinent research findings and recommendations of other agencies of this State or of the federal government.

(b)   The Board may by regulation require that notice of a proposed application of a pesticide be given to landowners adjoining the property to be treated or in the immediate vicinity thereof, if it finds that such notice is necessary to carry out the purpose of this Article.

(c)   A pesticide applicator, a pesticide applicator's employee, or an agent of a pesticide applicator shall not apply any substance that:

(1)   Has the active ingredients contained in a pesticide that is registered pursuant to G.S. 143-442, and

(2)   Is not registered as a pesticide pursuant to G.S. 143-442.

(d)   A pesticide applicator, a pesticide applicator's employee, or an agent of a pesticide applicator shall not combine any substance whose application is prohibited under subsection (c) of this section with any other substance to apply as a pesticide or to apply for any other reason, whether the combination occurs before, during, or after the application.

(e)   Any person who violates subsection (c) or (d) of this section shall be guilty of a Class 2 misdemeanor, which shall include a fine of up to one thousand dollars ($1,000) per violation. (1971, c. 832, s. 1; 1987, c. 827, s. 43; 1995, c. 478, s. 1.)

§ 143-459. Reporting of shipments and volumes of pesticides.

Every person selling pesticides directly to the consumer shall file with the Board, in such manner and with such frequency as the Board may prescribe, reports of purchases, sales and shipments of restricted use pesticides and other pesticides designated by the Board. Failure to file any report when due shall be cause for suspension or revocation of any license or registration issued under this Article, or for denial of the issuance or renewal of any such license or registration, and shall be a misdemeanor, punishable as provided by G.S. 143-469. The time for reporting may be extended for an additional 15 days for cause, upon written request to the Board. All reports provided under this Part are provided solely for the purposes of the Board. (1971, c. 832, s. 1; 1987, c. 559, s. 2.)

Part 5. General Provisions.

§ 143-460. Definitions.

As used in this Article, unless the context otherwise requires:

(1)   The term "active ingredient" means

a.   In the case of a pesticide other than a plant regulator, defoliant, or desiccant, an ingredient which will prevent, destroy, repel, or mitigate insects, nematodes, fungi, rodents, weeds, or other pests;

b.   In the case of a plant regulator, an ingredient which, through physiological action, will accelerate or retard the rate of growth or rate of maturation or otherwise alter the behavior of ornamental or crop plants or the produce thereof;

c.   In the case of a defoliant, an ingredient which will cause the leaves or foliage to drop from a plant;

d.   In the case of a desiccant, an ingredient which will artificially accelerate the drying of a plant tissue.

(2)   The term "adulterated" shall apply to any pesticide if its strength or purity falls below the professed standard or quality as expressed on labeling or under which it is sold, or if any substance has been substituted wholly or in part for the

article, or if any valuable constituent of the article has been wholly or in part abstracted.

(2a)   "Antimicrobial pesticide" means any substance or mixture of substances intended for preventing, destroying, repelling, or mitigating any microorganism pest.

(3)   Reserved.

(4)   "Board" means the North Carolina Pesticide Board.

(5)   "Commissioner" means the North Carolina Commissioner of Agriculture.

(6)   "Committee" means the Pesticide Advisory Committee.

(7)   The term "defoliant" means any substance or mixture of substances intended for causing the leaves or foliage to drop from a plant, with or without causing abscission.

(8)   The term "desiccant" means any substance or mixture of substances intended for artificially accelerating the drying of plant tissues.

(9)   The term "device" means any instrument or contrivance intended for trapping, destroying, repelling, or mitigating insects or rodents or destroying, repelling, or mitigating fungi, weeds, nematodes, or such other pests as may be designated by the Board, but not including equipment used for the application of pesticides when sold separately therefrom.

(10)   Repealed by Session Laws 1995, c. 445, s. 6.

(11)   "Equipment" means any type of ground, water or aerial equipment, device, or contrivance using motorized, mechanical or pressurized power and used to apply any pesticide on land and anything that may be growing, habitating or stored on or in such land, but shall not include any pressurized hand-sized household device used to apply any pesticide or any equipment, device or contrivance of which the person who is applying the pesticide is the source of power or energy in making such pesticide application.

(12)   The term "fungus" means any non-chlorophyll-bearing thallophyte (that is any non-chlorophyll-bearing plant of a lower order than mosses and liverworts), as for example, rust, smut, mildew, mold, yeast, and bacteria, except

those on or in living man or other animals and those on or in processed food, beverages, or pharmaceuticals.

(13)   The term "fungicide" means any substance or mixture of substances intended for preventing, destroying, repelling or mitigating any fungi.

(14)   The term "herbicide" means any substance or mixture of substances intended for preventing, destroying, repelling or mitigating any weed.

(15)   The term "inert ingredient" means an ingredient which is not an active ingredient.

(16)   The term "ingredient statement" means

a.   A statement of the name and percentage of each active ingredient, together with the total percentage of the inert ingredients, in the pesticide; and

b.   In case the pesticide contains arsenic in any form, a statement of the percentages of total and water-soluble arsenic, each calculated as elemental arsenic.

(17)   The term "insect" means any of the numerous small invertebrate animals generally having the body more or less obviously segmented, for the most part belonging to the class Insecta, comprising six-legged, usually winged forms, as, for example, beetles, bugs, wasps, flies, and to other allied classes of arthropods whose members are wingless and usually have more than six legs, as, for example, spiders, mites, ticks, centipedes, and wood lice.

(18)   The term "insecticide" means any substance or mixture of substances intended for preventing, destroying, repelling, or mitigating any insects which may be present in any environment whatsoever.

(19)   The term "label" means the written, printed, or graphic matter on, or attached to, the pesticide (or device) or the immediate container thereof, and the outside container or wrapper of the retail package, if any there be, of the pesticide (or device).

(20)   The term "labeling" means all labels and other written, printed, or graphic matter:

a.   Upon the pesticide (or device) or any of its containers or wrappers;

96

b. Accompanying the pesticide (or device) at any time;

c. To which reference is made on the label or in literature accompanying the pesticide (or device) except when accurate, nonmisleading reference is made to current official publications of the United States Department of Agriculture or Interior, the United States Public Health Service, state experiment stations, state agricultural colleges, or other similar federal institutions or official agencies of this State or other states authorized by law to conduct research in the field of pesticides.

(21) "Land" means all land and water areas, including airspace, and all plants, animals, structures, buildings, devices and contrivances, appurtenant thereto or situated thereon, fixed or mobile, including any used for transportation.

(22) "Manufacturer" includes any person engaged in the business of importing, producing, preparing, formulating, mixing, or processing pesticides.

(22a) "Material Safety Data Sheet" or "MSDS" means a chemical information sheet which would satisfy the requirements of the Hazardous Chemicals Right-to-Know Act, Article 18, Chapter 95 of the General Statutes, or any law enacted in substitution therefor.

(23) The term "misbranded" shall apply:

a. To any pesticide or device if its labeling bears any statement, design, or graphic representation relative thereto or to its ingredients which is false or misleading in any particular;

b. To any pesticide:

1. If it is an imitation of or is offered for sale under the name of another pesticide;

2. If its labeling bears any reference to registration under this Article;

3. If the labeling accompanying it does not contain instructions for use which are necessary and, if complied with, adequate for the protection of the public;

97

4.   If the label does not contain a warning or caution statement which may be necessary and, if complied with, adequate to prevent injury to living man and other vertebrate animals;

5.   If the label does not bear an ingredient statement on that part of the immediate container and on the outside container or wrapper, if there be one, through which the ingredient statement on the immediate container cannot be clearly read, of the retail package which is presented or displayed under customary conditions of purchase except that the Board may permit the statement to appear prominently on some other part of the container, if the size or form of the container make it impractical to comply with the requirements of this subparagraph;

6.   If any word, statement, or other information required by or under the authority of this Article to appear on the labeling is not prominently placed thereon with such conspicuousness (as compared with other words, statements, designs, or graphic matter in the labeling) and in such terms as to render it likely to be read and understood by the ordinary individual under customary conditions of purchase and use; or

7.   If in the case of an insecticide, nematicide, fungicide, or herbicide, when used as directed or in accordance with commonly recognized practice, it shall be injurious to living man or other vertebrate animals or vegetation, except weeds, to which it is applied, or to the person applying such pesticides or

8.   In the case of a plant regulator, defoliant, or desiccant when used as directed it shall be injurious to living man or other vertebrate animals, or vegetation to which it is applied, or to the person applying such pesticides, except that physical or physiological effects on plants or parts thereof shall not be deemed to be injury, when this is the purpose for which the plant regulator, defoliant, or desiccant was applied, in accordance with the label claims and recommendations.

(24)   The term "nematicide" means any substance or mixture of substances intended for preventing, destroying, repelling, or mitigating nematodes.

(25)   The term "nematode" means invertebrate animals of the phylum nemathelminthes and class Nematoda, that is, unsegmented round worms with elongated, fusiform, or saclike bodies covered with cuticle, and inhabiting soil, water, plants or plant parts; may also be called nemas or eelworms.

(25a)   The phrase "packaged, labeled and released for shipment" means the point in the production and marketing process of a pesticide where the pesticide has been produced, and it is the intent of the producer that such product be introduced into commerce for direct retail sale.

(26)   A "person" is any person, including (but not limited to) an individual, firm, partnership, association, company, joint-stock association, public or private institution, municipality or county or local government unit (as defined in G.S. 143-215.40(b)), state or federal governmental agency, or private or public corporation organized under the laws of this State or the United States or any other state or country.

(26a)   The term "pest" means any insect, rodent, nematode, fungus, weed or any other noxious or undesirable microorganism or macroorganism, except viruses, bacteria, or other microorganisms on or in living persons or other living animals.

(27)   "Pest control consultant" means any person, who, for a fee, offers or supplies technical advice, supervision, or aid, or recommends the use of specific pesticides for the purpose of controlling insects, plant diseases, weeds, and other pests, but does not include any person regulated by the North Carolina Structural Pest Control Act (G.S. Chapter 106, Article 4C).

(28)   The term "pesticide" means:

a.   Any substance or mixture of substances intended for preventing, destroying, repelling, or mitigating any pest, and

b.   Any substance or mixture of substances intended for use as a plant regulator, defoliant, or desiccant.

(29)   "Pesticide applicator" means any person who owns or operates a pesticide application business or who provides, for compensation, a service that includes the application of pesticides upon the lands or properties of another; any public operator; any golf course operator; any seed treater; any person engaged in demonstration or research pest control; and any other person who applies pesticides for compensation and is not exempt from this definition. It does not include:

a.   Any person who uses or supervises the use of a pesticide (i) only for the purpose of producing an agricultural commodity on property owned or rented by him or his employer, or (ii) only (if applied without compensation other than trading of personal services between producers of agricultural commodities) on the property of another person, or (iii) only for the purposes set forth in (i) and (ii) above.

b.   Any person who applies pesticides for structural pest control, as defined in the North Carolina Structural Pest Control Law (G.S. Chapter 106, Article 4C).

c.   Any person certified by the Water Treatment Facility Operators Board of Certification under Article 2 of Chapter 90A of the General Statutes or by the Wastewater Treatment Operators Plant Certification Commission under Article 3 of Chapter 90A of the General Statutes who applies pesticides labeled for the treatment of water or wastewater.

d.   Any person who applies antimicrobial pesticides that are not classified for restricted use and are not being used for agricultural, horticultural, or forestry purposes.

e.   Any person who applies a general use pesticide to the property of another as a volunteer, without compensation.

f.   Any person who is employed by a licensed pesticide applicator.

(30)   The term "pesticide dealer" means any person who is engaged in the business of distributing, selling, offering for sale, or holding for sale restricted use pesticides for distribution directly to users. The term pesticide dealer does not include:

a.   Persons whose sales of pesticides are limited to pesticides in consumer-sized packages (as defined by the Board) which are labeled and intended for home and garden use only and are not restricted use pesticides, or

b.   Practicing veterinarians and physicians who prescribe, dispense, or use pesticides in the performance of their professional services.

(31)   Repealed by Session Laws 1973, c. 389, s. 3.

(32)   The term "plant regulator" means any substance or mixture of substances, intended through physiological action, for accelerating or retarding the rate of growth or rate of maturation, or for otherwise altering the behavior of ornamental or crop plants or the produce thereof, but shall not include

100

substances to the extent that they are intended as plant nutrients, trace elements, nutritional chemicals, plant inoculants, and soil amendments.

(33) "Public operator" means any person in charge of any equipment used by public utilities (as defined by General Statutes Chapter 62), State agencies, municipal corporations, or other governmental agencies applying pesticides.

(34) The term "registrant" means the person registering any pesticide pursuant to the provisions of this Article.

(35) The term "restricted use pesticide" or "pesticide classified for restricted use" means any pesticide or use classified as restricted by the Administrator of the United States Environmental Protection Agency or other pesticide or use which the Board has designated as such pursuant to G.S. 143-440.

(36) The term "rodenticide" means any substance or mixture of substances intended for preventing, destroying, repelling, attracting, or mitigating rodents or any other vertebrate animal which the Board shall declare to be a pest.

(36a) The phrase "to use any pesticide in a manner inconsistent with its labeling" means to use any pesticide in a manner not permitted by the labeling; provided that the phrase shall not include:

a. Applying a pesticide at any dosage, concentration, or frequency less than that specified on the labeling,

b. Applying a pesticide against any target pest not specified on the labeling if the application is to the crop, animal, or site specified on the labeling, unless the labeling specifically states that the pesticide may be used only for the pests specified on the labeling,

c. Employing any method of application not prohibited by the labeling, or

d. Mixing pesticides or mixing a pesticide with a fertilizer when such mixture is not prohibited by the labeling.

(37) The term "weed" means any plant or part thereof which grows where not wanted.

(38) "Wildlife" means all living things that are neither human, domesticated, nor, as defined in this Article, pests; including but not limited to mammals, birds,

and aquatic life. (1971, c. 832, s. 1; 1973, c. 389, s. 3; 1975, c. 425, s. 11; 1979, c. 448, ss. 9, 10; 1981, c. 592, ss. 9-11; 1987, c. 559, ss. 2, 18-20; 1991, c. 87, ss. 1, 2; 1995, c. 445, ss. 6, 7.)

§ 143-461. General powers of Board.

In addition to the specific powers prescribed elsewhere in this Article, and for the purpose of carrying out its duties, the Board shall have the power, at any time and from time to time:

(1)   To adopt from time to time and to modify and revoke official regulations interpreting and applying the provisions of this Article and rules of procedure establishing and amplifying the procedures to be followed in the administration of this Article. Unless the Board deems there are overriding policy considerations involved, any regulation of the Board, which will in the judgment of the Board result in severe curtailment of the usefulness or value of inventories or equipment in the hands of persons licensed under this Article, should be given a future effective date so as to minimize undue potential economic loss to licensees;

(2)   To authorize the Commissioner by proclamation (i) to suspend or implement, in whole or in part, particular regulations of the Board which may be affected by variable conditions, or (ii) to suspend the application of any provision of this Part to any federal or State agency if it is determined by the Commissioner that emergency conditions require such action.

(3)   To conduct such investigations as it may reasonably deem necessary to carry out its duties as prescribed by this Article;

(4)   To conduct public hearings in accordance with the procedures prescribed by this Article;

(5)   To delegate such of the powers of the Board as the Board deems necessary (other than its powers to adopt rules and regulations of any kind) to one or more of its members, to the Commissioner, or to any qualified employee of the Board or of the Commissioner; provided, that the provisions of any such delegation of power shall be set forth in the official regulations of the Board. Any person to whom a delegation of power is made to conduct a hearing shall report the hearing with its evidence and record to the Board for decision;

(6)   To call upon the Attorney General for such legal advice and assistance as is necessary to the functioning of the Board;

(7)   To institute such actions in the superior court in the county in which any defendant resides, or has his or its principal place of business, as the Board may deem necessary for the enforcement of any of the provisions of this Article or of any official actions of the Board, including proceedings to enforce subpoenas or for the punishment of contempt of the Board. Upon violation of any of the provisions of this Article, or of any regulation of the Board adopted under the authority of this Article the Board may, either before or after the institution of any other proceedings (civil or criminal), institute a civil action in the superior court in the name of the State for injunctive relief to restrain the violation and for such other or further relief in the premises as said court shall deem proper. Neither the institution of the action nor any of the proceedings thereon shall relieve any party to such proceedings from any other penalty or remedy prescribed by this Article for any violation of same;

(8)   To agree upon or enter into any settlements or compromises of any actions and to prosecute any appeals or other proceedings. (1971, c. 832, s. 1; 1973, c. 389, s. 6; 1987, c. 827, s. 44.)

§ 143-462. Procedures for revocations and related actions affecting licenses.

In all proceedings, the effect of which would be to revoke, suspend, deny, or withhold renewal of a license issued under Part 3 or Part 4 of this Article, or to deny permission to take an examination for such a license, the provisions of Chapter 150B of the General Statutes shall be applicable. (1971, c. 832, s. 1; 1987, c. 827, s. 1.)

§ 143-463. Adoption and publication of rules.

Chapter 150B of the General Statutes governs the adoption of rules under this Article and the publication of those rules. (1971, c. 832, s. 1; 1975, 2nd Sess., c. 983, s. 84; 1979, c. 448, s. 11; 1987, c. 827, s. 45.)

§ 143-464. Procedures concerning registration of pesticides.

A denial, suspension, or cancellation of a registration of a pesticide shall be made in accordance with the procedures in Chapter 150B of the General Statutes for denying, suspending, or canceling a license. (1971, c. 832, s. 1; 1979, c. 448, s. 12; 1987, c. 827, s. 46.)

§ 143-465. Reciprocity; intergovernmental cooperation.

(a)   The Board may issue any license required by this Article on a reciprocal basis with other states without examination to a nonresident who is licensed in another state substantially in accordance with any of the provisions of the Article, provided that financial security as provided for in G.S. 143-467 is met.

(b)   The Board may cooperate or enter into formal agreements with any other agency of this State or its subdivisions or with any agency of any other state or of the federal government for the purpose of enforcing any of the provisions of this Article.

(c)   In order to avoid confusion resulting from diverse requirements and to avoid increased costs to the people of this State due to the necessity of complying with such diverse requirements in the manufacture and sale of such pesticides, it is desirable that there should be uniformity between the requirements of the several states and the federal government relating to such pesticides. To this end the Board is authorized, after public hearing, to adopt by regulation such regulations, applicable to and in conformity with the primary standards established by this Article, as have been or may be prescribed with respect to pesticides by departments or agencies of the United States government.

(d)   No county, city, or other political subdivision of the State shall adopt or continue in effect any ordinance, rule, regulation, or resolution regulating the use, sale, distribution, storage, transportation, disposal, formulation, labeling, registration, manufacture, or application of pesticides in any area subject to regulation by the Board pursuant to this Article. Nothing in this section shall prohibit a county, city, or other political subdivision of the State from exercising its planning and zoning authority under Article 19 of Chapter 160A of the General Statutes or Article 18 of Chapter 153A of the General Statutes, or from exercising its fire prevention or inspection authority. (1971, c. 832, s. 1; 1995, c. 445, s. 8.)

§ 143-466. Records; information; inspection; enforcement.

(a)   The Board shall require licensees to maintain records with respect to the sale and application of such pesticides as it may from time to time prescribe. Such relevant information as the Board may deem necessary may be specified by rule. The records shall be kept for a period of three years from the date of the application of the pesticide to which the records refer, and shall be available for inspection and copying by the Board or its agents at its request.

(b)   The Board may publish information regarding injury which may result from improper application or use of pesticides and the methods and precautions designed to prevent such injury.

(c)   The Board may provide for inspection of any equipment used for application of pesticides and may require repairs or other changes before its further use for pesticide application. A list of requirements that equipment shall meet may be adopted by the Board by regulation.

(d)   The Board may provide for inspection of any place of business where pesticides are stored or sold and may require changes in methods of handling, displaying and storing of all pesticides. A list of requirements that places of business must meet may be adopted by regulation of the Board.

(e)   For the purpose of carrying out the provisions of this Article, inspectors designated by the Board may enter upon any public or private premises at reasonable times, in order:

(1)   To have access for the purpose of inspecting the premises and any equipment subject to this Article and such premises on which such equipment is kept or stored;

(2)   To inspect lands actually or reported to be exposed to pesticides;

(3)   To inspect storage or disposal areas;

(4)   To inspect or investigate complaints of injury to humans, land or plants; or

(5)   To sample pesticides being applied, or to be applied.

No person shall refuse entry or access to any authorized representative of the Board who requests entry for purposes of inspection, and who presents appropriate credentials, nor shall any person obstruct, hamper or interfere with any such representative while in the process of carrying out his official duties. Should the Board or its designated agent be denied access to any land where such access was sought for the purposes set forth in this Article, the Board may apply to any court of competent jurisdiction for a search warrant authorizing access to such land for said purposes. The court may upon such application issue the search warrant for the purposes requested. (1971, c. 832, s. 1; 1995, c. 445, s. 9.)

§ 143-467. Financial responsibility.

(a)   The Board may require from a licensee or an applicant for a license under this Article evidence of his financial ability to properly indemnify persons suffering damage from the use or application of pesticides, in the form of a surety bond, liability insurance or cash deposit. The amount of this bond, insurance or deposit shall be determined by the Board, in light of the risk of damage. The indemnification requirements may extend to damage to persons and property from equipment used (including aircraft).

(b)   The Board may also require a reasonable performance bond with satisfactory surety to secure the performance of contractual obligations of the licensee, with respect to application of pesticides. Any person injured by the breach of any such obligation or any person damaged by pesticides or by equipment used in their application shall be entitled to sue on the bond in his own name in any court of competent jurisdiction to recover the damages he may have sustained.

(c)   Any regulations adopted by the Board pursuant to G.S. 143-461 to implement this section may provide for such conditions, limitations and requirements concerning the financial responsibility required by this section as the Board deems necessary, including but not limited to notice of reduction or cancellation of coverage, deductible provisions, and acceptability of surety.

Such regulations may classify financial responsibility requirements according to the separate license classifications and subclassifications prescribed by the Board pursuant to G.S. 143-452 and the dealer category (Part 3 of this Article). (1971, c. 832, s. 1.)

§ 143-468. Disposition of fees and charges.

(a)   Except as provided in G.S. 143-469 and in subsection (b), all fees and charges received by the Board under this Article shall be credited to the Department of Agriculture and Consumer Services for the purpose of administration and enforcement of this Article.

(b)   The Pesticide Environmental Trust Fund is established as a nonreverting account within the Department of Agriculture and Consumer Services. The Department of Agriculture and Consumer Services shall administer the Fund. The additional assessment imposed by G.S. 143-442(b) on the registration of a brand or grade of pesticide shall be credited to the Fund. The Department shall distribute money in the Fund as follows:

(1)   Two and one-half percent (2.5%) to North Carolina State University Cooperative Extension Service to enhance its agromedicine efforts in cooperation with East Carolina University School of Medicine.

(2)   Two and one-half percent (2.5%) to East Carolina University School of Medicine to enhance its agromedicine efforts in cooperation with North Carolina State University Cooperative Extension Service.

(3)   Twenty percent (20%) to North Carolina State University, Department of Toxicology, to establish and maintain an extension agromedicine specialist position.

(4)   Seventy-five percent (75%) to the Department of Agriculture and Consumer Services for the costs of administering its pesticide disposal program, including the salaries and support of staff for the pesticide disposal program, and for its environmental programs, as directed by the Board, including establishing a pesticide container management program to enhance its pesticide disposal program and its water quality initiatives. (1971, c. 832, s. 1; 1993, c. 481, s. 1; 1997-261, s. 92; 1998-215, s. 26(b); 2005-276, s. 11.1.)

§ 143-469. Penalties.

(a)   Any person who shall be adjudged to have violated any provision of this Article, or any regulation of the Board adopted pursuant to this Article, shall be guilty of a Class 2 misdemeanor. In addition, if any person continues to violate or further violates any provision of this Article after written notice from the Board, the court may determine that each day during which the violation continued or is repeated constitutes a separate violation subject to the foregoing penalties.

(b)   A civil penalty of not more than two thousand dollars ($2,000) may be assessed by the Board against any person who violates or directly causes a violation of any provision of this Article or any rule adopted pursuant to this Article.

(c)   Proceedings for the assessment of civil penalties under this section shall be governed by Chapter 150B of the North Carolina General Statutes. If the person assessed a civil penalty fails to pay the penalty to the North Carolina Department of Agriculture and Consumer Services, the Board may institute an action in the superior court of the county in which the person resides or has his principal place of business to recover the unpaid amount of said penalty. An action to recover a civil penalty under this section shall not relieve any party from any other penalty prescribed by law.

(d)   Notwithstanding any other provision of this Article, the maximum penalty which may be assessed under this section against any person referred to in G.S. 143-460(29)a shall not exceed five hundred dollars ($500.00). Penalties may be assessed under this section against a person referred to in G.S. 143-460(29)a only for willful violations.

(e)   The clear proceeds of civil penalties assessed pursuant to this section shall be remitted to the Civil Penalty and Forfeiture Fund in accordance with G.S. 115C-457.2. (1971, c. 832, s. 1; 1981, c. 592, s. 12; 1987, c. 559, s. 21; c. 827, s. 1; 1993, c. 539, s. 1035; 1994, Ex. Sess., c. 24, s. 14(c); 1995, c. 445, s. 10; 1997-261, s. 109; 1998-215, s. 26(a).)

§ 143-470: Repealed by Session Laws 1981, c. 592, s. 13, effective July 1, 1981.

§ 143-470.1. Report of minor violations in discretion of Board or Commissioner.

Nothing in this Article shall be construed to require the Board or the Commissioner to initiate, or attempt to initiate, any criminal or administrative proceedings under this Article for minor violations of this Article whenever the Board or Commissioner believes that the public interest will be adequately served in the circumstances by a suitable written notice or warning. (1979, c. 448, s. 13.)

Article 53.

Commission for Mental Health, Mental Retardation and Substance Abuse Services.

§§ 143-471 through 143-475. Repealed by Session Laws 1975, c. 879, s. 18.

§ 143-475.1: Repealed by Session Laws 1985, c. 589, s. 44.

Article 54.

North Carolina Council on State Goals and Policy Act.

§§ 143-476 through 143-489. Repealed by Session Laws 1975, c. 879, s. 9.

Article 55.

The Southern Growth Policies Agreement.

§ 143-490. Compact enacted into law.

The Southern Growth Policies Agreement is hereby enacted into law and entered into by this State with all other states legally joining therein in the form substantially as follows. (1973, c. 200, s. 1.)

§ 143-491. Article I. Findings and Purposes.

(a)   The party states find that the South has a sense of community based on common social, cultural and economic needs and fostered by a regional tradition. There are vast potentialities for mutual improvement of each state in the region by cooperative planning for the development, conservation and efficient utilization of human and natural resources in a geographic area large enough to afford a high degree of flexibility in identifying and taking maximum advantage of opportunities for healthy and beneficial growth. The independence of each state and the special needs of subregions are recognized and are to be safeguarded. Accordingly, the cooperation resulting from this Agreement is intended to assist the states in meeting their own problems by enhancing their abilities to recognize and analyze regional opportunities and take account of regional influences in planning and implementing their public policies.

(b)   The purposes of this Agreement are to provide:

(1)   Improved facilities and procedures for study, analysis and planning of governmental policies, programs and activities of regional significance.

(2)   Assistance in the prevention of interstate conflicts and the promotion of regional cooperation.

(3)   Mechanisms for the coordination of state and local interests on a regional basis.

(4)   An agency to assist the states in accomplishing the foregoing. (1973, c. 200, s. 1.)

§ 143-492. Article II. The Board.

(a)   There is hereby created the Southern Growth Policies Board, hereinafter called "the Board."

(b)   The Board shall consist of five members from each party state, as follows:

(1)   The governor.

(2)   Two members of the state legislature, one appointed by the presiding officer of each house of the legislature or in such other manner as the legislature may provide. For the Senate of North Carolina, the General Assembly provides that the appointment shall be made by the President Pro Tempore of the Senate.

(3)   Two residents of the state who shall be appointed by the governor to serve at his pleasure.

(c)   In making appointments pursuant to paragraph (b)(3), a governor shall, to the greatest extent practicable, select persons who, along with the other members serving pursuant to paragraph (b), will make the state's representation on the Board broadly representative of the several socioeconomic elements within his state.

(d)   (1)   A governor may be represented by an alternate with power to act in his place and stead, if notice of the designation of such alternate is given to the Board in such manner as its bylaws may provide.

(2)   A legislative member of the Board may be represented by an alternate with power to act in his place and stead, unless the laws of his state prohibit such representation and if notice of the designation of such alternate is given to the Board in such manner as its bylaws may provide. An alternate for a legislative member of the Board shall be selected by the member from among the members of the legislative house in which he serves.

(3)   A member of the Board serving pursuant to paragraph (b)(3) of this Article may be represented by another resident of his state who may participate in his place and stead, except that he shall not vote: Provided that notice of the identity and designation of the representative selected by the member is given to the Board in such manner as its bylaws may provide. (1973, c. 200, s. 1; 1995, c. 490, s. 50.)

§ 143-493. Article III. Powers.

(a)   The Board shall prepare and keep current a statement of regional objectives, including recommended approaches to regional problems. The statement may also identify projects deemed by the Board to be of regional significance. The statement shall be available in its initial form two years from

111

the effective date of this Agreement and shall be amended or revised no less frequently than once every six years. The statement shall be in such detail as the Board may prescribe. Amendments, revisions, supplements or evaluations may be transmitted at any time. An annual commentary on the statement shall be submitted at a regular time to be determined by the Board.

(b)   In addition to powers conferred on the Board elsewhere in this Agreement, the Board shall have the power to make or commission studies, investigations and recommendations with respect to:

(1)   The planning and programming of projects of interstate or regional significance.

(2)   Planning and scheduling of governmental services and programs which would be of assistance to the orderly growth and prosperity of the region, and to the well-being of its population.

(3)   Effective utilization of such federal assistance as may be available on a regional basis or as may have an interstate or regional impact.

(4)   Measures for influencing population distribution, land use, development of new communities and redevelopment of existing ones.

(5)   Transportation patterns and systems of interstate and regional significance.

(6)   Improved utilization of human and natural resources for the advancement of the region as a whole.

(7)   Any other matters of a planning, data collection or informational character that the Board may determine to be of value to the party states. (1973, c. 200, s. 1.)

§ 143-494. Article IV. Avoidance of Duplication.

(a)   To avoid duplication of effort and in the interest of economy, the Board shall make use of existing studies, surveys, plans and data and other materials in the possession of the governmental agencies of the party states and their respective subdivisions or in the possession of other interstate agencies. Each such agency, within available appropriations and if not expressly prevented or limited by law, is hereby authorized to make such materials available to the Board and to otherwise assist it in the performance of its functions. At the request of the Board, each such agency is further authorized to provide information regarding plans and programs affecting the region, or any subarea thereof, so that the Board may have available to it current information with respect thereto.

(b)   The Board shall use qualified public and private agencies to make investigations and conduct research, but if it is unable to secure the undertaking of such investigations or original research by a qualified public or private agency, it shall have the power to make its own investigations and conduct its own research. The Board may make contracts with any public or private agencies or private persons or entities for the undertaking of such investigations or original research within its purview.

(c)   In general, the policy of paragraph (b) of this Article shall apply to the activities of the Board relating to its statement of regional objectives, but nothing herein shall be construed to require the Board to rely on the services of other persons or agencies in developing the statement of regional objectives or any amendment, supplement or revision thereof. (1973, c. 200, s. 1.)

§ 143-495. Article V. Advisory Committees.

The Board shall establish a Local Governments Advisory Committee. In addition, the Board may establish advisory committees representative of subregions of the South, civic and community interests, industry, agriculture, labor or other categories or any combinations thereof. Unless the laws of a party state contain a contrary requirement, any public official of the party state or a subdivision thereof may serve on an advisory committee established pursuant hereto and such service may be considered as a duty of his regular office or employment. (1973, c. 200, s. 1.)

§ 143-496. Article VI. Internal Management of the Board.

(a)   The members of the Board shall be entitled to one vote each. No action of the Board shall be binding unless taken at a meeting at which a majority of the total number of votes on the Board are cast in favor thereof. Action of the Board shall be only at a meeting at which a majority of the members or their alternates are present. The Board shall meet at least once a year. In its bylaws, and subject to such directions and limitations as may be contained therein, the Board may delegate the exercise of any of its powers relating to internal administration and management to an Executive Committee or the Executive Director. In no event shall any such delegation include final approval of:

(1)   A budget or appropriation request.

(2)   The statement of regional objectives or any amendment, supplement or revision thereof.

(3)   Official comments on or recommendations with respect to projects of interstate or regional significance.

(4)   The annual report.

(b)   To assist in the expeditious conduct of its business when the full Board is not meeting, the Board shall elect an Executive Committee of not to exceed 23 members, including at least one member from each party state. The Executive Committee, subject to the provisions of this Agreement and consistent with the policies of the Board, shall be constituted and function as provided in the bylaws of the Board. One half of the membership of the Executive Committee shall consist of governors, and the remainder shall consist of other members of the Board, except that at any time when there is an odd number of members on the Executive Committee, the number of governors shall be one less than half of the total membership. The members of the Executive Committee shall serve for terms of two years, except that members elected to the first Executive Committee shall be elected as follows: One less than half of the membership for two years and the remainder for one year. The Chairman, Chairman-Elect, Vice-Chairman and Treasurer of the Board shall be members of the Executive Committee and anything in this paragraph to the contrary notwithstanding shall serve during their continuance in these offices. Vacancies in the Executive Committee shall not affect its authority to act, but the Board at its next regularly ensuing meeting following the occurrence of any vacancy shall fill it for the unexpired term.

(c)   The Board shall have a seal.

114

(d)   The Board shall elect, from among its members, a Chairman, a Chairman-Elect, a Vice-Chairman and a Treasurer. Elections shall be annual. The Chairman-Elect shall succeed to the office of chairman for the year following his service as Chairman-Elect. For purposes of the election and service of officers of the Board, the year shall be deemed to commence at the conclusion of the annual meeting of the Board and terminate at the conclusion of the next annual meeting thereof. The Board shall provide for the appointment of an Executive Director. Such Executive Director shall serve at the pleasure of the Board, and together with the Treasurer and such other personnel as the Board may deem appropriate shall be bonded in such amounts as the Board shall determine. The Executive Director shall be Secretary.

(e)   The Executive Director, subject to the policy set forth in this Agreement and any applicable directions given by the Board, may make contracts on behalf of the Board.

(f)   Irrespective of the civil service, personnel or other merit system laws of any of the party states, the Executive Director, subject to the approval of the Board, shall appoint, remove or discharge such personnel as may be necessary for the performance of the functions of the Board, and shall fix the duties and compensation of such personnel. The Board in its bylaws shall provide for the personnel policies and programs of the Board.

(g)   The Board may borrow, accept or contract for the services of personnel from any party jurisdiction, the United States, or any subdivision or agency of the aforementioned governments, or from any agency of two or more of the party jurisdictions or their subdivisions.

(h)   The Board may accept for any of its purposes and functions under this Agreement any and all donations, and grants of money, equipment, supplies, materials, and services, conditional or otherwise, from any state, the United States, or any other governmental agency, or from any person, firm, association, foundation, or corporation, and may receive, utilize and dispose of the same. Any donation or grant accepted by the Board pursuant to this paragraph or services borrowed pursuant to paragraph (g) of this Article shall be reported in the annual report of the Board. Such report shall include the nature, amount and conditions, if any, of the donation, grant, or services borrowed, and the identity of the donor or lender.

(i)   The Board may establish and maintain such facilities as may be necessary for the transacting of its business. The Board may acquire, hold, and convey real and personal property and any interest therein.

(j)   The Board shall adopt bylaws for the conduct of its business and shall have the power to amend and rescind these bylaws. The Board shall publish its bylaws in convenient form and shall file a copy thereof and a copy of any amendment thereto, with the appropriate agency or officer in each of the party states.

(k)   The Board annually shall make to the governor and legislature of each party state a report covering the activities of the Board for the preceding year. The Board at any time may make such additional reports and transmit such studies as it may deem desirable.

(l)   The Board may do any other or additional things appropriate to implement powers conferred upon it by this Agreement. (1973, c. 200, s. 1; 1979, c. 35, s. 1.)

§ 143-497. Article VII. Finance.

(a)   The Board shall advise the governor or designated officer or officers of each party state of its budget of estimated expenditures for such period as may be required by the laws of that party state. Each of the Board's budgets of estimated expenditures shall contain specific recommendations of the amount or amounts to be appropriated by each of the party states.

(b)   The total amount of appropriation requests under any budget shall be apportioned among the party states. Such apportionment shall be in accordance with the following formula:

(1)   One third in equal shares,

(2)   One third in the proportion that the population of a party state bears to the population of all party states, and

(3)   One third in the proportion that the per capita income in a party state bears to the per capita income in all party states.

116

In implementing this formula, the Board shall employ the most recent authoritative sources of information and shall specify the sources used.

(c)   The Board shall not pledge the credit of any party state. The Board may meet any of its obligations in whole or in part with funds available to it pursuant to Article VI(h) of this Agreement, provided that the Board takes specific action setting aside such funds prior to incurring an obligation to be met in whole or in part in such manner. Except where the Board makes use of funds available to it pursuant to Article VI(h), or borrows pursuant to this paragraph, the Board shall not incur any obligation prior to the allotment of funds by the party states adequate to meet the same. The Board may borrow against anticipated revenues for terms not to exceed two years, but in any such event the credit pledged shall be that of the Board and not of a party state.

(d)   The Board shall keep accurate accounts of all receipts and disbursements. The receipts and disbursements of the Board shall be subject to the audit and accounting procedures established by its bylaws. However, all receipts and disbursements of funds handled by the Board shall be audited yearly by a certified or licensed public accountant, and the report of the audit shall be included in and become part of the annual report of the Board.

(e)   The accounts of the Board shall be open at any reasonable time for inspection by duly constituted officers of the party states and by any persons authorized by the Board.

(f)   Nothing contained herein shall be construed to prevent Board compliance with laws relating to audit or inspection of accounts by or on behalf of any government contributing to the support of the Board. (1973, c. 200, s. 1.)

§ 143-498. Article VIII. Cooperation with the Federal Government and Other Governmental Entities.

Each party state is hereby authorized to participate in cooperative or joint planning undertakings with the federal government, and any appropriate agency or agencies thereof, or with any interstate agency or agencies. Such participation shall be at the instance of the governor or in such manner as state law may provide or authorize. The Board may facilitate the work of state representatives in any joint interstate or cooperative federal-state undertaking authorized by this Article, and each such state shall keep the Board advised of its activities in respect of such undertakings, to the extent that they have interstate or regional significance. (1973, c. 200, s. 1.)

§ 143-499. Article IX. Subregional Activities.

The Board may undertake studies or investigations centering on the problems of one or more selected subareas within the region: Provided that in its judgment, such studies or investigations will have value as demonstrations for similar or other areas within the region. If a study or investigation that would be of primary benefit to a given state, unit of local government, or intrastate or interstate area is proposed, and if the Board finds that it is not justified in undertaking the work for its regional value as a demonstration, the Board may undertake the study or investigation as a special project. In any such event, it shall be a condition precedent that satisfactory financing and personnel arrangements be concluded to assure that the party or parties benefited bear all costs which the Board determines that it would be inequitable for it to assume. Prior to undertaking any study or investigation pursuant to this Article as a special project, the Board shall make reasonable efforts to secure the undertaking of the work by another responsible public or private entity in accordance with the policy set forth in Article IV(b). (1973, c. 200, s. 1.)

§ 143-500. Article X. Comprehensive Land Use Planning.

If any two or more contiguous party states desire to prepare a single or consolidated comprehensive land use plan, or a land use plan for any interstate area lying partly within each such state, the governors of the states involved may designate the Board as their joint agency for the purpose. The Board shall accept such designation and carry out such responsibility: Provided that the states involved make arrangements satisfactory to the Board to reimburse it or otherwise provide the resources with which the land use plan is to be prepared. Nothing contained in this Article shall be construed to deny the availability for use in the preparation of any such plan of data and information already in the possession of the Board or to require payment on account of the use thereof in addition to payments otherwise required to be made pursuant to other provisions of this Agreement. (1973, c. 200, s. 1.)

§ 143-501. Article XI. Compacts and Agencies Unaffected.

Nothing in this Agreement shall be construed to:

(1)   Affect the powers or jurisdiction of any agency of a party state or any subdivision thereof.

(2)   Affect the rights or obligations of any governmental units, agencies or officials, or of any private persons or entities conferred or imposed by any interstate or interstate-federal compacts to which any one or more states participating herein are parties.

(3)   Impinge on the jurisdiction of any existing interstate-federal mechanism for regional planning or development. (1973, c. 200, s. 1.)

§ 143-502. Article XII. Eligible Parties; Entry into and Withdrawal.

(a)   This Agreement shall have as eligible parties the states of Alabama, Arkansas, Delaware, Florida, Georgia, Kentucky, Louisiana, Maryland, Mississippi, Missouri, North Carolina, Oklahoma, South Carolina, Tennessee, Texas, Virginia, West Virginia, the Commonwealth of Puerto Rico, and the Territory of the Virgin Islands, hereinafter referred to as party states.

(b)   Any eligible state may enter into this Agreement and it shall become binding thereon when it has adopted the same: Provided that in order to enter into initial effect, adoption by at least five states shall be required.

(c)   Adoption of the Agreement may be either by enactment thereof or by adherence thereto by the governor; provided that in the absence of enactment, adherence by the governor shall be sufficient to make his state a party only until December 31, 1973. During any period when a state is participating in this Agreement through gubernatorial action, the governor may provide to the Board an equitable share of the financial support of the Board from any source available to him. Nothing in this paragraph shall be construed to require a governor to take action contrary to the constitution or laws of his state.

(d)   Except for a withdrawal effective on December 31, 1973, in accordance with paragraph (c) of this Article, any party state may withdraw from this Agreement by enacting a statute repealing the same, but no such withdrawal shall take effect until one year after the governor of the withdrawing state has given notice in writing of the withdrawal to the governors of all other party states. No withdrawal shall affect any liability already incurred by or chargeable to a party state prior to the time of such withdrawal. (1973, c. 200, s. 1; 1979, c. 35, s. 2.)

§ 143-503. Article XIII. Construction and Severability.

This Agreement shall be liberally construed so as to effectuate the purposes thereof. The provisions of this Agreement shall be severable and if any phrase, clause, sentence, or provision of this Agreement is declared to be contrary to the constitution of any state or of the United States, or the application thereof to any government, agency, person or circumstance is held invalid, the validity of the remainder of this Agreement and the applicability thereof to any government, agency, person or circumstance shall not be affected thereby. If this Agreement shall be held contrary to the constitution of any state participating therein, the Agreement shall remain in full force and effect as to the state affected as to all severable matters. (1973, c. 200, s. 1.)

§ 143-504. Copies of bylaws and amendments to be filed.

Copies of bylaws and amendments to be filed pursuant to Article VI(j) of the Agreement shall be filed with chief state records-keeping agency. (1973, c. 200, s. 2.)

§ 143-505. Continuance of states as parties.

Nothing contained in the Southern Growth Policies Agreement as enacted by this Article shall in any event be construed to terminate the participation of this State with any state which adopted the Southern Growth Policies Agreement prior to the effective date of this Article, except that the provisions of Article XII(c) shall govern with respect to the continuance of states as parties thereto after December 31, 1973. (1973, c. 200, s. 3.)

§ 143-506. Rights of State and local governments not restricted.

No section, Article, or provision contained herein shall be construed so as to prohibit, restrict or restrain the actions of any individual member state or the actions of any county or municipal government within the boundaries of any individual member state nor shall any delegate from the State of North Carolina be authorized by this General Assembly to cast any vote that would in any manner restrict the sovereign rights presently granted to or retained by this State under the United States Constitution, or the rights of any local governments granted by the Constitution of the State of North Carolina or by statutory acts of the General Assembly. (1973, c. 200, s. 4.)

§§ 143-506.1 through 143-506.5. Reserved for future codification purposes.

Article 55A.

Balanced Growth Policy Act.

§ 143-506.6. Title.

This Article shall be known as the North Carolina Balanced Growth Policy Act. (1979, c. 412, s. 1.)

§ 143-506.7. Purposes.

The purposes of this Article are to declare as a policy that the State of North Carolina shall encourage economic progress and job opportunities throughout the State; support growth trends which are favorable to maintain a dispersed population, to maintain a healthy and pleasant environment and to preserve the natural resources of the State. (1979, c. 412, s. 2.)

§ 143-506.8. Declaration of State Balanced Growth Policy.

The General Assembly of North Carolina recognizes the importance of reaching a higher standard of living throughout North Carolina by maintaining a balance of people, jobs, public services and the environment, supported by the growing network of small and large cities in the State. The General Assembly of North Carolina, in order to assure that opportunities for a higher standard of living are available all across the State, declares that it shall be the policy of the State to bring more and better jobs to where people live; to encourage the development of adequate public services on an equitable basis for all of the State's people at an efficient cost; and to maintain the State's natural environmental heritage while accommodating urban and agricultural growth. (1979, c. 412, s. 3.)

§ 143-506.9. Cooperation of agencies.

The General Assembly encourages, to the fullest extent possible, all State agencies to review their existing policies, procedures and regulations to bring them into conformity with the provisions of this Balanced Growth Policy. (1979, c. 412, s. 4.)

§ 143-506.10. Designation of growth centers; achieving balanced growth.

It shall be the policy of the State of North Carolina to support the expansion of the State and to designate growth areas or centers with the potential, capacity and desire for growth. The Governor, with the advice of county and municipal government officials and citizens, is charged with designating growth areas or centers, which shall include at least one center in each North Carolina county. Designation of growth areas or centers shall be reviewed annually. These designations may be used for the purpose of establishing priority consideration for State and federal assistance for growth.

Progress toward achieving balanced growth shall be measured by the strengthening of economic activity and the adequacy of public services within each of the State's multi-county regions and, as to the geographical area included, the Southeastern Economic Development Commission. The Governor, with the advice of county and municipal government officials and citizens, shall develop measures of progress toward achieving balanced growth. (1979, c. 412, s. 5.)

§ 143-506.11. Citizen participation.

The Governor shall establish a process of citizen participation that assures the expression of needs and aspirations of North Carolina's citizens in regard to the purposes of this Article. (1979, c. 412, s. 6.)

§ 143-506.12. Policy areas.

The following program area guidelines shall become the policy for the State of North Carolina:

(1)   To encourage diversified job growth in different areas of the State, with particular attention to those groups which have suffered from high rates of unemployment or underemployment, so that sufficient work opportunities at high wage levels can exist where people live;

(2)   To encourage the development of transportation systems that link growth areas or centers together with appropriate levels of service;

(3)   To encourage full support for the expansion of family-owned and operated units in agriculture, forestry and the seafood industry as the basis for increasing productive capacity;

(4)   To encourage the development and use of the State's natural resources wisely in support of Balanced Growth Policy while fulfilling the State's constitutional obligation to protect and preserve its natural heritage;

(5)   To promote the concept that a full range of human development services shall be available and accessible to persons in all areas of the State;

(6)   To encourage the continued expansion of early childhood, elementary, secondary and higher education opportunities so that they are improving in both quality and availability;

(7)   To encourage excellent technical training for North Carolina workers that prepares them to acquire and hold high-skill jobs and that encourages industries which employ high-skill workers to locate in the State;

(8)   To encourage the availability of cultural opportunities to people where they live;

(9)   To encourage the expansion of local government capacity for managing growth consistent with this Balanced Growth Policy; and

(10)   To encourage conservation of existing energy resources and provide for the development of an adequate and reliable energy supply, while protecting the environment. (1979, c. 412, s. 7.)

§ 143-506.13. Implementation of a State-local partnership.

The Governor, with the advice of the State Goals and Policy Board, shall establish a statewide policy-setting process for Balanced Growth, in partnership with local government, that brings about full participation of both the State and local government. The purpose of this State-local partnership is to arrive at joint strategies and objectives for balanced statewide development and ensure consistent action by the State and local government for jointly agreed upon strategies and objectives. (1979, c. 412, s. 8.)

§ 143-506.14: Repealed by Session Laws 2011-266, s. 1.12, effective July 1, 2011.

Article 55B.

North Carolina Commission on Jobs and Economic Growth.

§ 143-506.15: Expired.

Article 56.

Emergency Medical Services Act of 1973.

§ 143-507. Establishment of Statewide Emergency Medical Services System.

(a)   There is established a comprehensive Statewide Emergency Medical Services System in the Department of Health and Human Services. All responsibility for this System shall be vested in the Secretary of the Department of Health and Human Services and other officers, boards, and commissions specified by law or regulation.

(b)   The Statewide Medical Services System includes Emergency Medical Services and also includes first aid by members of the community; public knowledge and easy access into the system; prompt emergency medical dispatch of well-designed, equipped, and staffed ambulances; effective care by trained and credentialed personnel with appropriate disposition at the scene of the emergency and while in transit; communications with the treatment center while at the scene and while in transit; routing and referral to the appropriate treatment facility; injury prevention initiatives; wellness initiatives within the community and the public health system; and follow-up lifesaving and restorative care.

(c)   The purpose of this Article is to enable and assist providers of Emergency Medical Services in the delivery of adequate emergency medical services for all people of North Carolina and the provision of medical care during a disaster.

(d)   Emergency Medical Services as referred to in this Article include all services rendered by emergency medical services personnel as defined in G.S. 131E-155(7) in responding to improve the health and wellness of the community and to address the individual's need for immediate emergency medical care in order to prevent loss of life or further aggravation of physiological or psychological illness or injury. (1973, c. 208, s. 1; 1997-443, s. 11A.118(a); 2001-220, s. 1.)

§ 143-508. Department of Health and Human Services to establish program; rules and regulations of North Carolina Medical Care Commission.

(a)   The State Department of Health and Human Services shall establish and maintain a program for the improvement and upgrading of emergency medical services throughout the State. The Department shall consolidate all

State functions relating to emergency medical services, both regulatory and developmental, under the auspices of this program.

(b)   The North Carolina Medical Care Commission shall adopt, amend, and rescind rules to carry out the purpose of this Article and Articles 7 and 7A of Chapter 131E of the General Statutes regardless of other provisions of rule or law. These rules shall be adopted with the advice of the Emergency Medical Services Advisory Council. The Department of Health and Human Services shall enforce all rules adopted by the Commission. Nothing in this Chapter shall be construed to authorize the North Carolina Medical Care Commission to establish or modify the scope of practice of emergency medical personnel.

(c)   The North Carolina Medical Care Commission may adopt rules with regard to emergency medical services, not inconsistent with the laws of this State, that may be required by the federal government for grants-in-aid for emergency medical services and licensure which may be made available to the State by the federal government. This section is to be liberally construed in order that the State and its citizens may benefit from such grants-in-aid.

(d)   The North Carolina Medical Care Commission shall adopt rules to do all of the following:

(1)   Establish standards and criteria for the credentialing of emergency medical services agencies to carry out the purpose of Article 7 of Chapter 131E of the General Statutes.

(2)   Establish standards and criteria for the credentialing of trauma centers to carry out the purpose of Article 7A of Chapter 131E of the General Statutes.

(3)   Establish standards and criteria for the education and credentialing of emergency medical services personnel to carry out the purpose of Article 7 of Chapter 131E of the General Statutes.

(4)   Establish standards and criteria for the credentialing of EMS educational institutions to carry out the purpose of Article 7 of Chapter 131E of the General Statutes.

(5)   Establish standards and criteria for data collection as part of the statewide emergency medical services information system to carry out the purpose of G.S. 143-509(5).

(6)   Implement the scope of practice of credentialed emergency medical services personnel as determined by the North Carolina Medical Board.

(7)   Define the practice settings of credentialed emergency medical services personnel.

(8)   Establish standards for vehicles and equipment used within the emergency medical services system.

(9)   Establish standards for a statewide EMS communications system.

(10)   Establish standards and criteria for the denial, suspension, or revocation of emergency medical services credentials for emergency medical services agencies, educational institutions, and personnel including the establishment of fines for credentialing violations.

(11)   Establish standards and criteria for the education and credentialing of persons trained to administer lifesaving treatment to a person who suffers a severe adverse reaction to agents that might cause anaphylaxis.

(12)   Establish standards for the voluntary submission of hospital emergency medical care data.

(13)   Establish occupational standards for EMS systems, EMS educational institutions, and specialty care transport programs. (1973, c. 208, s. 2; c. 1224, s. 2; 1997-443, s. 11A.118(a); 2001-220, s. 1; 2002-179, s. 13; 2003-392, s. 2(d).)

§ 143-509. Powers and duties of Secretary.

The Secretary of the Department of Health and Human Services has full responsibilities for supervision and direction of the emergency medical services program and, to that end, shall accomplish all of the following:

(1)   After consulting with the Emergency Medical Services Advisory Council and with any local governments that may be involved, seek the establishment of a Statewide Emergency Medical Services System, integrated with other health care providers and networks including, but not limited to, public health, community health monitoring activities, and special needs populations.

(2)   Repealed by Session Laws 1989, c. 74.

(3)   Establish and maintain a comprehensive statewide trauma system in accordance with the provisions of Article 7A of Chapter 131E of the General Statutes and the rules of the North Carolina Medical Care Commission.

(4)   Establish and maintain a statewide emergency medical services communications system including designation of EMS radio frequencies and coordination of EMS radio communications networks within FCC rules and regulations.

(5)   Establish and maintain a statewide emergency medical services information system that provides information linkage between various public safety services and other health care providers.

(6)   Credential emergency medical services providers, vehicles, EMS educational institutions, and personnel after documenting that the requirements of the North Carolina Medical Care Commission are met.

(7),   (8) Repealed by Session Laws 2001-220, s. 1, effective January 1, 2002.

(9)   Promote a means of training individuals to administer life-saving treatment to persons who suffer a severe adverse reaction to agents that might cause anaphylaxis. Individuals, upon successful completion of this training program, may be approved by the North Carolina Medical Care Commission to administer epinephrine to these persons, in the absence of the availability of physicians or other practitioners who are authorized to administer the treatment. This training may also be offered as part of the emergency medical services training program.

(10)   Establish and maintain a collaborative effort with other community resources and agencies to educate the public regarding EMS systems and issues.

(11)   Collaborate with community agencies and other health care providers to integrate the principles of injury prevention into the Statewide EMS System to improve community health.

(12)   Establish and maintain a means of medical direction and control for the Statewide EMS System.

(13)   Establish programs for aiding in the recovery and rehabilitation of EMS personnel who experience chemical addiction or abuse and programs for monitoring these EMS personnel for safe practice. (1973, c. 208, s. 3; 1981, c. 927; 1989, c. 74; 1995, c. 94, s. 34; 1997-443, s. 11A.118(a); 2001-220, s. 1; 2003-392, s. 2(e); 2009-363, s. 1.)

§ 143-510. North Carolina Emergency Medical Services Advisory Council.

(a)   There is created the North Carolina Emergency Medical Services Advisory Council to consult with the Secretary of the Department of Health and Human Services in the administration of this Article.

The North Carolina Emergency Medical Services Advisory Council shall consist of 25 members.

(1)   Twenty-one of the members shall be appointed by the Secretary of the Department of Health and Human Services as follows:

a.   Three of the members shall represent the North Carolina Medical Society and include one licensed pediatrician, one surgeon, and one public health physician.

b.   Three members shall represent the North Carolina College of Emergency Physicians, two of whom shall be current local EMS Medical Directors.

c.   One member shall represent the North Carolina Chapter of the American College of Surgeons Committee on Trauma.

d.   One member shall represent the North Carolina Association of Rescue and Emergency Medical Services.

e.   One member shall represent the North Carolina Association of EMS Administrators.

f.   One member shall represent the North Carolina Hospital Association.

g.   One member shall represent the North Carolina Nurses Association.

129

h.   One member shall represent the North Carolina Association of County Commissioners.

i.   One member shall represent the North Carolina Medical Board.

j.   One member shall represent the American Heart Association, North Carolina Council.

k.   One member shall represent the American Red Cross.

l.   The remaining six members shall be appointed so as to fairly represent the general public, credentialed and practicing EMS personnel, EMS educators, local public health officials, and other EMS interest groups in North Carolina.

(2)   Two members shall be appointed by the General Assembly upon the recommendation of the Speaker of the House of Representatives.

(3)   Two members shall be appointed by the General Assembly upon the recommendation of the President Pro Tempore of the Senate.

The membership of the Council shall, to the extent possible, reflect the gender and racial makeup of the population of the State.

(b)   The members of the Council appointed pursuant to subsection (a) of this section shall serve initial terms as follows:

(1)   The members appointed by the Secretary of the Department of Health and Human Services shall serve initial terms as follows:

a.   Five members shall serve initial terms of one year;

b.   Five members shall serve initial terms of two years;

c.   Five members shall serve initial terms of three years; and

d.   Six members shall serve initial terms of four years.

(2)   The members appointed by the General Assembly upon the recommendation of the President Pro Tempore of the Senate shall serve initial terms as follows:

a.   One member shall serve an initial term of two years; and

b.   One member shall serve an initial term of four years.

(3)   The members appointed by the General Assembly upon the recommendation of the Speaker of the House of the Representatives shall serve initial terms as follows:

a.   One member shall serve an initial term of two years; and

b.   One member shall serve an initial term of four years. Thereafter, all terms shall be four years.

(c)   Any appointment to fill a vacancy on the Council created by the resignation, dismissal, death, or disability of a member shall be for the balance of the unexpired term. Vacancies on the Council among the membership nominated by a society, association, or foundation as provided in subsection (a) of this section shall be filled by appointment of the Secretary upon consideration of a nomination by the executive committee or other authorized agent of the society, association, or foundation until the next meeting of the society, association, or foundation at which time the society, association, or foundation shall nominate a member to fill the vacancy for the unexpired term.

(d)   The members of the Council shall receive per diem and necessary travel and subsistence expenses in accordance with the provisions of G.S. 138-5.

(e)   A majority of the Council shall constitute a quorum for the transaction of business. All clerical and other services required by the Council shall be supplied by the Department of Health and Human Services, Division of Health Service Regulation, Office of Emergency Medical Services.

(f)   The Council shall elect annually from its membership a chairperson and vice-chairperson upon a majority vote of the quorum present. (1973, c. 208, s. 4; 1977, c. 509; 1991, c. 739, s. 24; 1997-443, s. 11A.118(a); 2001-220, s. 1; 2003-392, s. 2(f); 2007-182, s. 1.)

§ 143-511. Powers and duties of the Council.

The North Carolina Emergency Medical Services Advisory Council may advise the Secretary of the Department of Health and Human Services on policy issues regarding the Statewide Emergency Medical Services System, including all rules proposed to be adopted by the North Carolina Medical Care Commission. (1973, c. 208, s. 5; 1997-443, s. 11A.118(a); 2001-220, s. 1.)

§ 143-512. Regional demonstration plans.

The Secretary of the Department of Health and Human Services may develop and implement, in conjunction with any local sponsors that may agree to participate, regional emergency medical services systems in order to demonstrate the desirability of comprehensive regional emergency medical services systems and to determine the optimum characteristics of such plans. The Secretary may make special grants-in-aid to participants. (1973, c. 208, s. 6; 1997-443, s. 11A.118(a); 2001-220, s. 1.)

§ 143-513. Regional emergency medical services councils.

The Secretary of the Department of Health and Human Services may establish emergency medical services regional councils to implement and coordinate emergency medical services programs within regions. (1973, c. 208, s. 7; 1997-443, s. 11A.118(a).)

§ 143-514. Scope of practice for credentialed emergency medical services personnel.

The North Carolina Medical Board shall determine the scope of practice for credentialed emergency medical services personnel regardless of other provisions of law by establishing the medical skills and medications that may be used by credentialed emergency medical services personnel at each level of patient care. No provision of Article 56 of Chapter 143 or Article 7 of Chapter 131E of the General Statutes shall be interpreted to require the North Carolina Medical Board to include any service within the scope of practice of any Emergency Medical Services provider, unless the North Carolina Medical Board determines that the emergency medical service personnel in question have the

132

experience and training necessary to ensure the service can be provided in a safe manner. (1973, c. 208, s. 8; c. 1121; 1995, c. 94, s. 35; 1997-443, s. 11A.118(a); 2001-220, s. 1.)

§ 143-515. Establishment of regions.

The Secretary may establish an appropriate number of multicounty emergency medical services regions. (1973, c. 208, s. 9; 2001-220, s. 1.)

§ 143-516. Single State agency.

The Department of Health and Human Services is hereby designated as the single agency for North Carolina for the purposes of all federal emergency medical services legislation as has or may be hereafter enacted to assist in development of emergency medical services plans and programs. (1973, c. 208, s. 10; 1997-443, s. 11A.118(a).)

§ 143-517. Ambulance support; free enterprise.

Each county shall ensure that emergency medical services are provided to its citizens. Nothing in this Article affects the power of local governments to finance ambulance operations or to support rescue squads. Nothing in this Article shall be construed to allow infringement on the private practice of medicine or the lawful operation of health care facilities. (1973, c. 208, s. 11; 2001-220, s. 1.)

§ 143-518. Confidentiality of patient information.

(a)   Medical records compiled and maintained by the Department, hospitals participating in the statewide trauma system, or EMS providers in connection with dispatch, response, treatment, or transport of individual patients or in connection with the statewide trauma system pursuant to Article 7 of Chapter 131E of the General Statutes may contain patient identifiable data which will

133

allow linkage to other health care-based data systems for the purposes of quality management, peer review, and public health initiatives.

These medical records and data shall be strictly confidential and shall not be considered public records within the meaning of G.S. 132-1 and shall not be released or made public except under any of the following conditions:

(1)   Release is made of specific medical or epidemiological information for statistical purposes in a way that no person can be identified.

(2)   Release is made of all or part of the medical record with the written consent of the person or persons identified or their guardians.

(3)   Release is made to health care personnel providing medical care to the patient.

(4)   Release is made pursuant to a court order. Upon request of the person identified in the record, the record shall be reviewed in camera. In the trial, the trial judge may, during the taking of testimony concerning such information, exclude from the courtroom all persons except the officers of the court, the parties, and those engaged in the trial of the case.

(5)   Release is made to a Medical Review Committee as defined in G.S. 131E-95, 90-21.22A, or 130A-45.7 or to a peer review committee as defined in G.S. 131E-108, 131E-155, 131E-162, 122C-30, or 131D-21.1.

(6)   Release is made for use in a health research project under rules adopted by the North Carolina Medical Care Commission. The Commission shall adopt rules that allow release of information when an institutional review board, as defined by the Commission, has determined that the health research project:

a.   Is of sufficient scientific importance to outweigh the intrusion into the privacy of the patient that would result from the disclosure;

b.   Is impracticable without the use or disclosure of identifying health information;

c.   Contains safeguards to protect the information from redisclosure;

d. Contains safeguards against identifying, directly or indirectly, any patient in any report of the research project; and

e. Contains procedures to remove or destroy at the earliest opportunity, consistent with the purposes of the project, information that would enable the patient to be identified, unless an institutional review board authorizes retention of identifying information for purposes of another research project.

(7) Release is made to a statewide data processor, as defined in Article 11A of Chapter 131E of the General Statutes, in which case the data is deemed to have been submitted as if it were required to have been submitted under that Article.

(8) Release is made pursuant to any other law.

(b) Charges, accounts, credit histories, and other personal financial records compiled and maintained by the Department or EMS providers in connection with the admission, treatment, and discharge of individual patients are strictly confidential and shall not be released. (2001-220, s. 1; 2002-179, s. 11; 2003-392, ss. 2(g), 2(h).)

§ 143-519. Emergency Medical Services Disciplinary Committee.

(a) There is created the Emergency Medical Services Disciplinary Committee. The Committee shall review and make recommendations to the Department regarding all disciplinary matters relating to credentialing of emergency medical services personnel. At the request of the Department, the Committee shall review criminal background information and make a recommendation regarding the eligibility of an individual to obtain initial EMS credentials, renew EMS credentials, or maintain EMS credentials.

(b) The Emergency Medical Services Disciplinary Committee shall consist of seven members appointed by the Secretary of the Department of Health and Human Services to serve four-year terms. Two of the members shall be currently practicing local EMS physician medical directors. One member each shall be a current physician member of the North Carolina Medical Board, a current EMS administrator, a current EMS educator, and two currently practicing and credentialed EMS personnel, one of whom shall be an emergency medical technician-paramedic.

(c)   In order to stagger the terms of the membership of the Committee, the initial appointment for one of the local EMS physician medical directors and the currently practicing and credentialed emergency medical technician-paramedic shall be for a three-year term. The other three initial appointments and all future appointments shall be for four-year terms.

(d)   Any appointment to fill a vacancy on the Committee created by a resignation, dismissal, death, or disability of a member shall be for the balance of the unexpired term.

(e)   A majority of the Committee shall constitute a quorum for the transaction of business. The Department of Health and Human Services, Division of Health Service Regulation, Office of Emergency Medical Services, shall supply all clerical and other services required by the Committee.

(f)   The Committee shall elect annually from its membership a chairperson and vice-chairperson upon a majority vote of the quorum present. (2001-220, s. 1; 2003-392, s. 2(i); 2007-182, s. 1.1; 2007-411, s. 3.)

§ 143-520. Reserved for future codification purposes.

Article 57.

Crime Study Commission.

§§ 143-521 through 143-531. Repealed by Session Laws 1979, c. 504, s. 3.

Article 58.

Committee on Inaugural Ceremonies.

§ 143-532. Definitions.

For the purposes of this Article:

(1)   The term "inaugural period" means the period which includes the day on which the ceremony inaugurating the Governor is held, the seven calendar days immediately preceding such day, and the seven calendar days immediately subsequent to such day; and

(2)   The term "inaugural planning period" means the period beginning July 1 of the year in which the Governor is elected and ending the last day in the inaugural period. (1975, c. 816.)

§ 143-533. Creation, appointment of members; members ex officio.

There is hereby created a Committee on Inaugural Ceremonies to consist of three representatives to be appointed by the Speaker of the House, (or a person designated by the Speaker) three senators to be appointed by the President Pro Tempore of the Senate, three citizens to be appointed by the Governor, and three citizens to be appointed by the Governor-elect upon certification of his election. Of the three citizens appointed to the Committee by the Governor, only two may be of the same political party. The Speaker of the House, the President of the Senate, (or a person designated by the President of the Senate), the Governor, and, upon certification of their election, all members-elect of the Council of State, shall be ex officio members of the Committee on Inaugural Ceremonies. (1975, c. 816; 1981, c. 47, s. 2; 1991, c. 739, s. 25.)

§ 143-534. Time of appointments; terms of office.

Appointments to the Committee on Inaugural Ceremonies shall be made on or before July 1 of years in which there is an election of the Governor. The term of office of the Committee members, the Speaker of the House, the President of the Senate and the Governor who are members ex officio, shall begin on the first day of the inaugural planning period, and shall end on the last day of the inaugural period. The term of office of the members-elect of the Council of State, who are ex officio members of the Committee, shall begin upon certification of their election, and shall end on the last day of the inaugural period. (1975, c. 816.)

§ 143-535. Vacancies.

Vacancies in the appointive membership of the Committee on Inaugural Ceremonies occurring during a term shall be filled for the unexpired term by appointment by the officer who made the original appointment. Vacancies in the ex officio membership shall be filled for the unexpired term by election by the remaining members of the Committee. A legislative vacancy on the Committee shall be filled by a member of the same house in which the vacancy occurred. (1975, c. 816.)

§ 143-536. Chairman; rules of procedure; quorum.

At its first meeting the Committee on Inaugural Ceremonies shall, by majority vote, elect a chairman from within the Committee membership. There shall also be a vice-chairman who shall be designated by the Governor-elect from among his appointees on the Committee who shall assume his duties upon appointment. The chairman, and in his absence the vice-chairman, shall preside over meetings of the Committee. The Committee shall adopt rules of procedure governing its meetings. Six members, excluding ex officio members, shall constitute a quorum of the Committee. (1975, c. 816.)

§ 143-537. Meetings.

The first meeting of the Committee on Inaugural Ceremonies shall be held during the inaugural planning period at the call of the President of the Senate. Thereafter the Committee shall meet at the call of the chairman. (1975, c. 816.)

§ 143-538. Powers and duties.

During the inaugural planning period the Committee on Inaugural Ceremonies shall plan and sponsor official parades, swearing-in ceremonies and other formal occasions connected with the swearing-in and installation of the Governor and other members of the Council of State. Throughout the inaugural planning period the Committee shall consult with and remain in close contact with the Governor-elect and all of the other members-elect of the Council of

State upon certification of their election. Balls, dinners, testimonials, parties and other informal occasions shall be coordinated with official events by the Committee; however, nothing in this Article shall preclude any group or person from conducting private events during the inaugural period. (1975, c. 816.)

§ 143-539. Offices; per diem and allowances of members; payments from appropriations.

The Department of Administration shall provide office space to the Committee. The members of the Committee, including ex officio members, shall be paid such per diem, subsistence and travel allowances as are prescribed by law for State boards and commissions generally. All payments for purposes authorized by this Article shall be paid by the State Treasurer upon written authorization of the chairman of the Committee, from funds appropriated to the Contingency and Emergency Budget. (1975, c. 816; 1991, c. 739, s. 26.)

§§ 143-540 through 143-544. Reserved for future codification purposes.

Article 59.

Vocational Rehabilitation Services.

§ 143-545: Repealed by Session Laws 1995, c. 403, s. 1.

§ 143-545.1. Purpose, establishment and administration of program; services.

(a)   Policy. - Recognizing that disability is a natural part of human experience, the State establishes as its policy that individuals with physical and mental disabilities should be able to participate to the maximum extent of their abilities in the economic, educational, cultural, social, and political activities available to all citizens of the State. To implement this policy, the Department of Health and Human Services shall establish and operate comprehensive and accountable programs of vocational rehabilitation and independent living for

139

persons with disabilities. These programs are to be administered by the Division of Vocational Rehabilitation Services in collaboration with the Division of Services for the Blind, which conducts vocational rehabilitation and independent living programs for individuals who are blind or visually impaired, pursuant to Chapter 111 of the General Statutes and the rules of the Commission for the Blind adopted pursuant to G.S. 143B-157. The programs so provided shall be administered according to the following principles:

(1)   The opportunity and ability to work and to live independently are important activities that enhance not only the lives of individuals with disabilities but also the greater society in which they live. These activities fulfill the need to be productive, promote self-esteem, and allow for participation in the full array of activities of daily living;

(2)   Eligible individuals with disabilities shall be provided individualized training, independent living services, and educational and support services that prepare them for independent living and competitive employment opportunities in integrated settings with reasonable accommodations;

(3)   Individuals with disabilities shall be active participants in their own vocational rehabilitation/independent living programs and shall be involved in making meaningful and informed choices about vocational/independent living goals and objectives and the related services they receive; and

(4)   As full partners in their vocational rehabilitation and independent living programs, participants in the programs shall provide information required by the Department to determine eligibility and the nature of their disabilities, shall use other resources that are available to assist in their programs, and shall assume joint responsibility with departmental staff for planning and implementing their programs.

(b)   Services: -

(1)   Vocational rehabilitation and independent living services provided by the Department shall address comprehensively the needs of each individual to the maximum extent possible within available resources. These services shall contain labor force development and training components and services that enhance the independence and full participation of citizens with disabilities in community life. Specific services shall include assessment services to determine eligibility and rehabilitation needs; counseling, guidance, and referral services; physical and mental restoration services; reader services; vocational

140

and other training services; job development and job placement services; interpreter services; on-the-job or other related personal assistance services including attendant care services; mobility and rehabilitation technology services; training services necessary for living in the community; and supported employment services.

(2)   The Secretary of the Department of Health and Human Services shall adopt rules to establish eligibility for services, the nature and scope of services to be provided, standards for community rehabilitation programs and qualified personnel to provide services and conditions, criteria, and procedures under which services may be provided including financial need for services. Rules governing financial need for services shall meet the requirements set in federal law and regulations.

(3)   The Secretary of the Department of Health and Human Services or, when appropriate, the Commission for the Blind, shall establish by rule a formula for a schedule of rates and fees to be paid by clients and other third party purchasers for services.

(4)   The Secretary of the Department of Health and Human Services or, when appropriate, the Commission for the Blind, shall establish formal appeals procedures that are consistent with those required by federal regulations so that any applicant for or client of vocational rehabilitation or independent living services who is dissatisfied with any determinations made by rehabilitation counselors or coordinators concerning the furnishing or denial of services may request a timely review of those determinations. The appeal procedures shall be the same regardless of whether federal funds are included in the particular services. (1995, c. 403, s. 1(b); 1997-443, s. 11A.118(a); 1997-456, s. 27; 1999-161, s. 1.)

§ 143-546: Repealed by Session Laws 1995, c. 403, s. 2(a).

§ 143-546.1. Duties of Secretary; cooperation with federal rehabilitation services administration or successor.

(a)   [Duties of Secretary]. - In carrying out the purposes of this Article, the Secretary of the Department of Health and Human Services shall:

(1)   Ensure the cooperation of other divisions in the Department of Health and Human Services in implementing the provisions of this Article;

(2)   Cooperate with other departments, agencies, and institutions, both public and private, in providing for the vocational rehabilitation and independent living of individuals with disabilities, in studying the problems involved, and in establishing, developing, and providing the programs, facilities, and services necessary to implement this Article;

(3)   Conduct research and gather statistical data related to the vocational rehabilitation and independent living needs of individuals with disabilities; and

(4)   Administer the expenditure of funds made available by appropriations by the General Assembly by grants from the federal government, and by gifts, grants, or reimbursements from private or public sources, or other sources, and any combination thereof for vocational rehabilitation and independent living services. Gifts or donations, from either public or private sources, as may be offered unconditionally or under conditions that are proper and consistent with this Article, shall be deposited in the State treasury in a fund to be known as the "Vocational Rehabilitation and Independent Living State Program Fund".

(b)   Federal Funds. - In accepting federal funds provided under the Rehabilitation Act of 1973, as amended, the State accepts all of the provisions and benefits of the Act. The Department of Health and Human Services shall:

(1)   Cooperate with the Federal Rehabilitation Services Administration or its successor agency in the administration of the Rehabilitation Act of 1973, as amended;

(2)   Administer vocational rehabilitation and independent living services provided in cooperation with the Federal Rehabilitation Services Administration or its successor agency through an approved State plan;

(3)   Adopt rules as required by the Rehabilitation Act of 1973, as amended, and federal regulations promulgated pursuant to it. (1995, c. 403, s. 2(b); 1997-443, s. 11A.118(a).)

§ 143-547. Subrogation rights; withholding of information a misdemeanor.

(a)   Notwithstanding any other provisions of law, to the extent of payments under this Article, the State Vocational Rehabilitation program shall be subrogated to all rights of recovery, contractual or otherwise, of the beneficiary of the assistance, or his personal representative, his heirs, or the administrator or executor of his estate, against any person; provided, however, that any attorney retained by the beneficiary of the assistance shall be compensated for his services in accordance with the following schedule and in the following order of priority from any amount obtained on behalf of the beneficiary by settlement with, judgment against, or otherwise from a third party by reason of such injury or death:

(1)   First to the payment of any court costs taxed by the judgment;

(2)   Second to the payment of the fee of the attorney representing the beneficiary making the settlement or obtaining the judgment, but this fee shall not exceed one-third of the amount obtained or recovered to which the right of subrogation applies;

(3)   Third to the payment of the amount of assistance received by the beneficiary as prorated with other claims against the amount obtained or received from the third party to which the right of subrogation applies, but the amount shall not exceed one-third of the amount obtained or recovered to which the right of subrogation applies; and

(4)   Fourth to the payment of any amount remaining to the beneficiary or his personal representative.

The United States and the State of North Carolina shall be entitled to shares in each net recovery under this section. Their shares shall be promptly paid under this section and their proportionate parts of such sum shall be determined in accordance with the matching formulas in use during the period for which assistance was paid to the recipient.

(b)   In furnishing a person rehabilitation services, including medical case services under this Chapter, the Division of Vocational Rehabilitation Services is subrogated to the person's right of recovery from:

(1)   Personal insurance;

(2)   Worker's Compensation;

(3)   Any other person or personal injury caused by the other person's negligence or wrongdoing; or

(4)   Any other source.

(c)   The Division of Vocational Rehabilitation Services' right to subrogation is limited to the cost of the rehabilitation services provided by or through the Division for which a financial needs test is a condition of the service provisions. Those services that are provided without a financial needs test are excluded from these subrogation rights.

(d)   The Division of Vocational Rehabilitation Services may totally or partially waive subrogation rights when the Division finds that enforcement would tend to defeat the client's process of rehabilitation or when client assets can be used to offset additional Division costs.

(e)   The Division of Vocational Rehabilitation Services may adopt rules for the enforcement of its rights of subrogation.

(f)   It is a Class 1 misdemeanor for a person seeking or having obtained assistance under this Part for himself or another to willfully fail to disclose to the Division of Vocational Rehabilitation Services or its attorney the identity of any person or organization against whom the recipient of assistance has a right of recovery, contractual or otherwise. (1989, c. 552; 1993, c. 539, s. 1036; 1994, Ex. Sess., c. 24, s. 14(c).)

§ 143-548. Vocational Rehabilitation Council.

(a)   There is established the Vocational Rehabilitation Council within the Division of Vocational Rehabilitation Services to be composed of not more than 18 appointed members. Appointed members shall be voting members except where prohibited by federal law or regulations. The Director of the Division of Vocational Rehabilitation Services and one vocational rehabilitation counselor who is an employee of the Division shall serve ex officio as nonvoting members. The President Pro Tempore of the Senate shall appoint six members, the Speaker of the House of Representatives shall appoint six members, and the Governor shall appoint five or six members. The appointing authorities shall appoint members of the Council after soliciting recommendations from representatives of organizations representing a broad range of individuals with

144

disabilities. Terms of appointment shall be as specified in subsection (d1) of this section. Appointments shall be made as follows:

(1)   The six members appointed by the President Pro Tempore of the Senate shall include one member recommended by the North Carolina Chamber, one other representing providers of community rehabilitation services, one other who is a vocational rehabilitation counselor, with knowledge of and experience with vocational rehabilitation programs, who is not an employee of the Division, one other representing the Commission on Workforce Preparedness, and two others representing disability advocacy groups representing a cross-section of individuals with physical, cognitive, sensory, and mental disabilities. Of the six members appointed by the President Pro Tempore of the Senate, three shall be individuals with disabilities;

(2)   The six members appointed by the Speaker of the House of Representatives shall include one member representing the business and industry sector, one other representing labor, one other representing a parent training and information center established pursuant to section 631(c) of the Individuals with Disabilities Education Act, 20 U.S.C. § 1431(c), one other representing the Department of Public Instruction, and two others representing disability advocacy groups representing a cross-section of individuals with physical, cognitive, sensory, and mental disabilities. Of the six members appointed by the Speaker of the House of Representatives, three shall be individuals with disabilities; and

(3)   The five or six members appointed by the Governor shall include one member representing the business and industry sector, one other representing the regional rehabilitation centers for the physically disabled, one other representing the Division's Statewide Independent Living Council, one other representing the State's Client Assistance Program, one other representing the directors of projects carried out under section 121 of the Rehabilitation Act of 1973, 29 U.S.C. § 741, as amended, if there are any of these projects in the State, and one other current or former applicant for or recipient of vocational rehabilitation services. If five members are appointed by the Governor, three shall be individuals with disabilities. If six members are appointed by the Governor, four shall be individuals with disabilities.

(b)   Repealed by Session Laws 1993, c. 248, s. 1.

(b1)   Additional Qualifications. - In addition to ensuring the qualifications for membership prescribed in subsection (a) of this section, the appointing authorities shall ensure that a majority of Council members are individuals with disabilities and are not employed by the Division of Vocational Rehabilitation Services.

(c)   The Council shall elect one of the voting members of the Council as Chair of the Council. The Chair's term shall not exceed a single three-year term.

(d)   The Council shall meet at least quarterly and at other times at the call of the Chair. A majority of the voting members of the Council constitutes a quorum.

(d1)   Terms of Appointment. -

(1)   Length of Term. - Each member of the Council shall serve for a term of not more than three years, except that:

a.   A member appointed to fill a vacancy occurring prior to the expiration of the term for which a predecessor was appointed shall be appointed for the remainder of that term;

b.   The terms of service of the members initially appointed are as specified by the appointing authority for a fewer number of years as will provide for the expiration of terms on a staggered basis and shall include the members of the existing Council to the extent possible with appropriate adjustments to their terms;

c.   The appointing authority shall have the power to remove any member of the Council from office in accordance with the provisions of G.S. 143B-16; and

d.   A member may continue to serve until a successor for the position is appointed;

(2)   Number of Terms. - No member of the Council other than the representative of the Client Assistance Program and the representative of the directors of projects carried out under section 121 of the Rehabilitation Act of 1973, 29 U.S.C. § 741, as amended, may serve more than two consecutive full terms.

(d2)   Vacancies. - Any vacancy occurring in the membership of the Council shall be filled in the same manner as the original appointment. The vacancy shall not affect the power of the remaining members to execute the duties of the Council.

(d3)   Functions of Council. - The Council shall, after consulting with the Commission on Workforce Preparedness:

(1)   Review, analyze, and advise the Division regarding the performance of its responsibilities under Title I of the Rehabilitation Act of 1973, Pub. L. No. 93-112, 29 U.S.C. § 720, et seq., as amended, particularly responsibilities relating to:

a.   Eligibility, including order of selection;

b.   The extent, scope, and effectiveness of services provided; and

c.   Functions performed by State agencies that affect or that potentially affect the ability of individuals with disabilities in achieving employment outcomes under Title I of the Rehabilitation Act of 1973, Pub. L. No. 93-112, 29 U.S.C. § 720, et seq.;

(1a)   In partnership with the Division:

a.   Develop, agree to, and review State goals and priorities in accordance with section 101(a)(15)(C) of the Rehabilitation Act of 1973, 29 U.S.C. § 721(a)(15)(C); and

b.   Evaluate the effectiveness of the vocational rehabilitation program and submit reports of progress to the Commissioner of the Rehabilitation Services Administration of the U.S. Department of Education in accordance with section 101(a)(15)(E) of the Rehabilitation Act of 1973, 29 U.S.C. § 721(a)(15)(E);

(2)   Advise the Department of Health and Human Services and the Division regarding activities authorized to be carried out under Title I of the Rehabilitation Act of 1973, Pub. L. No. 93-112, 29 U.S.C. § 720, et seq., as amended and assist in the preparation of applications, the State Plan, amendments to the plans, reports, needs assessments, and evaluations required by Title I of the Rehabilitation Act of 1973;

(3)   To the extent feasible, conduct a review and analysis of the effectiveness of, and consumer satisfaction with:

a.   Vocational rehabilitation functions and services provided by the Department of Health and Human Services and other State agencies and public and private entities responsible for providing vocational rehabilitation services to

147

individuals with disabilities under the Rehabilitation Act of 1973, Pub. L. No. 93-112, 87 Stat. 355, 29 U.S.C. § 701, et seq.; and

b.   Repealed by Session Laws 1999-161, s. 2, effective June 8, 1999.

c.   Employment outcomes achieved by eligible individuals receiving services under Title I of the Rehabilitation Act of 1973, Pub. L. No. 93-112, 29 U.S.C. § 720, et seq., as amended, including the availability of health and other employment benefits in connection with those employment outcomes;

(4)   Prepare and submit an annual report to the Governor and the Commissioner of the Rehabilitation Services Administration of the U.S. Department of Education on the status of vocational rehabilitation programs operated within the State and make the report available to the public;

(5)   Coordinate activities with the activities of other councils within the State, including the Division's Statewide Independent Living Council established under section 705 of the Rehabilitation Act of 1973, 29 U.S.C. § 742, the advisory panel established under section 612(a)(21) of the Individuals with Disabilities Education Act, 20 U.S.C. § 1413(a)(12), the State Development Disabilities Council described in section 124 of the Developmental Disabilities Assistance and Bill of Rights Act, 42 U.S.C. § 6024, the State Mental Health Planning Council established under section 1914(a) of the Public Health Service Act, 42 U.S.C. § 300x-4(e), and the Commission on Workforce Preparedness;

(6)   Provide for coordination and the establishment of working relationships between the Department and the Statewide Independent Living Council and centers for independent living within the State; and

(7)   Perform such other functions, consistent with the purpose of Title I of the Rehabilitation Act of 1973, Pub. L. No. 93-112, 29 U.S.C. § 720, et seq., as amended, as the Council determines to be appropriate, that are comparable to other functions performed by the Council.

(d4)   Resources. -

(1)   The Division shall supply all necessary clerical and staff support to the Council pursuant to G.S. 143B-14(a) and (d). The Council shall prepare, in conjunction with the Division, a plan for the provision of such resources as may be necessary and sufficient to carry out the functions of the Council under this

148

Part. The resource plan shall, to the maximum extent possible, rely on the use of resources in existence during the period of implementation of the plan.

(2)   To the extent that there is a disagreement between the Council and the Division in regard to the resources necessary to carry out the functions of the Council as set forth in this Part, the disagreement shall be resolved by the Governor.

(3)   While assisting the Council in carrying out its duties, staff and other personnel shall not be assigned duties by the Division or any other agency of the State that would create a conflict of interest.

(d5)   Member Conflict of Interest. - No member of the Council shall cast a vote on any matter that would provide direct financial benefit to the member or otherwise give the appearance of a conflict of interest under State law.

(e)   Council members shall be reimbursed for expenses incurred in the performance of their duties in accordance with G.S. 138-5. In addition, Council members may be reimbursed for personal assistance services that are necessary for members to attend Council meetings and perform Council duties. These expenses shall not exceed whichever is lower, the actual cost of the services or the Medicaid rate per day for personal assistance services, in addition to subsistence and travel expenses at the State rate for the attendant.

(f)   Repealed by Session Laws 1993, c. 248, s. 1. (1991 (Reg. Sess., 1992), c. 900, s. 150; 1993, c. 248, s. 1; 1997-443, s. 11A.118(a); 1997-509, s. 1; 1999-161, s. 2; 2009-570, s. 8(e).)

§§ 143-549 through 143-551. Reserved for future codification purposes.

Article 60.

State and Certain Local Educational Entity Employees, Nonsalaried Public Officials, and Legislators Required to Repay Money Owed to State.

Part 1. State and Local Educational Entity Employees.

§ 143-552. Definitions.

As used in this Part:

(1)   "Employing entity" means and includes:

a.   Any State entity enumerated in G.S. 143B-3 of the Executive Organization Act of 1973;

b.   Any city or county board of education under Chapter 115 of the General Statutes; or

c.   Any board of trustees of a community college under Chapter 115D of the General Statutes.

(2)   "Employee" means any person who is appointed to or hired and employed by an employing entity under this Part and whose salary is paid in whole or in part by State funds.

(3)   "Net disposable earnings" means the salary paid to an employee by an employing entity after deduction of withholdings for taxes, social security, State retirement or any other sum obligated by law to be withheld. (1979, c. 864, s. 1; 1987, c. 564, s. 29.)

§ 143-553. Conditional continuing employment; notification among employing entities; repayment election.

(a)   All persons employed by an employing entity as defined by this Part who owe money to the State and whose salaries are paid in whole or in part by State funds must make full restitution of the amount owed as a condition of continuing employment; provided, however, that no employing entity shall terminate for failure to make full restitution the employment of such an employee who owes money to the University of North Carolina Health Care System or to East Carolina University's Division of Health Sciences for health care services.

(b)   Whenever a representative of any employing entity as defined by this Part has knowledge that an employee owes money to the State and is delinquent in satisfying this obligation, the representative shall notify the employing entity. Upon receipt of notification an employing entity shall terminate the employee's employment if after written notice of his right to do so he does not repay the money within a reasonable period of time; provided, however, that where there is a genuine dispute as to whether the money is owed or how much is owed, or there is an unresolved issue concerning insurance coverage, the employee shall not be dismissed as long as he is pursuing administrative or judicial remedies to have the dispute or the issue resolved.

(c)   An employee of any employing entity who has elected in writing to allow not less than ten percent (10%) of his net disposable earnings to be periodically withheld for application towards a debt to the State shall be deemed to be repaying the money within a reasonable period of time and shall not have his employment terminated so long as he is consenting to repayment according to such terms. Furthermore, the employing entity shall allow the employee who for some extraordinary reason is incapable of repaying the obligation to the State according to the preceding terms to continue employment as long as he is attempting repayment in good faith under his present financial circumstances, but shall promptly terminate the employee's employment if he ceases to make payments or discontinues a good faith effort to make repayment. (1979, c. 864, s. 1; 2007-306, s. 2; 2012-194, s. 68(a).)

§ 143-554. Right of employee appeal.

(a)   Any employee or former employee of an employing entity within the meaning of G.S. 143-552(1)a whose employment is terminated pursuant to the provisions of this Part shall be given the opportunity to appeal the employment termination to the State Human Resources Commission according to the normal appeal and hearing procedures provided by Chapter 126 and the State Human Resources Commission rules adopted pursuant to the authority of that Chapter; however, nothing herein shall be construed to give the right to termination reviews to anyone exempt from that right under G.S. 126-5.

(b)   Before the employment of an employee of a local board of education within the meaning of G.S. 143-552(1)b who is either a superintendent, supervisor, principal, teacher or other professional person is terminated pursuant to this Part, the local board of education shall comply with the provisions of G.S. 115-142. If an employee within the meaning of G.S. 143-552(1)b is other than one whose termination is made reviewable pursuant to G.S. 115-142, he shall be given the opportunity for a hearing before the local board of education prior to the termination of his employment.

(c)   Before the employment of an employee of a board of trustees of a community college within the meaning of G.S. 143-552(1)c is finally terminated pursuant to this Part, he shall be given the opportunity for a hearing before the board of trustees. (1979, c. 864, s. 1; 1987, c. 564, s. 12; 2013-382, s. 9.1(c).)

Part 2. Public Officials.

§ 143-555. Definitions.

As used in this Part:

(1)   "Appointing authority" means the Governor, Chief Justice of the Supreme Court, Lieutenant Governor, Speaker of the House, President pro tempore of the Senate, members of the Council of State, all heads of the executive departments of State government, the Board of Governors of The University of North Carolina, and any other State person or group of State persons authorized by law to appoint to a public office.

(2)   "Employing entity" means and includes:

a.   Any State entity enumerated in G.S. 143B-3 of the Executive Organization Act of 1973;

b.   Any city or county board of education under Chapter 115 of the General Statutes; or

c.   Any board of trustees of a community college under Chapter 115D of the General Statutes.

(3)   "Public office" means appointive membership on any State Commission, council, committee, board, including occupational licensing boards as defined in G.S. 93B-1, board of trustees, including boards of constituent institutions of The University of North Carolina and boards of community colleges under Chapter 115D of the General Statutes, and any other State agency created by law; provided that "public office" does not include an office for which a regular salary is paid to the holder as an employee of the State or of one of its departments, agencies, or institutions.

152

(4)   "Public official" means any person who is a member of any public office as defined by this Part. (1979, c. 864, s. 1; 1987, c. 564, ss. 29, 30.)

§ 143-556. Notification of the appointing authority; investigation.

Whenever a representative of an employing entity as defined by this Part has knowledge that a public official owes money to the State and is delinquent in satisfying this obligation, the representative shall notify the appointing authority who appointed the public official in question. Upon receipt of notification the appointing authority shall investigate the circumstances of the claim of money owed to the State for purposes of determining if a debt is owed and its amount. (1979, c. 864, s. 1.)

§ 143-557. Conditional continuing appointment; repayment election.

If after investigation under the terms of this Part an appointing authority determines the existence of a delinquent monetary obligation owed to the State by a public official, he shall notify the public official that his appointment will be terminated 60 days from the date of notification unless repayment in full is made within that period. Upon determination that any public official has not made repayment in full after the expiration of the time prescribed by this section, the appointing authority shall terminate the appointment of the public official; provided however, the appointing authority shall allow the public official who for some extraordinary reason is incapable of repaying the obligation according to the preceding terms to continue his appointment as long as he is attempting repayment in good faith under his present financial circumstances, but shall promptly terminate the public official's appointment if he ceases to make payments or discontinues a good faith effort to make repayment. (1979, c. 864, s. 1.)

Part 3. Legislators.

§ 143-558. Definition of employing entity.

153

For the purposes of this Part "employing entity" shall have the same meaning as provided in G.S. 143-552(1) and 143-555(2). (1979, c. 864, s. 1.)

§ 143-559. Notification to the Legislative Ethics Committee; investigation.

Whenever a representative of any employing entity as defined by this Part has knowledge that a legislator owes money to the State and is delinquent in satisfying this obligation, this information shall be reported to the Legislative Ethics Committee established pursuant to Chapter 120, Article 14 of the General Statutes for disposition. (1979, c. 864, s. 1.)

Part 4. Confidentiality Exemption, Preservation of Federal Funds, and Limitation of Actions.

§ 143-560. Confidentiality exemption.

Notwithstanding the provisions of any law of this State making confidential the contents of any records or prohibiting the release or disclosure of any information, all information exchange among the employing entities defined under this Article necessary to accomplish and effectuate the intent of this Article is lawful. (1979, c. 864, s. 1.)

§ 143-561. Preservation of federal funds.

Nothing in this Article is intended to conflict with any provision of federal law or to result in the loss of federal funds. If the exchange among employing entities of information necessary to effectuate the provisions of this Article would conflict with this intention, the exchange of information shall not be made. (1979, c. 864, s. 1.)

§ 143-562. Applicability of a statute of limitations.

Payments on obligations to the State collected under the procedures established by this Article shall not be construed to revive obligations or any part thereof already barred by an applicable statute of limitations. Furthermore, payments made as a result of collection procedures established by the terms of this Article shall not be construed to extend an applicable statute of limitations. (1979, c. 864, s. 1.)

Article 61.

Commission on the Bicentennial of the United States Constitution.

§§ 143-563 through 143-570: Expired.

Article 62.

North Carolina Child Fatality Prevention System.

§§ 143-571 through 143-579: Repealed by Session Laws 1998-202, s. 5, effective July 1, 1999.

Article 63.

State Employees Workplace Requirements Program for Safety and Health.

Part 1. Executive Branch Programs.

§ 143-580. Definition.

As used in this Article, "State agency" means any department, commission, division, board, or institution of the State within the executive branch of government and the Office of Administrative Hearings. (1991 (Reg. Sess., 1992), c. 994, s. 1.)

§ 143-581. Program goals.

Each State agency shall establish a written program for State employee workplace safety and health. The program shall promote safe and healthful working conditions and shall be based on clearly stated goals and objectives for meeting the goals. The program shall provide managers, supervisors, and employees with a clear and firm understanding of the State's concern for protecting employees from job-related injuries and health impairment; preventing accidents and fires; planning for emergencies and emergency medical procedures; identifying and controlling physical, chemical, and biological hazards in the workplace; communicating potential hazards to employees; and assuring adequate housekeeping and sanitation. (1991 (Reg. Sess., 1992), c. 994, s. 1.)

§ 143-582. Program requirements.

The written program required under this Article shall describe at a minimum:

(1)   The methods to be used to identify, analyze, and control new or existing hazards, conditions, and operations.

(2)   How managers, supervisors, and employees are responsible for implementing the program, controlling accident-related expenditures, and how continued participation of management and employees will be established, measured, and maintained.

(3)   How the plan will be communicated to all affected employees so that they are informed of work-related physical, chemical, or biological hazards, and controls necessary to prevent injury or illness.

(4)   How managers, supervisors, and employees will receive training in avoidance of job-related injuries and health impairment.

(5)   How workplace accidents will be reported and investigated and how corrective actions will be implemented.

(6)   How safe work practices and rules will be communicated and enforced.

(7)   The safety and health training program that will be made available to employees.

156

(8)   How employees can make complaints concerning safety and health problems without fear of retaliation.

(9)   How employees will receive medical attention following a work-related injury or illness. (1991 (Reg. Sess., 1992), c. 994, s. 1.)

§ 143-583. Model program; technical assistance; reports.

(a)   The State Human Resources Commission, through the Office of State Human Resources, shall:

(1)   Maintain a model program of safety and health requirements to guide State agencies in the development of their individual programs and in complying with the provisions of G.S. 95-148 and this Article.

(2)   Establish guidelines for the creation and operation of State agency safety and health committees.

(b)   The Office of State Human Resources shall:

(1)   Provide consultative and technical services to assist State agencies in establishing and administering their workplace safety and health programs and to address specific technical problems.

(2)   Monitor compliance with this Article.

(c)   The State Human Resources Commission shall report annually to the Joint Legislative Commission on Governmental Operations on the safety and health activities of State agencies, compliance with this Article, and the fines levied against State agencies pursuant to Article 16 of Chapter 95 of the General Statutes. (1991 (Reg. Sess., 1992), c. 994, s. 1; 2013-382, s. 9.1(c).)

§ 143-584. State agency safety and health committees.

Each State agency shall create, pursuant to guidelines adopted under subsection (a) of G.S. 143-583, safety and health committees to perform workplace inspections, review injury and illness records, make advisory

157

recommendations to the agency's managers, and perform other functions determined by the State Human Resources Commission to be necessary for the effective implementation of the State Employees Workplace Requirements Program for Safety and Health. (1991 (Reg. Sess., 1992), c. 994, s. 1; 2013-382, s. 9.1(c).)

§§ 143-585 through 143-588. Reserved for future codification purposes.

Part 2. Legislative and Judicial Branch Programs.

§ 143-589. Legislative and judicial branch safety and health programs.

The Legislative Services Commission and the Administrative Office of the Courts are authorized to separately establish safety and health programs for their employees. (1991 (Reg. Sess., 1992), c. 994, s. 3; 2001-424, s. 22.6(c).)

§§ 143-590 through 143-594. Reserved for future codification purposes.

Article 64.

Smoking in Public Places.

§ 143-595. Legislative intent.

It is the intent of the General Assembly to address the needs and concerns of both smokers and nonsmokers in public places by providing for designated smoking and nonsmoking areas. (1993, c. 367, s. 1.)

§ 143-596. Definitions.

As used in this Article, unless the context clearly provides otherwise:

(1)   Constituent institution. - As defined in G.S. 116-2(4) and G.S. 116-4.

158

(1a)   Grounds. - The area located and controlled by State government that is within 100 linear feet of any of the following:

a.   A State-owned building allocated to and occupied by State government.

b.   A State-owned building leased to a third party.

c.   A building owned by a third party and leased to State government.

(1b)   Local government. - The local political subdivision of the State or any authority or body created by any ordinance or rules of any such entity.

(1c)   Medical Faculty Practice Plan. - As defined in G.S. 116-40.6.

(2)   Nonsmoking area. - Any designated area where smoking is not permitted.

(3)   Public meeting. - Any assemblage authorized by State or local government or any subdivision of State or local government.

(4)   Restaurant. - Any building, structure, or area having a seating capacity of 50 or more patrons where food is available for eating on the premises in consideration of payment. The following are not included in determining seating capacity:

a.   Seats in any bar or lounge area of a restaurant.

b.   Seats in any separate room or section of a restaurant which is used exclusively for private functions.

c.   Seats in any open outside area.

(5)   Smoke, smokes, or smoking. - The use or possession of a lighted cigarette, lighted cigar, lighted pipe, or any other lighted tobacco product.

(6)   State government. - The political unit for the State of North Carolina; including all agencies of the executive, judicial, and legislative branches of government.

(7)   The University of North Carolina. - As defined in Chapter 116 of the General Statutes.

159

(8)   The University of North Carolina Health Care System. - As defined in G.S. 116-37. (1993, c. 367, s. 1; 2007-114, s. 1.)

§ 143-597. Nonsmoking areas in State-controlled buildings.

(a)   All of the following areas may be designated as nonsmoking in buildings owned, leased, or occupied by State government:

(1)   Any library open to the public.

(2)   Any museum open to the public.

(3)   Any area established as a nonsmoking area, so long as at least twenty percent (20%) of the interior space of equal quality to that of the nonsmoking area shall be designated as a smoking area, unless physically impracticable. If physically impracticable, the person in charge of the facility shall provide an adequate smoking area within the facility as near as feasible to twenty percent (20%) of the interior space.

(4)   Any indoor space in a State-controlled building such as an auditorium, arena, or coliseum, or an appurtenant building thereof; except that a designated area for smoking shall be established in lobby areas.

(5)   Any educational buildings primarily involved in health care instruction and the grounds of those buildings.

(6)   Except as provided in G.S. 143-599(11), any facilities of The University of North Carolina and the grounds of those facilities. Each constituent institution, except for the North Carolina School of Science and Mathematics, shall make a reasonable effort to provide residential smoking rooms in residence halls in proportion to student demand for those rooms. For purposes of this subdivision, the term "facilities" includes all of the following:

a.   State-owned buildings allocated to and occupied by The University of North Carolina.

b.   State-owned buildings allocated to The University of North Carolina and leased to a third party.

160

c.   The area of any building owned by a third party and occupied by The University of North Carolina as lessee.

(7)   Repealed by Session Laws 2007-114, s. 2, effective July 1, 2007.

(a1)   All areas of any building occupied by the General Assembly shall be designated as nonsmoking areas.

(b)   Any area designated as nonsmoking or smoking shall be established by the appropriate department, institution, agency, or person in charge of the State-controlled building or area, except as specified in subsection (a1). The person in charge of the building shall conspicuously post or cause to be posted, in any area designated as a smoking or nonsmoking area, one or more signs stating that smoking is or is not permitted in the area.

(c)   Where a nonsmoking area is designated, existing physical barriers and ventilation systems shall be used where appropriate to minimize smoke from adjacent areas. This subsection shall not be construed to require fixed structural or other physical modification in providing these areas or to require installation or operation of any heating, ventilating, or air-conditioning system in any manner which adds expense. (1993, c. 367, s. 1; 2003-292, s. 1; 2006-66, s. 9.11(cc); 2006-76, s. 1; 2007-114, s. 2.)

§ 143-598. Prohibited acts related to nonsmoking areas.

(a)   No person shall smoke in a nonsmoking area in a State-controlled building or area pursuant to G.S. 143-597.

(b)   Any person who continues to smoke in a nonsmoking area described in this section following notice by the person in charge of the State-controlled building or area or their designee that smoking is not permitted shall be guilty of an infraction and punished by a fine of not more than twenty-five dollars ($25.00). (1993, c. 367, s. 1.)

§ 143-599. Exemptions.

All of the following facilities shall be exempt from the provisions of this Article:

161

(1)   Any primary or secondary school or child care center, except for a teacher's lounge.

(2)   An enclosed elevator.

(3)   Public school bus.

(4)   Hospital, nursing home, rest home, and State facility operated under the authority of G.S. 122C-181.

(5)   Local health department and local department of social services and the building and grounds where the local health department or local department of social services, as applicable, is located. For the purposes of this subdivision, "grounds" means the area located within 50 linear feet of a local health department or a local department of social services.

(6)   Any nonprofit organization or corporation whose primary purpose is to discourage the use of tobacco products by the general public.

(7)   Tobacco manufacturing, processing, and administrative facilities.

(8)   Indoor arenas with a seating capacity greater than 23,000.

(9)   State correctional facilities operated by the Division of Adult Correction of the Department of Public Safety.

(10)   Community colleges.

(11)   The buildings, grounds, and walkways of the University of North Carolina Health Care System and of the East Carolina University School of Medicine, Health Sciences Complex, and Medical Faculty Practice Plan. (1993, c. 367, s. 1; 1997-506, s. 53; 2005-19, s. 1; 2005-168, s. 1; 2005-239, s. 1; 2005-372, s. 1; 2006-133, s. 1; 2007-114, s. 3; 2011-145, s. 19.1(h).)

§ 143-600. Construction of Article.

Nothing in this Article shall be construed to permit smoking in any area where smoking is prohibited by any other law or rule for fire safety purposes, including the State minimum fire safety standards pursuant to Chapter 58, Chapter 153A, or Chapter 160A of the General Statutes; provided, however, this Article shall not be construed to recognize any authority of a local government to restrict smoking other than as provided in this Article, for fire safety purposes as specified herein, and for the facilities exempt pursuant to G.S. 143-599. (1993, c. 367, s. 1.)

§ 143-601. Applicability of Article; local government may enact.

(a)   This Article shall not supersede nor prohibit the enactment or enforcement of any otherwise valid local law, rule, or ordinance enacted prior to October 15, 1993, regulating the use of tobacco products. However, no local law, rule, or ordinance enacted and placed in operation prior to October 15, 1993, shall be amended to impose a more stringent standard than in effect on the date of ratification of this Article.

(b)   Any local ordinance, law, or rule that regulates smoking adopted on or after October 15, 1993, shall not contain restrictions regulating smoking which exceed those established in this Article. Any such local ordinance, law, or rule may restrict smoking in accordance with this subsection and pursuant to G.S. 143-597 only in the following facilities that are not owned, leased, or occupied by local government:

(1)   Repealed by Session Laws 2007-193, s. 3, effective January 1, 2008.

(2)   A public meeting.

(3)   The indoor space in an auditorium, arena, or coliseum, or an appurtenant building thereof.

(4)   A library or museum open to the public.

(5)   Repealed by Session Laws 2007-193, s. 3, effective January 1, 2008.

If any of the facilities listed in this subsection are owned, leased as lessor, or the area leased as lessee and occupied by local government, then the local ordinance, law, or rule restricting smoking shall be governed by Article 23 of Chapter 130A of the General Statutes. (1993, c. 367, s. 1; 2007-193, s. 3.)

163

§§ 143-602 through 143-609. Reserved for future codification purposes.

Article 65.

Medical Education and Primary Care.

§§ 143-610 through 143-611: Repealed by Session Laws 1996, Second Extra Session, c. 17, s. 16.2.

§ 143-612: Repealed by Session Laws 1995, c. 507, s. 23A.3(d).

§ 143-612A: Repealed by Session Laws 1996, Second Extra Session, c. 17, s. 16.2.

§ 143-613. Medical education; primary care physicians and other providers.

(a)   In recognition of North Carolina's need for primary care physicians, Bowman Gray School of Medicine and Duke University School of Medicine shall each prepare a plan with the goal of encouraging North Carolina residents to enter the primary care disciplines of general internal medicine, general pediatrics, family medicine, obstetrics/gynecology, and combined medicine/pediatrics and to strive to have at least fifty percent (50%) of North Carolina residents graduating from each school entering these disciplines. These schools of medicine shall present their plans to the Board of Governors of The University of North Carolina by April 15, 1996, and shall update and present their plans every two years thereafter. The Board of Governors shall report to the Joint Legislative Education Oversight Committee by May 15, 1996, and every two years thereafter on the status of these efforts to strengthen primary health care in North Carolina.

(b)   The Board of Governors of The University of North Carolina shall set goals for the Schools of Medicine at the University of North Carolina at Chapel Hill and the School of Medicine at East Carolina University for increasing the percentage of graduates who enter residencies and careers in primary care. A minimum goal should be at least sixty percent (60%) of graduates entering primary care disciplines. Each school shall submit a plan with strategies to reach these goals of increasing the number of graduates entering primary care disciplines to the Board by April 15, 1996, and shall update and present the

164

plans every two years thereafter. The Board of Governors shall report to the Joint Legislative Education Oversight Committee by May 15, 1996, and every two years thereafter on the status of these efforts to strengthen primary health care in North Carolina.

Primary care shall include the disciplines of family medicine, general pediatric medicine, general internal medicine, internal medicine/pediatrics, and obstetrics/gynecology.

(b1)   The Board of Governors of The University of North Carolina shall set goals for State-operated health professional schools that offer training programs for licensure or certification of physician assistants, nurse practitioners, and nurse midwives for increasing the percentage of the graduates of those programs who enter clinical programs and careers in primary care. Each State-operated health professional school shall submit a plan with strategies for increasing the percentage to the Board by April 15, 1996, and shall update and present the plan every two years thereafter. The Board of Governors shall report to the Joint Legislative Education Oversight Committee by May 15, 1996, and every two years thereafter on the status of these efforts to strengthen primary health care in North Carolina.

(c)   The Board of Governors of The University of North Carolina shall further initiate whatever changes are necessary on admissions, advising, curriculum, and other policies for State-operated medical schools and State-operated health professional schools to ensure that larger proportions of students seek residencies and clinical training in primary care disciplines. The Board shall work with the Area Health Education Centers and other entities, adopting whatever policies it considers necessary to ensure that residency and clinical training programs have sufficient residency and clinical positions for graduates in these primary care specialties. As used in this subsection, health professional schools are those schools or institutions that offer training for licensure or certification of physician assistants, nurse practitioners, and nurse midwives.

(d)   The progress of the private and State-operated medical schools and State-operated health professional schools towards increasing the number and proportion of graduates entering primary care shall be monitored annually by the Board of Governors of The University of North Carolina. Monitoring data shall include (i) the entry of State-supported graduates into primary care residencies and clinical training programs, and (ii) the specialty practices by a physician and each midlevel provider who were State-supported graduates as of a date five years after graduation. The Board of Governors shall certify data on graduates,

165

their residencies and clinical training programs, and subsequent careers by November 15 of each calendar year, beginning in November of 2012, to the Fiscal Research Division of the Legislative Services Office and to the Joint Legislative Education Oversight Committee.

(e)   The information provided in subsection (d) of this section shall be made available to the Appropriations Committees of the General Assembly for their use in future funding decisions on medical and health professional education. (1993, c. 321, ss. 78(a1)-(e); c. 529, s. 1.3; c. 561, s. 10; 1995, c. 507, s. 23A.5; 2012-142, s. 9.5.)

§ 143-614: Repealed by Session Laws 1996, Second Extra Session, c. 17, s. 16.2.

§§ 143-615 through 143-620. Reserved for future codification purposes.

Article 66.

Health Care Purchasing Alliance Act

§§ 143-621 through 143-639: Repealed by Session Laws 2000-67, s. 21.2.

Article 67.

First Flight Centennial Commission.

§ 143-640. Commission established; purpose; members; terms of office; quorum; compensation; termination.

(a)   Establishment. - There is established the First Flight Centennial Commission. The Commission shall be located within the Department of Cultural Resources for organizational, budgetary, and administrative purposes.

(b)   Purpose. - The purpose of the Commission is to develop and plan activities to commemorate the centennial of the first successful manned, controlled, heavier-than-air, powered flight (in this Article referred to as "the First Flight") and other historical events related to the development of powered flight.

166

(c)   Membership. - The Commission shall consist of 29 members, as follows:

(1)   Four persons appointed by the Governor.

(2)   Five persons appointed by the President Pro Tempore of the Senate.

(3)   Five persons appointed by the Speaker of the House of Representatives.

(4)   The following persons or their designees, ex officio:

a.   The Governor.

b.   The President Pro Tempore of the Senate.

c.   The Speaker of the House of Representatives.

d.   The United States Senators from this State.

e.   The member of the United States House of Representatives for the Third Congressional District.

f.   The Governor of the State of Ohio.

g.   The Secretary of the Department of Cultural Resources.

h.   The Superintendent of the Cape Hatteras National Seashore of the United States National Park Service.

i.   The chair of the Centennial of Flight Commemoration Commission.

j.   The President of the First Flight Society.

k.   The chair of the Dare County Board of Commissioners.

l.   The Mayor of the Town of Kill Devil Hills.

m.   The chair of the Dare County Tourism Board.

n.   The Mayor of the Town of Kitty Hawk.

The members appointed to the First Flight Centennial Commission shall be chosen from among individuals who have the ability and commitment to promote and fulfill the purposes of the Commission, including individuals who have demonstrated expertise in the fields of aeronautics, aerospace science, or history, who have contributed to the development of the fields of aeronautics or aerospace science, or who have demonstrated a commitment to serving the public.

(d)   Terms. - Members shall serve for two-year terms, with no prohibition against being reappointed, except initial appointments shall be for terms as follows:

(1)   The Governor shall initially appoint two members for a term of two years and two members for a term of three years.

(2)   The President Pro Tempore of the Senate shall initially appoint two members for a term of two years and two members for a term of three years.

(3)   The Speaker of the House of Representatives shall initially appoint two members for a term of two years and two members for a term of three years.

Initial terms shall commence on July 1, 1994.

(e)   Cochairs. - The Governor shall select the cochairs biennially from among the membership of the Commission. The initial term shall commence on July 1, 2001.

(f)   Vacancies. - A vacancy in the Commission or as chair of the Commission resulting from the resignation of a member or otherwise shall be filled in the same manner in which the original appointment was made and the term shall be for the balance of the unexpired term.

(g)   Compensation. - The Commission members shall receive no salary as a result of serving on the Commission but shall receive per diem, subsistence, and travel expenses in accordance with the provisions of G.S. 120-3.1, 138-5, and 138-6, as applicable. When approved by the Commission, members may be reimbursed for subsistence and travel expenses in excess of the statutory amount.

(h)   Removal. - Members may be removed in accordance with G.S. 143B-13 as if that section applied to this Article.

168

(i)   Meetings. - The chair shall convene the Commission. Meetings shall be held as often as necessary, but not less than four times a year.

(j)   Quorum. - A majority of the members of the Commission shall constitute a quorum for the transaction of business. The affirmative vote of a majority of the members present at meetings of the Commission shall be necessary for action to be taken by the Commission.

(k)   Termination of Commission. - The Commission shall terminate June 30, 2004, which is six months after the 100th anniversary of the First Flight. (1993 (Reg. Sess., 1994), c. 777, s. 7(a); 1999-431, s. 3.2(a); 2001-486, ss. 2.12(a), 2.12(b); 2002-159, s. 20.)

§ 143-641. Powers and duties of the Commission.

(a)   Powers and Duties. - The Commission shall have the following powers and duties:

(1)   To plan and develop activities appropriate to commemorate the centennial of the First Flight, including the coordination of activities throughout the State and nation.

(2)   To coordinate with the national Centennial of Flight Commemoration Commission and the 2003 Fund Commission of Ohio in planning and promoting commemorative events and activities.

(3)   To appoint a director, who shall be exempt from the North Carolina Human Resources Act, to employ other staff as it deems necessary, subject to the North Carolina Human Resources Act, and to fix their compensation.

(4)   To adopt bylaws by a majority vote of the Commission.

(5)   To accept grants, contributions, devises, gifts, and services for the purpose of providing support to the Commission. The funds and property shall be retained by the Commission, and the Commission shall prescribe rules under which the Commission may accept donations of money, property, or personal services, and determine the value of donations of property or personal services.

169

(6)   To design, seek clearance for, and register with the Secretary of State a logo as the official emblem of the First Flight celebration, in coordination with the federal advisory commission. The Commission shall issue rules regarding the use of the logo.

(b)   Commemoration Activities. - In planning and implementing appropriate activities to commemorate the centennial of the First Flight, the Commission shall give due consideration to:

(1)   The historical setting in which the First Flight of the Wright Brothers took place.

(2)   The contribution of powered flight to the development of transportation worldwide.

(3)   The contribution that powered flight has made to worldwide trade and the economic development of the United States and all nations.

(4)   The contribution that powered flight has made to world peace and security.

(5)   The need to educate the public regarding the research and development of powered flight, and to acknowledge the development of aeronautics, aerospace science, and the aerospace industry, including the development of the glider and Orville and Wilbur Wright's contribution to the development of the glider.

(6)   The development of aerospace science and the aerospace industry since the First Flight, including the development of space exploration.

(7)   The importance of activities to commemorate the First Flight and to honor Orville and Wilbur Wright and their contribution to powered flight.

(8)   The need to expand the facilities of the Wright Brothers National Memorial to honor Orville and Wilbur Wright and to educate the public regarding the development of powered flight and the development of aeronautics and aerospace science since the First Flight.

(9)   The commitment and efforts of the First Flight Society and the National Park Service to preserving the Wright Brothers National Memorial and to honoring Orville and Wilbur Wright on the centennial of the First Flight.

(c)   Contract Authority. - The Commission may procure supplies, services, and property as appropriate, and may enter into contracts, leases, or other legal agreements to carry out the purposes of this Article. All contracts, leases, or legal agreements entered into by the Commission shall terminate on the date of termination of the Commission. Termination shall not affect any disputes or causes of action of the Commission that arise before the date of termination, and the Department of Cultural Resources may prosecute or defend any causes of action arising before the date of termination. All property acquired by the Commission that remains in the possession of the Commission on the date of termination shall become the property of the Department of Cultural Resources. (1993 (Reg. Sess., 1994), c. 777, s. 7(a); 2011-284, s. 95; 2013-382, s. 9.1(c).)

§ 143-642. Assignment of property; offices.

(a)   Assignment of Property. - Upon request of the Commission, the head of any State agency may assign property, equipment, and personnel of such agency to the Commission to assist the Commission in carrying out its duties under this Article. Assignments under this subsection shall be without reimbursement by the Commission to the agency from which the assignment was made. Property and equipment that remains in the possession of the Commission on the date of the termination of the Commission shall revert to the agency from which the property was acquired.

(b)   Office Space. - The Department of Cultural Resources shall provide office space in Raleigh for use as offices by the First Flight Centennial Commission, and the Department of Cultural Resources shall receive no reimbursement from the Commission for the use of the property during the life of the Commission. (1993 (Reg. Sess., 1994), c. 777, s. 7(a).)

§ 143-643. Commission reports.

(a)   Annual Report. - Before July 1, 1995, the Commission shall submit to the General Assembly a comprehensive report incorporating specific recommendations of the Commission for commemoration of the First Flight and other historical events related to the development of powered flight. After the initial report, the Commission shall submit a report to the General Assembly

171

within 30 days of the convening of each Regular Session of the General Assembly until the Commission terminates. The report shall include:

(1)   Recommendations for appropriate activities for the commemoration, including:

a.   Publications, both printed and electronic, of books, periodicals, films, videotapes, and other promotional and educational materials.

b.   Scholarly projects, conferences, lectures, seminars, and programs.

c.   Libraries, exhibits, and museums.

d.   Competitions and awards for historical, scholarly, artistic, and other works and projects related to the centennial.

e.   Ceremonies and celebrations, including a calendar of major activities, commemorating the centennial and other related historical events and achievements.

(2)   Recommendations for legislation and administrative action to promote and develop the commemoration.

(3)   An accounting of funds received and expended.

(b)   Final Report. - The Commission shall submit a final report to the General Assembly no later than June 30, 2004. The final report shall include:

(1)   A summary of the activities of the Commission.

(2)   A final accounting of funds received and expended by the Commission.

(3)   Recommendations concerning the disposition of historically significant property donated to or acquired by the Commission. (1993 (Reg. Sess., 1994), c. 777, s. 7(a).)

§§ 143-644 through 143-649. Reserved for future codification purposes.

Article 68.

Regulation of Boxing.

§ 143-650: Repealed by Session Laws 2004-124, s. 18.2(a), effective July 1, 2004.

§ 143-651. Definitions.

The following definitions apply in this Article:

(1)   Amateur. - A person who is not receiving or competing for and has never received or competed for any purse or other article or thing of value for participating in a match.

(2)   Announcer. - Any person who engages in the act of announcing a match.

(3)   Boxer. - Any person who engages as a participant in a boxing match.

(4)   Boxing match. - A match where the participants engage in the use of full contact boxing techniques (using the fist only), and where the object of a match is to win by decision, knockout (KO), or technical knockout (TKO).

(5)   Repealed by Session Laws 2004-124, s. 18.2.(a), effective July 1, 2004.

(6)   Contest. - A match in which the participants strive to win.

(7)   Contestant. - Any person who engages as a participant in a boxing, kickboxing, or mixed martial arts match, or toughman event.

(8)   Exhibition. - A match where the participants display their skills and technique without necessarily striving to win.

(9)   Judge. - A person who has a vote in determining the winner of any match or contest.

(10)   Kickboxer. - Any person who engages as a participant in a kickboxing match.

173

(11)   Kickboxing match. - A match in which the participants engage in full contact martial arts fighting techniques using the hands and the feet, and where the object of the match is to win by decision, knockout (KO), or technical knockout (TKO).

(12)   Licensee. - Any person, club, corporation, organization, or association to whom a license has been issued pursuant to the provisions of this Article.

(13)   Manager. - Any person who controls or administers the affairs of any contestant, and who:

a.   By contract, agreement, or other arrangement with any person undertakes or has undertaken to represent in any way the interest of the contestant in any professional contest in which the contestant is to participate and is entitled under that contract, agreement, or arrangement to receive monetary or other compensation for his or her services, without regard to the sources of the compensation. The term "manager" shall not be construed to mean any attorney licensed to practice in this State whose participation in the activities is restricted solely to representing the interests of a professional contestant as a client.

b.   Directs or controls the professional activities of any professional contestant.

c.   Receives or is entitled to receive a percentage of the gross purse or gross income of any professional contest.

(14)   Match. - Any boxing, kickboxing, or mixed martial arts contest or exhibition, or toughman event, and includes any event, engagement, sparring or practice session, show or program where the public is admitted and in which there is intended to be physical contact, whether an exhibition or contest. This definition does not include training or practice sessions when no admission is charged.

(15)   Matchmaker. - A person through whom matches are arranged for participants and who otherwise assists participants in procuring engagement dates.

(15a)   Mixed martial artist. - Any person who engages as a participant in a mixed martial arts match.

174

(15b)   Mixed martial arts. - A form of sporting martial arts that uses a variety of martial arts techniques to deliver blows with the hands, elbows, and any part of the leg below the hip, including the knee and foot, and also uses boxing, wrestling, and grappling techniques.

(16)   Natural person. - An individual.

(17)   Participant. - Any person who engages in a match or exhibition and performs as a boxer, kickboxer, or mixed martial artist.

(18)   Person. - An individual, group of individuals, business, corporation, limited liability company, partnership, or any other individual or collective entity.

(19)   Physician. - An individual licensed to practice medicine in this State.

(20)   Professional. - Any person who is licensed as a contestant and receives compensation for participating in matches.

(21)   Promoter. - Any person who produces, arranges, stages, holds, or gives any match in North Carolina involving a professional participant.

(22)   Referee. - The official who shall enter and remain in the ring for the duration of a match and shall enforce the rules and maintain order in the ring.

(23)   Ring official. - Any person who performs an official function for the duration of a match.

(23a)   Sanctioned amateur. - A person who competes in a sanctioned amateur match.

(23b)   Sanctioned amateur match. - Any match regulated by an amateur sports organization that has been recognized and approved by the Section.

(24)   Second. - Any person who will work or be present in the corner of a participant for the duration of a match.

(24a)   Section. - The Alcohol Law Enforcement Section of the Department of Public Safety.

(25)   Timekeeper. - Any person who will operate the clock or watch for the duration of a match for the purpose of keeping the official time of the match.

(25a)　Toughman contestant. - Any person who competes in a toughman event.

(25b)　Toughman event. - An elimination program of matches in which (i) the contestants are not professional boxers, (ii) the finalist receives a purse or other article of value, (iii) the participants engage in the use of full contact boxing techniques, and (iv) the object of each match is to win by decision, knockout (KO), or technical knockout (TKO).

(26)　Repealed by Session Laws 2007-490, s. 1, effective August 30, 2007.

(27)　Unarmed combat. - A match consisting of any combination of boxing, kicking, wrestling, hitting, punching, or other combative contact techniques which may reasonably be expected to inflict injury to opponents. (1995, c. 499, s. 1; 1997-504, s. 1; 1998-23, s. 18; 1998-212, s. 19.11(g); 2004-124, ss. 18.2(a), (b), (e); 2006-264, s. 22(c); 2007-490, s. 1; 2011-145, s. 19.1(g), (n).)

§ 143-652:　Repealed by Session Laws 2004-124, s. 18.2.(a), effective July 1, 2004.

§ 143-652.1.　Regulation of boxing, kickboxing, mixed martial arts, and toughman events.

The Alcohol Law Enforcement Section of the Department of Public Safety shall regulate live boxing, kickboxing, and mixed martial arts matches, whether professional, amateur, or sanctioned amateur, or toughman events, in which admission is charged for viewing, or the contestants compete for a purse or prize of value greater than twenty-five dollars ($25.00). The Section shall have the exclusive authority to approve and issue rules for the regulation of the conduct, promotion, and performances of live boxing, kickboxing, and mixed martial arts matches and exhibitions, whether professional, amateur, or sanctioned amateur, and toughman events in this State. The rules shall be issued pursuant to the provisions of Chapter 150B of the General Statutes and may include, without limitation, the following subjects:

176

(1)   Requirements for issuance of licenses and permits required by this Article.

(2)   Regulation of ticket sales.

(3)   Physical requirements for contestants, including classification by weight and skill.

(4)   Supervision of matches and exhibitions by licensed physicians and referees.

(5)   Insurance and bonding requirements.

(6)   Compensation of participants and licensees.

(7)   Contracts and financial arrangements.

(8)   Prohibition of dishonest, unethical, and injurious practices.

(9)   Facilities.

(10)   Approval of sanctioning amateur sports organizations.

(11)   Procedures and requirements for compliance with the Professional Boxing Safety Act of 1996. (2004-124, s. 18.2(d); 2007-490, s. 2; 2011-145, s. 19.1(g), (n).)

§ 143-652.2. Boxing Advisory Commission.

(a)   Creation. - The Boxing Advisory Commission is created within the Department of Public Safety to advise the Alcohol Law Enforcement Section of the Department of Public Safety concerning matters regulated by this Article. The Commission shall consist of six voting members and two nonvoting advisory members. All the members shall be residents of North Carolina. The members shall be appointed as follows:

(1)   One voting member shall be appointed by the Governor for an initial term of two years.

(2)   One voting member shall be appointed by the President Pro Tempore of the Senate for an initial term of three years.

(3)   One voting member shall be appointed by the Speaker of the House of Representatives for an initial term of three years.

(4)   One voting member shall be appointed by the Secretary of Public Safety for an initial term of three years.

(5)   One voting member shall be appointed by the Lieutenant Governor for an initial term of two years.

(6)   One voting member shall be appointed by the Tribal Council of the Eastern Band of the Cherokee for an initial term of three years.

(7)   One nonvoting advisory member shall be appointed by the Speaker of the House of Representatives for an initial term of one year, from nominations made by the North Carolina Medical Society, which shall nominate two licensed physicians for the position.

(8)   One nonvoting advisory member shall be appointed by the President Pro Tempore of the Senate for an initial term of one year, from nominations made by the North Carolina Medical Society, which shall nominate two licensed physicians for the position.

Notwithstanding the schedule above in subdivisions (1), (5), (7), and (8) of this subsection, if any former member of the North Carolina Boxing Commission is appointed to the initial membership, that person shall serve an initial term of three years. The member appointed pursuant to subdivision (6) of this subsection may serve on the Commission only if an agreement exists and remains in effect between the Tribal Council of the Eastern Band of the Cherokee and the Commission authorizing the Commission to regulate professional boxing matches within the Cherokee Indian Reservation as provided by the Professional Boxing Safety Act of 1996.

The two nonvoting advisory members appointed pursuant to subdivisions (7) and (8) of this subsection shall advise the Commission and the Section on matters concerning the health and physical condition of boxers and health issues relating to the conduct of exhibitions and boxing matches. They may prepare and submit to the Commission for its consideration and to the Section

178

for its approval any rules that in their judgment will safeguard the physical welfare of all participants engaged in boxing.

Terms for all members of the Commission except for the initial appointments shall be for three years.

The Secretary of Public Safety shall designate which member of the Commission is to serve as chair. A member of the Commission may be removed from office by the Secretary of Public Safety for cause. Members of the Commission are subject to the conflicts of interest requirements of 15 U.S.C. § 6308 (contained in the Professional Boxing Safety Act of 1996, as amended). Each member, before entering upon the duties of a member, shall take and subscribe an oath to perform the duties of the office faithfully, impartially, and justly to the best of the member's ability. A record of these oaths shall be filed in the Department of Public Safety.

(b)   Vacancies. - Members shall serve until their successors are appointed and have been qualified. Any vacancy in the membership of the Commission shall be filled in the same manner as the original appointment. A vacancy in the membership of the Commission other than by expiration of term shall be filled for the unexpired term only.

(c)   Meetings. - Meetings of the Commission shall be called by the chair or by any two members of the Commission, and meetings shall be held at least quarterly. Any three voting members of the Commission shall constitute a quorum at any meeting. Action may be taken and motions and resolutions adopted by the Commission at any meeting by the affirmative vote of a majority of the members of the Commission present at a meeting at which a quorum exists.

(d)   Review Authority of the Commission. - The Commission shall review existing rules adopted under this Article and shall from time to time make recommendations to the Section for changes or addition to such rules. Any proposals for change, amendment, addition, or deletion to those rules shall be submitted by the Section to the Commission for its comments prior to approval.

(e)   Compensation. - None of the members of the Commission shall receive compensation for serving on the Commission. However, members of the Commission may be reimbursed for their expenses in accordance with the provisions of Chapter 138 of the General Statutes.

179

(f)   Staff Assistance. - The Secretary of Public Safety shall provide staff assistance to the Commission.

(g)   Initial appointments to the Commission under this section shall be for terms commencing July 1, 2007. (2007-528, s. 1; 2008-187, s. 22; 2011-145, ss. 19.1(g), 19.1(n).)

§ 143-653. Unauthorized matches prohibited.

No person shall promote, conduct, or engage in an unarmed combat match, whether the participants are professional or amateur, except as authorized by this Article. This section shall not preclude professional wrestling. (1995, c. 499, s. 1; 1997-504, s. 3; 1998-23, s. 18; 1998-212, s. 19.11(g); 2007-490, s. 3.)

§ 143-654. Licensing and permitting.

(a)   License and Permit Required. - Except for sanctioned amateur matches, it is unlawful for any person to act in this State as an announcer, contestant, judge, manager, matchmaker, promoter, referee, timekeeper, or second unless the person is licensed to do so under this Article. It is unlawful for a promoter to present a match in this State, other than a sanctioned amateur match, unless the promoter has a permit issued under this Article to do so. The Section has the exclusive authority to issue, deny, suspend, or revoke any license or permit provided for in this Article.

(b)   License. - All licenses issued under this Article shall be valid only during the calendar year in which they are issued, except contestant licenses shall be valid for one year from the date of issuance. A license for an announcer, contestant, judge, matchmaker, referee, timekeeper, or second shall be issued only to a natural person. A natural person shall not transfer or assign a license or change it into another name. A license for a manager or promoter may be issued to a corporation or partnership; provided, however, that all officers or partners shall submit an application for individual licensure, and only those officers or partners who are licensed shall be entitled to negotiate or sign contracts. The addition of a new officer or partner during the license period shall necessitate the filing of an application for individual licensure by the new officer or partner.

180

An applicant for a license shall file with the Section the appropriate nonrefundable fee and any forms, documents, medical examinations, or exhibits the Section may require in order to properly administer this Article. The information requested shall include the date of birth and social security number of each applicant as well as any other personal data necessary to positively identify the applicant and may include the requirement of verification of any documents the Section deems appropriate. A person may not participate under a fictitious or assumed name in any match unless the person has first registered the name with the Section.

(c)   Surety Bond. - An applicant for a promoter's license must submit, in addition to any other forms, documents, or exhibits requested by the Section, a surety bond payable to the Section for the benefit of any person injured or damaged by (i) the promoter's failure to comply with any provision of this Article or any rules adopted by the Section or (ii) the promoter's failure to fulfill the obligations of any contract related to the holding of a match. The surety bond shall be issued in an amount to be no less than ten thousand dollars ($10,000). The amount of the surety bond shall be negotiable upon the sole discretion of the Section. All surety bonds shall be upon forms approved by the Secretary of Public Safety and supplied by the Section.

(d)   Permit. - A permit issued to a promoter under this Article is valid for a single match. An applicant for a permit shall file with the Section the appropriate nonrefundable fee and any forms or documents the Section may require. (1995, c. 499, s. 1; 1997-504, s. 4; 1998-23, s. 18; 1998-212, s. 19.11(c), (g); 1999-237, s. 20.3(b); 2004-124, s. 18.2(e); 2006-264, s. 22(a); 2007-490, s. 4; 2011-145, s. 19.1(g), (n).)

§ 143-655. Fees; State Boxing Revenue Account.

(a)   License Fees. - The Section shall collect the following license fees:

Announcer	$75.00
Contestant	$50.00
Judge	$75.00
Manager	$150.00

Matchmaker	$300.00
Promoter	$450.00
Referee	$75.00
Timekeeper	$75.00
Second	$50.00.

The annual license renewal fees shall not exceed the initial license fees.

(b)   Permit Fees. - The Section may establish a fee schedule for permits issued under this Article. The fees may vary depending on the seating capacity of the facility to be used to present a match. The fee may not exceed the following amounts:

Seating Capacity	Fee Amount
Less than 2,000	$150.00
2,000 - 5,000	$300.00
Over 5,000	$450.00.

(b1)   Admission Fees. - The Section shall collect a fee in the amount of two dollars ($2.00) per each ticket sold to attend events regulated in this Article.

(c)   State Boxing Revenue Account. - There is created the State Boxing Revenue Account within the Department of Public Safety. Monies collected pursuant to the provisions of this Article shall be credited to the Account and applied to the administration of the Article. (1995, c. 499, s. 1; 1998-212, s. 19.11(d); 2004-124, s. 18.2(e); 2006-264, s. 22(b); 2007-490, s. 5; 2009-451, s. 17.7(a), (b); 2011-145, s. 19.1(g), (n).)

§ 143-656. Contracts and financial arrangements.

Any contract between licensees and related to a match or exhibition held or to be held in this State must meet the requirements of administrative rules as set forth by the Section. Any contract which does not satisfy the requirements of the administrative rules shall be void and unenforceable. All contracts shall be in writing. (1995, c. 499, s. 1; 1997-504, s. 5; 1998-23, s. 18; 1998-212, s. 19.11(g); 2004-124, s. 18.2(e); 2006-264, s. 22(a); 2007-490, s. 6; 2011-145, s. 19.1(n).)

§ 143-657: Repealed by Session Laws 1997-504, s. 6.

§ 143-657.1. Sanctioned amateur matches.

In addition to the other applicable provisions of this Article, a sanctioned amateur match shall be conducted pursuant to the rules of the sports organization sanctioning the match or exhibition. (1997-504, s. 7; 1998-23, s. 18; 1998-212, s. 19.11(g); 2007-490, s. 7.)

§ 143-658. Violations.

(a)   Civil Penalties. - The Secretary of Public Safety may issue an order against a licensee or other person who willfully violates any provision of this Article, imposing a civil penalty of up to five thousand dollars ($5,000) for a single violation or of up to twenty-five thousand dollars ($25,000) for multiple violations in a single proceeding or a series of related proceedings. No order under this subsection may be entered without giving the licensee or other person 15 days' prior notice and an opportunity for a contested case hearing conducted pursuant to Article 3 of Chapter 150B of the General Statutes.

The clear proceeds of civil penalties imposed pursuant to this subsection shall be remitted to the Civil Penalty and Forfeiture Fund in accordance with G.S. 115C-457.2.

(b)   Criminal Penalties. - A willful violation of any provision of this Article shall constitute a Class 2 misdemeanor. The Secretary of Public Safety may refer any available evidence concerning violations of this Article to the proper district attorney, who may, with or without such a reference, institute the appropriate criminal proceedings.

(c)   Injunction. - Whenever it appears to the Secretary of Public Safety that a person has engaged or is about to engage in an act or practice constituting a violation of any provision of this Article or any rule or order hereunder, the Secretary of Public Safety may bring an action in any court of competent jurisdiction to enjoin those acts or practices and to enforce compliance with this Article or any rule or order issued pursuant to this Article.

(d)   Repealed by Session Laws 1998-212, s. 19.11(e), effective July 1, 1998. (1995, c. 499, s. 1; 1997-504, s. 8; 1998-23, s. 18; 1998-212, s. 19.11(e), (g); 1998-215, s. 125; 2011-145, s. 19.1(g).)

§ 143-659. Reserved for future codification purposes.

Article 69.

Criminal Justice Information Network Governing Board.

§ 143-660. Definitions.

As used in this Article:

(1)   "Board" means the Criminal Justice Information Network Governing Board established by G.S. 143-661.

(2)   "Local government user" means a unit of local government of this State having authorized access to the Network.

(3)   "Network" means the Criminal Justice Information Network established by the Board pursuant to this Article.

(4)   "Network user" or "user" means any person having authorized access to the Network.

(5)   "State agency" means any State department, agency, institution, board, commission, or other unit of State government. (1996, 2nd Ex. Sess., c. 18, s. 23.3(a).)

184

§ 143-661. Criminal Justice Information Network Governing Board - creation; purpose; membership; conflicts of interest.

(a)   The Criminal Justice Information Network Governing Board is established within the Office of the State Chief Information Officer to operate the State's Criminal Justice Information Network, the purpose of which shall be to provide the governmental and technical information systems infrastructure necessary for accomplishing State and local governmental public safety and justice functions in the most effective manner by appropriately and efficiently sharing criminal justice and juvenile justice information among law enforcement, judicial, and corrections agencies. The Board is established within the Office of the State Chief Information Officer, for organizational and budgetary purposes only and the Board shall exercise all of its statutory powers in this Article independent of control by the Office of the State Chief Information Officer.

(b)   The Board shall consist of 21 members, appointed as follows:

(1)   Five members appointed by the Governor, including one member who is a director or employee of a State correction agency for a term to begin September 1, 1996 and to expire on June 30, 1997, one member who is an employee of the North Carolina Department of Public Safety for a term beginning September 1, 1996 and to expire on June 30, 1997, one member selected from the North Carolina Association of Chiefs of Police for a term to begin September 1, 1996 and to expire on June 30, 1999, one member who is an employee of the Division of Juvenile Justice of the Department of Public Safety, and one member who represents the Division of Motor Vehicles.

(2)   Six members appointed by the General Assembly in accordance with G.S. 120-121, as follows:

a.   Three members recommended by the President Pro Tempore of the Senate, including two members of the general public for terms to begin on September 1, 1996 and to expire on June 30, 1997, and one member selected from the North Carolina League of Municipalities who is a member of, or an employee working directly for, the governing board of a North Carolina municipality for a term to begin on September 1, 1996 and to expire on June 30, 1999; and

b.   Three members recommended by the Speaker of the House of Representatives, including two members of the general public for terms to begin on September 1, 1996 and to expire on June 30, 1999, and one member

185

selected from the North Carolina Association of County Commissioners who is a member of, or an employee working directly for, the governing board of a North Carolina county for a term to begin on September 1, 1996 and to expire on June 30, 1997.

(3)   Two members appointed by the Attorney General, including one member who is an employee of the Attorney General for a term to begin on September 1, 1996 and to expire on June 30, 1997, and one member from the North Carolina Sheriffs' Association for a term to begin on September 1, 1996 and to expire on June 30, 1999.

(4)   Six members appointed by the Chief Justice of the North Carolina Supreme Court, as follows:

a.   The Director of the Administrative Office of the Courts, or an employee of the Administrative Office of the Courts, for a term beginning July 1, 1997, and expiring June 30, 2001.

b.   One member who is a district attorney or an assistant district attorney upon the recommendation of the Conference of District Attorneys of North Carolina, for a term beginning July 1, 1998, and expiring June 30, 1999.

c.   Two members who are superior court or district court judges for terms beginning July 1, 1998, and expiring June 30, 2001.

d.   One member who is a magistrate upon the recommendation of the North Carolina Magistrates' Association, for a term beginning July 1, 1998, and expiring June 30, 1999.

e.   One member who is a clerk of superior court upon the recommendation of the North Carolina Association of Clerks of Superior Court, for a term beginning July 1, 1998, and expiring June 30, 1999.

(5)   One member appointed by the State Chief Information Officer.

(6)   One member appointed by the President of the North Carolina Chapter of the Association of Public Communications Officials International, who is an active member of the Association, for a term to begin on September 1, 1996 and to expire on June 30, 1999.

The respective appointing authorities are encouraged to appoint persons having a background in and familiarity with criminal information systems and networks generally and with the criminal information needs and capacities of the constituency from which the member is appointed.

As the initial terms expire, subsequent members of the Board shall be appointed to serve four-year terms. At the end of a term, a member shall continue to serve on the Board until a successor is appointed. A member who is appointed after a term is begun serves only for the remainder of the term and until a successor is appointed. Any vacancy in the membership of the Board shall be filled by the same appointing authority that made the appointment, except that vacancies among members appointed by the General Assembly shall be filled in accordance with G.S. 120-122.

(c)   Members of the Board shall not be employed by or serve on the board of directors or other corporate governing body of any information systems, computer hardware, computer software, or telecommunications vendor of goods and services to the State or to any unit of local government in the State. No member of the Board shall vote on an action affecting solely the member's own State agency or local governmental unit or specific judicial office. (1996, 2nd Ex. Sess., c. 18, s. 23.3(a); 1998-202, s. 9; 1998-212, s. 18.2(b); 2001-424, s. 23.6(b); 2001-487, s. 90; 2003-284, s. 17.1(a); 2004-129, s. 42; 2011-145, ss. 6A.11(b), 19.1(g), (l).)

§ 143-662. Compensation and expenses of Board members; travel reimbursements.

Members of the Board shall serve without compensation but may receive travel and subsistence as follows:

(1)   Board members who are officials or employees of a State agency or unit of local government, in accordance with G.S. 138-6.

(2)   All other Board members, at the rate established in G.S. 138-5. (1996, 2nd Ex. Sess., c. 18, s. 23.3(a).)

§ 143-663. Powers and duties.

187

(a)   The Board shall have the following powers and duties:

(1)   To establish and operate the Network as an integrated system of State and local government components for effectively and efficiently storing, communicating, and using criminal justice information at the State and local levels throughout North Carolina's law enforcement, judicial, juvenile justice, and corrections agencies, with the components of the Network to include electronic devices, programs, data, and governance and to set the Network's policies and procedures.

(2)   To develop and adopt uniform standards and cost-effective information technology, after thorough evaluation of the capacity of information technology to meet the present and future needs of the State and, in consultation with the Office of Information Technology Services, to develop and adopt standards for entering, storing, and transmitting information in criminal justice databases and for achieving maximum compatibility among user technologies.

(3)   To identify the funds needed to establish and maintain the Network, identify public and private sources of funding, and secure funding to:

a.   Create the Network and facilitate the sharing of information among users of the Network; and

b.   Make grants to local government users to enable them to acquire or improve elements of the Network that lie within the responsibility of their agencies or State agencies; provided that the elements developed with the funds must be available for use by the State or by local governments without cost and the applicable State agencies join in the request for funding.

(4)   To provide assistance to local governments for the financial and systems planning for Network-related automation and to coordinate and assist the Network users of this State in soliciting bids for information technology hardware, software, and services in order to assure compliance with the Board's technical standards, to gain the most advantageous contracts for the Network users of this State, and to assure financial accountability where State funds are used.

(5)   To provide a liaison among local government users and to advocate on behalf of the Network and its users in connection with legislation affecting the Network.

(6)   To facilitate the sharing of knowledge about information technologies among users of the Network.

(7)   To take any other appropriate actions to foster the development of the Network.

(b)   All grants or other uses of funds appropriated or granted to the Board shall be conditioned on compliance with the Board's technical and other standards. (1996, 2nd Ex. Sess., c. 18, s. 23.3(a); 2003-284, s. 17.2(b); 2004-129, s. 43.)

§ 143-664. Election of officers; meetings; staff, etc.

(a)   The Governor shall call the first meeting of the Board. At the first meeting, the Board shall elect a chair and a vice-chair, each to serve a one-year term, with subsequent officers to be elected for one-year terms. The Board shall hold at least two regular meetings each year, as provided by policies and procedures adopted by the Board. The Board may hold additional meetings upon the call of the chair or any three Board members. A majority of the Board membership constitutes a quorum.

(b)   The staff of the Criminal Justice Information Network shall provide the Board with professional and clerical support and any additional support the Board needs to fulfill its mandate. The Board's staff shall use space provided by the Office of the State Chief Information Officer. (1996, 2nd Ex. Sess., c. 18, s. 23.3(a); 2003-284, s. 17.1(b); 2011-145, ss. 6A.11(c), 19.1(g).)

§§ 143-665 through 143-669. Reserved for future codification purposes.

Article 70.

Adopt-A-Beach Program.

§§ 143-670 through 143-674: Repealed by Session Laws 2001-452, s. 1.1.

§ 143-677. Assignment of property; offices.

(a)   Assignment of Property. - Upon request of the Commission, the head of any State agency may assign property, equipment, and personnel of such agency to the Commission to assist the Commission in carrying out its duties under this Article. Assignments under this subsection shall be without reimbursement by the Commission to the agency from which the assignment was made. Property and equipment that remain in the possession of the Commission on the date of the termination of the Commission shall revert to the agency from which the property was acquired.

(b)   Office Space. - The Department of Cultural Resources shall provide office space in Raleigh for use as offices by the North Carolina Postal History Commission, and the Department of Cultural Resources shall receive no reimbursement from the Commission for the use of the property during the life of the Commission. (1997-443, s. 30.5.)

§ 143-678. Commission reports.

(a)   Annual Report. - Before July 1, 1998, the Commission shall submit to the General Assembly a comprehensive report incorporating specific recommendations of the Commission. After the initial report, the Commission shall submit a report to the General Assembly within 30 days of the convening of each regular session of the General Assembly.

(b)   Final Report. - The Commission shall submit a final report to the General Assembly no later than June 30, 2000. The final report shall include:

(1)   A summary of the activities of the Commission.

(2)   A final accounting of funds received and expended by the Commission. (1997-443, s. 30.5.)

§ 143-679. Application of Article.

The provisions of Article 1 of Chapter 121 of the General Statutes apply to the Commission. (1997-443, s. 30.5.)

§ 143-680. Reserved for future codification purposes.

§ 143-681. Reserved for future codification purposes.

§ 143-676. Powers and duties of the Commission.

(a)   Powers and Duties. - The Commission shall have the following powers and duties:

(1)   To advise the Secretary of Cultural Resources on the collection, preservation, cataloging, publication, and exhibition of materials associated with North Carolina's postal history in cooperation with the North Carolina Museum of History.

(2)   To adopt bylaws by a majority vote of the Commission.

(3)   To accept grants, contributions, devises, gifts, and services for the purpose of providing support to the Commission. The funds and property shall be retained by the Commission, and the Commission shall prescribe rules under which the Commission may accept donations of money, property, or personal services, and determine the value of donations of property or personal services.

(b)   Contract Authority. - The Commission may procure supplies, services, and property as appropriate and may enter into contracts, leases, or other legal agreements within funds available to carry out the purposes of this Article. All contracts, leases, or legal agreements entered into by the Commission shall terminate on the date of termination of the Commission. Termination shall not affect any disputed or causes of action of the Commission that arise before the date of termination, and the Department of Cultural Resources may prosecute or defend any causes of action arising before the date of termination. All property acquired by the commission that remains in the possession of the Commission on the date of termination shall become the property of the Department of Cultural Resources. (1997-443, s. 30.5; 2011-284, s. 96.)

§ 143-677. Assignment of property; offices.

(a)   Assignment of Property. - Upon request of the Commission, the head of any State agency may assign property, equipment, and personnel of such

191

agency to the Commission to assist the Commission in carrying out its duties under this Article. Assignments under this subsection shall be without reimbursement by the Commission to the agency from which the assignment was made. Property and equipment that remain in the possession of the Commission on the date of the termination of the Commission shall revert to the agency from which the property was acquired.

(b)   Office Space. - The Department of Cultural Resources shall provide office space in Raleigh for use as offices by the North Carolina Postal History Commission, and the Department of Cultural Resources shall receive no reimbursement from the Commission for the use of the property during the life of the Commission. (1997-443, s. 30.5.)

§ 143-678. Commission reports.

(a)   Annual Report. - Before July 1, 1998, the Commission shall submit to the General Assembly a comprehensive report incorporating specific recommendations of the Commission. After the initial report, the Commission shall submit a report to the General Assembly within 30 days of the convening of each regular session of the General Assembly.

(b)   Final Report. - The Commission shall submit a final report to the General Assembly no later than June 30, 2000. The final report shall include:

(1)   A summary of the activities of the Commission.

(2)   A final accounting of funds received and expended by the Commission. (1997-443, s. 30.5.)

§ 143-679. Application of Article.

The provisions of Article 1 of Chapter 121 of the General Statutes apply to the Commission. (1997-443, s. 30.5.)

§ 143-680. Reserved for future codification purposes.

192

§ 143-681. Reserved for future codification purposes.

Article 72.

Commission On Children With Special Health Care Needs.

§ 143-682. Commission established.

(a)   There is established the Commission on Children With Special Health Care Needs. The Department of Health and Human Services shall provide staff services and space for Commission meetings. The purpose of the Commission is to monitor and evaluate the availability and provision of health services to special needs children in this State, and to monitor and evaluate services provided to special needs children under the Health Insurance Program for Children established under Part 8 of Article 2 of Chapter 108A of the General Statutes.

(b)   The Commission shall consist of nine members appointed by the Governor, as follows:

(1)   Two parents, not of the same family, each of whom has a special needs child. In appointing parents, the Governor shall consider appointing one parent of a child with chronic illness and one parent of a child with a developmental disability or behavioral disorder.

(2)   A licensed psychiatrist recommended by the North Carolina Psychiatric Association.

(3)   A licensed psychologist recommended by the North Carolina Psychological Association.

(4)   A licensed pediatrician whose practice includes services for special needs children, recommended by the Pediatric Society of North Carolina.

(5)   A representative of one of the children's hospitals in the State, recommended by the Pediatric Society of North Carolina.

(6)   A local public health director recommended by the Association of Local Health Directors.

(7)   An educator providing education services to special needs children, recommended by the North Carolina Council of Administrators of Special Education.

(8)   A licensed dentist who provides services to children with special needs, recommended by the North Carolina Dental Society.

(c)   The Governor shall appoint from among Commission members the person who shall serve as chair of the Commission. Of the initial appointments, two shall serve one-year terms, three shall serve two-year terms, and three shall serve three-year terms. Thereafter, terms shall be for two years. Vacancies occurring before expiration of a term shall be filled from the same appointment category in accordance with subsection (b) of this section. (1998-1, s. 3(a); 1998-212, s. 12.12(c); 2010-12, s. 1.)

§ 143-683. Powers and duties of the Commission.

The Commission shall have the following powers and duties:

(1)   Study the needs of children with special health care needs in this State for health care services not presently provided or regularly available through State or federal programs or through private or employer-sponsored health insurance plans;

(2)   Develop guidelines for case management services, quality assurance measures, and periodic evaluations to determine efficacy of health services provided to special needs children;

(3)   Develop and coordinate an outreach program of case managers to assist children with special health care needs and their families in accessing available State and federal resources for all health care services;

(4)   Review rules adopted by the Commission for Public Health pertaining to the provision of services for special needs children and make recommendations for modifications or additions to the rules necessary to improve services to these children or to make service delivery more efficient and effective;

(5)   Review policies and practices of the Department of Health and Human Services and recommend to the Secretary of Health and Human Services

194

changes that would improve implementation of health programs for children with special health care needs;

(6)   Report to each session of the General Assembly not later than the first day of its convening. The report shall include a summary of the Commission's work and any recommendations the Commission may have on ways to improve the efficiency and effectiveness of health services delivery to children with special health care needs in this State, The Commission shall provide a copy of its report to the General Assembly's Commission on Children With Special Needs;

(7)   Study the feasibility of establishing a privately funded risk pool to provide insurance coverage and services for children with special health care needs;

(8)   Make recommendations to the Department and to the Commission for Public Health regarding quality assurance measures and mechanisms to enhance the health outcomes of children with special health care needs;

(9)   Establish subcommittees as necessary to provide assistance and advice to the Commission in conducting its studies and other activities. The Commission may appoint non-Commission members to the subcommittees;

(10)   Seek grants and other funds from private and federal sources to carry out the purposes of this Article; and

(11)   Conduct other activities the Commission deems appropriate and necessary to carry out the purposes of this Article. (1998-1, s. 3(a); 2007-182, s. 2.)

§ 143-684. Compensation and expenses of Commission members; travel reimbursements.

Members of the Commission shall serve without compensation but may receive travel and subsistence as follows:

(1)   Commission members who are officials or employees of a State agency or unit of local government, in accordance with G.S. 138-6.

195

(2)   All other Commission members at the rate established in G.S. 138-5. (1998-1, s. 3(a).)

§§ 143-685 through 143-689. Reserved for future codification purposes.

Article 73.

Reserved.

§§ 143-690 through 143-693. Reserved for future codification purposes.

Article 74.

North Carolina Government Competition Act.

§§ 143-701 through 143-709. Repealed by Session Laws 1999-395, s. 18.1, effective July 1, 1999.

§§ 143-710 through 143-714. Reserved for future codification purposes.

Article 75.

Tobacco Trust Fund

§ 143-715. Policy; purpose.

The General Assembly finds:

(1)   For many years, the State and its prosperity have been supported by its agricultural economy and particularly by the tobacco-related segment of the agricultural economy. The Master Settlement Agreement is expected to cause

significant economic hardship upon the tobacco-related segment of the agricultural economy in that it is expected to result in reduced demand, sales, and prices for tobacco as an agricultural product.

(2)   Tobacco producers, tobacco allotment holders, and persons engaged in tobacco-related businesses are entitled to indemnification for the adverse economic effects in the State resulting from the Master Settlement Agreement, tobacco producers, allotment holders, and persons engaged in tobacco-related businesses are entitled to compensation for the economic losses resulting from lost quota in this State, and tobacco producers are entitled to compensation for the decline in value of tobacco-related personal property assets and declining market conditions in this State resulting from the Master Settlement Agreement, to the extent that funds are available in the Tobacco Trust Fund to address those purposes.

(3)   Even in the absence of the Master Settlement Agreement, the tobacco-related segment of the State's economy is experiencing severe economic hardship as it confronts a national decline in the use of, and demand for, tobacco products, which decline is expected to continue. At present, the tobacco producers, tobacco allotment holders, and persons engaged in tobacco-related businesses are facing an economic crisis that threatens their health and survival. Therefore, in addition to indemnification and compensation for losses in this State resulting from the Master Settlement Agreement, the public interest will be served by the funding of qualified agricultural programs that support, foster, encourage, and facilitate a strong agricultural economy in North Carolina. To the extent that funds are available in the Tobacco Trust Fund, expenditure of those funds to finance qualified agricultural programs is in the public interest.

(4)   It is a public purpose for these funds to be expended in this manner, and it is public service for these persons to accept these funds to the end that conditions of unemployment and fiscal distress may be alleviated or avoided, more stable local economies may be created, local tax bases may be stabilized and maintained, natural resources may be optimally used, and the general public may be benefited. (2000-147, s. 3.)

§ 143-716. Definitions.

The following definitions apply in this Article:

(1)   Commission. - The Tobacco Trust Fund Commission.

(2)   Compensatory programs. - Programs developed by the Commission to identify, locate, compensate, and indemnify tobacco producers, allotment holders, and persons engaged in tobacco-related businesses who have suffered actual economic losses in this State due to lost quota, the decline in value of tobacco-related personal property assets, and declining market conditions resulting from the Master Settlement Agreement or declines in the tobacco-related segment of the State's economy.

(3)   Fund. - The Tobacco Trust Fund.

(4)   Master Settlement Agreement. - The settlement agreement between certain tobacco manufacturers and the states, as incorporated in the consent decree entered in the action of State of North Carolina v. Philip Morris, Incorporated, et al., 98 CVS 14377, in the General Court of Justice, Superior Court Division, Wake County, North Carolina.

(5)   National Tobacco Grower Settlement Trust. - The trust established by tobacco companies to provide payments to tobacco growers and allotment holders in 14 states for the purposes of ameliorating potential adverse economic consequences of likely reduction in demand, sales, and prices for tobacco as an agricultural product as a result of the Master Settlement Agreement.

(6)   Qualified agricultural programs. - Programs developed by the Commission to support and foster the vitality and solvency of the tobacco-related segment of the State's agricultural economy, particularly the segment adversely affected by the Master Settlement Agreement, with the objective of alleviating and avoiding unemployment, preserving, and increasing local tax bases, and encouraging the economic stability of participants in the State's agricultural economy. Examples of qualified agricultural programs include programs to finance the modernization of farming equipment, programs to finance the conversion of existing equipment to conform to environmental and other regulatory requirements, and programs to finance the conversion or replacement of equipment in order to cultivate crops that are more profitable than are currently being cultivated.

(7)   Tobacco product component business. - An individual, partnership, limited liability company, corporation, or other commercial entity that engages in the manufacture of component products for use in the manufacture of tobacco products.

(8)   Tobacco-related business. - An individual, partnership, limited liability company, corporation, or other commercial entity that provides products or services used directly in (i) the production of tobacco, or (ii) support of the business of the production or sale of tobacco. The term does not include the manufacturing of tobacco products or the sale of tobacco products at wholesale or retail.

(9)   Tobacco-related employment. - Employment in a tobacco-related business, or in the manufacturing of tobacco products or the component products used in the manufacture of tobacco products. The term does not include persons employed in the sale of tobacco products at wholesale or retail. (2000-147, s. 3.)

§ 143-717. Commission.

(a)   Creation. - The Tobacco Trust Fund Commission is created. The Commission shall be administratively located within the Department of Agriculture and Consumer Services but shall exercise its powers independently of the Commissioner of Agriculture and the Department. All administrative expenses of the Commission shall be paid from the Fund.

(b)   Membership. - The Commission shall consist of 18 members. The Commission shall be appointed as follows: six members by the Governor, six members by the President Pro Tempore of the Senate, and six members by the Speaker of the House of Representatives. The members shall be appointed as follows:

(1)   The Governor shall make the following appointments:

a.   A flue-cured tobacco farmer.

b.   A flue-cured tobacco farmer.

c.   A person in or displaced from tobacco-related employment.

d.   An at-large appointee.

e.   An at-large appointee.

199

f.   An at-large appointee.

(2)   The President Pro Tempore of the Senate shall make the following appointments:

a.   A flue-cured tobacco farmer.

b.   A flue-cured tobacco farmer.

c.   A burley tobacco farmer.

d.   An at-large appointee.

e.   An at-large appointee.

f.   An at-large appointee.

(3)   The Speaker of the House of Representatives shall make the following appointments:

a.   A flue-cured tobacco farmer.

b.   A former flue-cured allotment holder who is not also a flue-cured tobacco farmer.

c.   A burley tobacco farmer.

d.   An at-large appointee.

e.   An at-large appointee.

f.   An at-large appointee.

It is the intent of the General Assembly that the appointing authorities, in appointing members, shall appoint members who represent the geographic, political, gender, and racial diversity of the State. It is the intent of the General Assembly that at least one-half of the members of the Commission be tobacco farmers.

Except as provided for the initial members under subsection (c) of this section, members shall serve four-year terms beginning July 1. No member may serve more than two full consecutive terms. Members may continue to serve beyond their terms until their successors are duly appointed, but any holdover shall not affect the expiration date of the succeeding term. Vacancies shall be filled by the designated appointing authority for the remainder of the unexpired term. A member may be removed from office for cause by the authority that appointed that member.

(c)   Initial Membership; Staggering. - To provide for a staggered membership, the members initially appointed to the Commission shall be appointed to staggered terms. Of the initial appointments to the Commission, the members initially appointed pursuant to sub-subdivisions (b)(1)a., (1)b., (2)d., and (3)d. of this section shall serve one-year terms ending on June 30, 2001. The members initially appointed pursuant to sub-subdivisions (b)(2)c., (2)e., (3)a., and (3)e. shall serve two-year terms ending on June 30, 2002. The members initially appointed pursuant to sub-subdivisions (b)(1)c., (1)d., (1)e., (2)b., and (3)c. of this section shall serve three-year terms ending June 30, 2003. The remaining members initially appointed pursuant to subsection (b) of this section shall serve four-year terms ending June 30, 2004.

(d)   Officers. - The Commission shall elect from its membership a chair, vice-chair, and other officers as necessary for two-year terms beginning July 1 at the first meeting of the Commission held on or after July 1 of every even-numbered year. The vice-chair may act for the chair in the absence of the chair as authorized by the Commission.

(e)   Frequency of Meetings. - The Commission shall meet at least quarterly each year and may hold special meetings at the call of the chair or a majority of members. The Governor shall call the initial meeting of the Commission.

(f)   Quorum; Majority. - Ten members shall constitute a quorum of the Commission. The Commission may act upon a majority vote of the members of the Commission on matters involving the disbursement of funds and personnel matters properly before the Commission. On all other matters, the Commission may act by majority vote of the members of the Commission at a meeting at which a quorum is present.

(g)   Per Diem and Expenses. - The members of the Commission shall receive per diem and necessary travel and subsistence expenses in accordance with the provisions of G.S. 138-5. Per diem, subsistence, and travel expenses of the members shall be paid from the Fund.

(h)   Conflict of Interest. - Members of the Commission shall comply with the provisions of G.S. 14-234 prohibiting conflicts of interest, except that G.S. 14-234(a) shall not apply to an application for or the receipt of a grant or other financial assistance award by a member of the Commission from the Fund created under this Article, or an entity in which a member of the Commission has an interest, if both of the following conditions are met:

(1)   A member does not vote on, participate in the deliberation of, or otherwise attempt through his or her official capacity to influence the vote on, a grant or other financial assistance award by the Commission to the member.

(2)   The Commissioner of Agriculture determines that any award to a member is in accordance with general criteria adopted by the Commission for the distribution of funds from the Fund.

(i)   Limit on Operating and Administrative Expenses. - No more than two and one-half percent (2 ½%) of the annual receipts of the Fund for the fiscal year beginning July 1 or a total sum of one million dollars ($1,000,000), whichever is less, may be used each fiscal year for administrative and operating expenses of the Commission and its staff. All administrative expenses of the Commission shall be paid from the Fund. (2000-147, s. 3; 2006-264, s. 68.)

§ 143-718. Powers and duties.

The Commission shall have the following powers and duties:

(1)   To administer the provisions of this Article.

(2)   To develop compensatory programs and qualified agriculture programs, including guidelines and criteria for eligibility for and disbursement of funds, the forms of direct and indirect economic assistance to be awarded, and procedures for applying for and reviewing applications for assistance from the Fund. In developing guidelines and criteria for eligibility and disbursement of funds, the Commission may consult with and otherwise obtain assistance from the State and local offices of the Farm Service Agency and other agencies of the United States Department of Agriculture.

(3)   To provide financial assistance to eligible recipients, in carrying out compensatory programs and qualified agricultural programs.

(4)   To hire staff for the administration of the Fund.

(5)   To contract with other persons to assist in the administration of the Commission's programs.

(6)   To accept gifts or grants from other sources.

(7)   To adopt rules to implement this Article. (2000-147, s. 3.)

§ 143-719. Tobacco Trust Fund; creation; investment; priority use.

(a)   Fund Established. - The Tobacco Trust Fund is established in the Office of the State Treasurer. The Fund shall be used for the purposes provided in this Article.

(b)   Fund Earnings, Assets, and Balances. - The State Treasurer shall hold the Fund separate and apart from all other moneys, funds, and accounts. The State Treasurer is the custodian of the Fund and shall invest the assets in accordance with G.S. 147-69.2 and G.S. 147-69.3. Investment earnings credited to the Fund become part of the Fund. Any balance remaining in the Fund at the end of any fiscal year is carried forward in the Fund for the next succeeding fiscal year. Payments from the Fund shall be made on the warrant of the chair of the Commission, pursuant to the directives of the Commission.

(c)   Priority Use of Funds. - As soon as practicable after the beginning of each fiscal year, the State Treasurer must certify in writing to the chair of the Commission the estimated amount of debt service anticipated to be paid during the fiscal year for special indebtedness authorized by the State Capital Facilities Act of 2004, Part 1 of S.L. 2004-179. The chair of the Commission must issue a warrant from the Fund to the General Fund for the lesser of (i) one-half of the amount certified by the Treasurer and (ii) the applicable percentage of the Fund's receipts for the current fiscal year. For fiscal years beginning before July 1, 2007, the applicable percentage is thirty percent (30%). For fiscal years beginning on or after July 1, 2007, the applicable percentage is sixty-five percent (65%). (2000-147, s. 3; 2004-179, s. 1.4.)

§ 143-720. Benefits and administration of Fund for compensatory programs.

(a)   Funds held in the Fund may be expended on compensatory programs as provided in this section.

(b)   The Fund may provide direct and indirect financial assistance, in accordance with criteria established by the Commission and to the extent allowed by law, to accomplish the following:

(1)   Indemnify tobacco producers, allotment holders, and persons engaged in tobacco-related businesses from the adverse economic effects in this State of the Master Settlement Agreement.

(2)   Compensate tobacco producers, allotment holders, and persons engaged in tobacco-related businesses for economic loss resulting from lost quota and compensate tobacco producers for the decline in value of tobacco-related personal property assets and declining market conditions resulting from the Master Settlement Agreement in this State.

(3)   Compensate individuals displaced from tobacco-related employment in this State as a result of the adverse economic effects of the Master Settlement Agreement.

(4)   Compensate tobacco product component businesses that are (i) adversely impacted by the Master Settlement Agreement and that (ii) need financial assistance to retool machinery or equipment or to retrain workers, in order to convert to the production of new products or nontobacco use of existing products, or to effect other similar changes.

(c)   Only tobacco producers, persons engaged in tobacco-related businesses, individuals displaced from tobacco-related employment, and tobacco product component businesses in this State, and holders of North Carolina tobacco allotments are eligible to apply for and receive assistance pursuant to subsection (b) of this section. Direct payments made to tobacco producers, tobacco allotment holders, and persons engaged in tobacco-related businesses shall be based on losses resulting in 1998 and thereafter. Lost quota shall be a primary determinative factor in calculating the amount of compensable economic loss for tobacco producers, allotment holders, and persons engaged in tobacco-related businesses.

(d)   The Commission shall determine the priority of awards among the categories in subsection (b) of this section and within each of those categories.

(e)   Financial assistance awards shall be for no more than one year at a time. An award may be renewed annually, without limitation.

(f)   The Commission may require applicants to provide copies of documents necessary to determine compensable economic loss.

(g)   In no event shall the amount paid to a tobacco producer or allotment holder pursuant to this Article, when combined with the amount received through the National Tobacco Grower Settlement Trust, exceed the compensable economic loss of the producer or allotment holder.

(h)   The Commission may consider the criteria used for National Tobacco Grower Settlement Trust payments and may correspond with the National Tobacco Grower Settlement Trust certification entity to ensure that tobacco farmers and allotment holders are treated fairly. (2000-147, s. 3.)

§ 143-721. Benefits and administration of Fund for qualified agricultural programs.

(a)   Funds held in the Fund may be expended on qualified agricultural programs as provided in this section.

(b)   In implementing qualified agricultural programs, the Commission shall endeavor to identify those areas of the tobacco-related segment of the State's economy in need of assistance to be provided by the Fund in order to assure the continued vitality and solvency of those areas. The Commission shall endeavor to select for funding qualified agricultural programs that will have the greatest favorable impact on the long-term health of the tobacco-related economy of the State.

(c)   The benefits of qualified agricultural programs are not limited to persons suffering economic loss resulting from the Master Settlement Agreement, but these programs shall be designed to foster, support, and assist the tobacco-related segment of the agricultural economy.

(d)   The Commission may solicit and accept proposals from agencies and departments of the State, including institutions of The University of North Carolina, local units of government, the federal government, and members of the private sector for qualified agricultural programs to be funded with money held in the Fund. (2000-147, s. 3.)

§ 143-722. Reporting.

(a)   The chair of the Commission shall report each year by November 1 to the Joint Legislative Commission on Governmental Operations and the chairs of the House and Senate Appropriations Committees regarding the implementation of this Article, including a report on funds disbursed during the fiscal year by amount, purpose, and category of recipient, and other information as requested by the Joint Legislative Commission on Governmental Operations. A written copy of the report shall also be sent to the Legislative Library by November 1 each year.

(b)   Any non-State entity as that term is defined in G.S. 143C-1-1 that receives, uses, or expends any funds from the Commission is subject to the applicable reporting requirements of G.S. 143C-6-14. (2000-147, s. 3; 2004-196, s. 4; 2006-203, s. 99; 2008-187, s. 23.)

§ 143-723. Open meetings; public records; audit.

The Open Meetings Law (Article 33 of Chapter 143 of the General Statutes) and the Public Records Act (Chapter 132 of the General Statutes) shall apply to the Fund and the Commission, and the Fund and the Commission shall be subject to audit by the State Auditor as provided by law. The Commission shall reimburse the State Auditor for the actual cost of the audit. (2000-147, s. 3.)

§ 143-724. Reserved for future codification purposes.

Article 76.

North Carolina Geographic Information Coordinating Council.

§ 143-725. Council established; role of the Center for Geographic Information and Analysis.

(a)   Council Established. - The North Carolina Geographic Information Coordinating Council ("Council") is established to develop policies regarding the utilization of geographic information, GIS systems, and other related technologies. The Council shall be responsible for the following:

(1)   Strategic planning.

(2)   Resolution of policy and technology issues.

(3)   Coordination, direction, and oversight of State, local, and private GIS efforts.

(4)   Advising the Governor, the General Assembly, and the State Chief Information Officer as to needed directions, responsibilities, and funding regarding geographic information.

The purpose of this statewide geographic information coordination effort shall be to further cooperation among State, federal, and local government agencies; academic institutions; and the private sector to improve the quality, access, cost-effectiveness, and utility of North Carolina's geographic information and to promote geographic information as a strategic resource in the State. The Council shall be located in the Office of the Governor for organizational, budgetary, and administrative purposes.

(b)   Role of CGIA. - The Center for Geographic Information and Analysis (CGIA) shall staff the Geographic Information and Coordinating Council and its committees. CGIA shall manage and distribute digital geographic information about North Carolina maintained by numerous State and local government agencies. It shall operate a statewide data clearinghouse and provide Internet access to State geographic information. (2001-359, s. 1; 2004-129, s. 44.)

§ 143-726. Council membership; organization.

(a)   Members. - The Council shall consist of up to 35 members, or their designees, as set forth in this section. An appointing authority may reappoint a Council member for successive terms.

(b)   Governor's Appointments. - The Governor shall appoint the following members:

(1)   The head of an at-large State agency not represented in subsection (d) of this section.

(2)   An employee of a county government, nominated by the North Carolina Association of County Commissioners.

(3)   An employee of a municipal government, nominated by the North Carolina League of Municipalities.

(4)   An employee of the federal government who is stationed in North Carolina.

(5)   A representative from the Lead Regional Organizations.

(6)   A member of the general public.

(7)   Other individuals whom the Governor deems appropriate to enhance the efforts of geographic information coordination.

Members appointed by the Governor shall serve three-year terms. The Governor shall appoint an individual from the membership of the Council to serve as Chair of the Council. The member appointed shall serve as Chair for a term of one year.

(c)   General Assembly Appointments. - The President Pro Tempore of the Senate and the Speaker of the House of Representatives shall each appoint three members to the Council. These members shall serve three-year terms.

(d)   Other Members. - Other Council members shall include:

(1)   The Secretary of State.

(2)   The Commissioner of Agriculture.

(3)   The Superintendent of Public Instruction.

(4)   The Secretary of Environment and Natural Resources.

(5)   The Secretary of the Department of Transportation.

(6)   The Secretary of the Department of Administration.

(7)   The Secretary of the Department of Commerce.

(8)   The Secretary of the Department of Public Safety.

(9)   The Secretary of the Department of Health and Human Services.

(10)   The Secretary of the Department of Revenue.

(11)   The President of the North Carolina Community Colleges System.

(12)   The President of The University of North Carolina System.

(13)   The Chair of the Public Utilities Commission.

(14)   The State Budget Officer.

(15)   The Executive Director of the North Carolina League of Municipalities.

(16)   The Executive Director of the North Carolina Association of County Commissioners.

(17)   One representative from the State Government GIS User Committee.

(18)   One representative elected annually from the Local Government Committee established pursuant to subdivision (h)(2) of this section.

(19)   The State Chief Information Officer who shall serve as a nonvoting member.

Council members serving ex officio pursuant to this subsection shall serve terms coinciding with their respective offices. Members serving by virtue of their appointment by a standing committee of the Council shall serve for the duration of their appointment by the standing committee.

(e)   Meetings. - The Council shall meet at least quarterly on the call of the Chair. The Management and Operations Committee shall conduct the Council's business between quarterly meetings.

(f)   Administration. - The Director of the CGIA shall be secretary of the Council and provide staff support as it requires.

(g)   Reports. - The Council shall report at least annually to the Governor and to the Joint Legislative Commission on Governmental Operations.

(h)   Committees. - The Council may establish work groups, as needed, and shall oversee the standing committees created in this subsection. Each standing committee shall adopt bylaws, subject to the Council's approval, to govern its proceedings. Except as otherwise provided, the Chair of the Council shall appoint the standing committee chairs from representatives listed in subsections (b), (c), or (d) of this section. The standing committees are as follows:

(1)   State Government GIS User Committee. - Membership shall consist of representatives from all interested State government departments. The Chair of the Council shall appoint the committee chair from one of the State agencies represented in subsection (d) of this section.

(2)   Local Government Committee. - Membership shall consist of representatives from organizations and professional associations that currently serve or represent local government GIS users, the North Carolina League of Municipalities, the North Carolina Association of County Commissioners, and Lead Regional Organizations. The committee shall elect one of its members to the Council.

(3)   Federal Interagency Committee. - Membership shall consist of representatives from all interested federal agencies and Tribal governments with an office located in North Carolina. The appointed federal representative serving pursuant to subdivision (b)(4) of this section shall serve as the Chair of the Federal Interagency Committee.

(4)   Statewide Mapping Advisory Committee. - This committee shall consolidate statewide mapping requirements and attempt to gain statewide support for financing cooperative programs. The committee shall also advise the Council on issues, problems, and opportunities relating to federal, State, and local government geospatial data programs.

(5)   GIS Technical Advisory Committee. - This committee shall develop the statewide technical architecture for GIS and anticipate and respond to GIS technical opportunities and issues affecting State, county, and local governments in North Carolina.

(6)   Management and Operations Committee. - This committee shall consider management and operational matters related to GIS and other matters that are formally requested by the Council. The committee membership shall consist of the Chair of the Council, the State Budget Officer, the chair of each of the standing committees of the Council, and other members of the Council appointed by the Chair. (2001-359, s. 1; 2003-340, s. 1.9; 2011-145, s. 19.1(g); 2012-120, s. 3.2.)

§ 143-727. Compensation and expenses of Council members; travel reimbursements.

Members of the Council shall serve without compensation but may receive travel and subsistence as follows:

(1)   Council members who are officials or employees of a State agency or unit of local government, in accordance with G.S. 138-6.

(2)   All other Council members at the rate established in G.S. 138-5. (2001-359, s. 1.)

§ 143-728. Reserved for future codification purposes.

§ 143-729. Reserved for future codification purposes.

Article 77.

Managed Care Patient Assistance Program.

§ 143-730. Health Insurance Smart NC.

(a)   The Office of Managed Care Patient Assistance Program shall hereafter be known as the Health Insurance Smart NC.

(b)   The Health Insurance Smart NC shall provide information and assistance to individuals enrolled in health care plans.

(c)   Health Insurance Smart NC shall have the responsibility and duty to:

(1)   Develop and distribute educational and informational materials for consumers, explaining their rights and responsibilities as health care plan enrollees.

(2)   Answer inquiries posed by consumers.

(3)   Advise health care plan enrollees about the utilization review process.

(4)   Assist enrollees with the grievance, appeal, and external review procedures established by Article 50 of Chapter 58 of the General Statutes.

(5)   Publicize the Health Insurance Smart NC.

(6)   Compile data on the activities of the Office and evaluate such data to make recommendations as to the needed activities of the Office.

(d)   Repealed by Session Laws 2013-199, s. 11, effective July 1, 2013.

(e)   All health information in the possession of the Health Insurance Smart NC is confidential and is not a public record pursuant to G.S. 132-1 or any other applicable statute.

For purposes of this section, "health information" means any of the following:

(1)   Information relating to the past, present, or future physical or mental health or condition of an individual.

(2)   Information relating to the provision of health care to an individual.

(3)   Information relating to the past, present, or future payment for the provision of health care to an individual.

(4)   Information, in any form, that identifies or may be used to identify an individual, that is created by, provided by, or received from any of the following:

a.   An individual or an individual's spouse, parent, legal guardian, or designated representative.

b.　　A health care provider, health plan, employer, health care clearinghouse, or an entity doing business with these entities. (2001-446, s. 1.6; 2002-159, s. 45; 2012-142, s. 15.3(b); 2013-199, s. 11.)

§ 143-731. Reserved for future codification purposes.

§ 143-732. Reserved for future codification purposes.

§ 143-733. Reserved for future codification purposes.

§ 143-734. Reserved for future codification purposes.

Article 78.

Commission on State Property.

§ 143-735: Repealed by Session Laws 2007-12, s. 1, effective April 12, 2007.

§ 143-736: Repealed by Session Laws 2007-12, s. 1, effective April 12, 2007.

§ 143-737: Repealed by Session Laws 2007-12, s. 1, effective April 12, 2007.

§ 143-738: Reserved for future codification purposes.

§ 143-739: Reserved for future codification purposes.

§ 143-740: Reserved for future codification purposes.

§ 143-741: Reserved for future codification purposes.

§ 143-742: Reserved for future codification purposes.

§ 143-743: Reserved for future codification purposes.

§ 143-744: Reserved for future codification purposes.

Article 79.

Internal Auditing.

§ 143-745. Definitions; intent; applicability.

(a)   For the purposes of this section:

(1)   "Agency head" means the Governor, a Council of State member, a cabinet secretary, the President of The University of North Carolina, the President of the Community College System, the State Controller, and other independent appointed officers with authority over a State agency. The agency head for the Department of Public Instruction shall be the State Board of Education.

(2)   "State agency" means each department created pursuant to Chapter 143A or 143B of the General Statutes, and includes all institutions, boards, commissions, authorities, by whatever name, that is a unit of the executive branch of State government, including The University of North Carolina, and the Community Colleges System Office. The term does not include a unit of local government.

(b)   This Article applies only to a State agency that:

(1)   Has an annual operating budget that exceeds ten million dollars ($10,000,000);

(2)   Has more than 100 full-time equivalent employees; or

(3)   Receives and processes more than ten million dollars ($10,000,000) in cash in a fiscal year. (2007-424, s. 1; 2009-516, s. 2; 2013-406, s. 1.)

§ 143-746. Internal auditing required.

(a)   Requirements. - A State agency shall establish a program of internal auditing that:

(1)   Promotes an effective system of internal controls that safeguards public funds and assets and minimizes incidences of fraud, waste, and abuse.

214

(2)   Determines if programs and business operations are administered in compliance with federal and state laws, regulations, and other requirements.

(3)   Reviews the effectiveness and efficiency of agency and program operations and service delivery.

(4)   Periodically audits the agency's major systems and controls, including:

a.   Accounting systems and controls.

b.   Administrative systems and controls.

c.   Information technology systems and controls.

(b)   Internal Audit Standards. - Internal audits shall comply with current Standards for the Professional Practice of Internal Auditing issued by the Institute for Internal Auditors or, if appropriate, Government Auditing Standards issued by the Comptroller General of the United States.

(c)   Appointment and Qualifications of Internal Auditors. - Any State employee who performs the internal audit function shall meet the minimum qualifications for internal auditors established by the Office of State Human Resources, in consultation with the Council of Internal Auditing.

(d)   Director of Internal Auditing. - The agency head shall appoint a Director of Internal Auditing who shall report to, as designated by the agency head, (i) the agency head, (ii) the chief deputy or chief administrative assistant, or (iii) the agency governing board, or subcommittee thereof, if such a governing board exists. The Director of Internal Auditing shall be organizationally situated to avoid impairments to independence as defined in the auditing standards referenced in subsection (b) of this section.

(e)   If a State agency has insufficient personnel to comply with this section, the Office of State Budget and Management shall provide technical assistance. (2007-424, s. 1; 2013-382, s. 9.1(c); 2013-406, s. 1.)

§ 143-747. Council of Internal Auditing.

(a)   The Council of Internal Auditing is created, consisting of the following members:

(1)   The State Controller who shall serve as Chair.

(2)   The State Budget Officer.

(3)   The Secretary of Administration.

(4)   The Attorney General.

(5)   The Secretary of Revenue.

(6)   The State Auditor who shall serve as a nonvoting member. The State Auditor may appoint a designee.

(b)   The Council shall be supported by the Office of State Budget and Management.

(c)   The Council shall:

(1)   Hold meetings at the call of the Chair or upon written request to the Chair by two members of the Council.

(2)   Keep minutes of all proceedings.

(3)   Promulgate guidelines for the uniformity and quality of State agency internal audit activities.

(4)   Recommend the number of internal audit employees required by each State agency.

(5)   Develop internal audit guides, technical manuals, and suggested best internal audit practices.

(6)   Administer an independent peer review system for each State agency internal audit activity; specify the frequency of such reviews consistent with applicable national standards; and assist agencies with selection of independent peer reviewers from other State agencies.

(7)   Provide central training sessions, professional development opportunities, and recognition programs for internal auditors.

(8)   Administer a program for sharing internal auditors among State agencies needing temporary assistance and assembly of interagency teams of internal auditors to conduct internal audits beyond the capacity of a single agency.

(9)   Maintain a central database of all annual internal audit plans; topics for review proposed by internal audit plans; internal audit reports issued and individual findings and recommendations from those reports.

(10)   Require reports in writing from any State agency relative to any internal audit matter.

(11)   If determined necessary by a majority vote of the council:

a.   Conduct hearings relative to any attempts to interfere with, compromise, or intimidate an internal auditor.

b.   Inquire as to the effectiveness of any internal audit unit.

c.   Authorize the Chair to issue subpoenas for the appearance of any person or internal audit working papers, report drafts, and any other pertinent document or record regardless of physical form needed for the hearing.

(12)   Issue an annual report including, but not limited to, service efforts and accomplishments of State agency internal auditors and to propose legislation for consideration by the Governor and General Assembly. (2007-424, s. 1; 2013-406, s. 1.)

§ 143-748. Confidentiality of internal audit work papers.

Internal audit work papers are confidential except as otherwise provided in this section or upon subpoena issued by a duly authorized court. A published internal audit report is a public record as defined in G.S. 132-1 to the extent it does not include information which is confidential under State or federal law or would compromise the security of a State agency. An internal auditor shall maintain for 10 years a complete file of all audit reports and reports of other examinations, investigations, surveys, and reviews conducted under the internal auditor's authority. Audit work papers and other evidence and related supportive material directly pertaining to the work of the internal auditor's office shall be retained in accordance with Chapter 132 of the General Statutes. Unless otherwise prohibited by law and to promote intergovernmental cooperation and avoid unnecessary duplication of audit effort, audit work papers related to released audit reports shall be made available for inspection by duly authorized representatives of the State and federal government in connection with some matter officially before them. (2013-406, s. 1.)

§ 143-749. Obstruction of audit.

It shall be a Class 2 misdemeanor for any officer, employee, or agent of a State agency subject to the provisions of this Article to willfully make or cause to be made to a State agency internal auditor or the internal auditor's designated representatives any false, misleading, or unfounded report for the purpose of interfering with the performance of any audit, special review, or investigation or to hinder or obstruct the State agency internal auditor or the internal auditor's designated representatives in the performance of their duties. (2013-406, s. 1.)

Chapter 143A.

State Government Reorganization.

Article 1.

General Provisions.

§ 143A-1. Short title.

This Chapter shall be known and may be cited as the "Executive Organization Act of 1971." (1971, c. 864, s. 1.)

§ 143A-2. Head of department defined.

Whenever the term "head of the department" is used it shall mean the head of one of the principal departments created by this Chapter. (1971, c. 864, s. 1.)

§ 143A-3. Agency defined.

Whenever the term "agency" is used it shall mean and include, as the context may require, an existing department, institution, commission, committee, board, division, bureau, officer or official. (1971, c. 864, s. 1.)

§ 143A-4. Policy-making authority and administrative powers of Governor; delegation.

The Governor, in accordance with Article III of the Constitution of North Carolina, shall be the chief executive officer of the State. Subject to the Constitution and laws of this State, the Governor shall be responsible for formulating and administering the policies of the executive branch of the State government. Where a conflict arises in connection with the administration of the policies of the executive branch of the State government with respect to the reorganization of State government, such conflict shall be resolved by the Governor, and the decision of the Governor shall be final. (1971, c. 864, s. 1.)

§ 143A-5. Office of the Lieutenant Governor.

The Lieutenant Governor shall maintain an office in a State building in the City of Raleigh which office shall be open during normal working hours throughout the year. The Lieutenant Governor shall serve as President of the Senate and perform such additional duties as the Governor or General Assembly may assign to him. This section shall become effective January 1, 1973. (1971, c. 864, s. 1.)

§ 143A-6. Types of transfers.

(a)   Under this Chapter, a Type I transfer means the transferring of all or part of an existing agency to a principal department established by this Chapter. When all or part of any agency is transferred to a principal department under a Type I transfer, its statutory authority, powers, duties, and functions, records, personnel, property, unexpended balances of appropriations, allocations or other funds, including the functions of budgeting and purchasing, are transferred to the principal department.

When any agency, or part thereof, is transferred by a Type I transfer to a principal department under the provisions of this Chapter, all its prescribed powers, duties, and functions, including but not limited to rule making, regulation, licensing, and promulgation of rules, rates, regulations, and standards, and the rendering of findings, orders, and adjudications are transferred to the head of the principal department into which the agency, or part thereof, has been transferred.

(b)   Under this Chapter, a Type II transfer means the transferring intact of an existing agency, or part thereof, to a principal department established by this Chapter. When any agency, or part thereof, is transferred to a principal department under a Type II transfer, that agency, or part thereof, shall be administered under the direction and supervision of that principal department, but shall exercise all its prescribed statutory powers independently of the head of the principal department, except that under a Type II transfer the management functions of any transferred agency, or part thereof, shall be performed under the direction and supervision of the head of the principal department.

(c)   Whenever the term "management functions" is used it shall mean planning, organizing, staffing, directing, coordinating, reporting and budgeting. (1971, c. 864, s. 1.)

§ 143A-7. Agencies not enumerated; continuation.

Any existing department, institution, board or commission not enumerated in this Chapter but established or created by the General Assembly shall continue to exercise all its powers, duties and functions. (1971, c. 864, s. 1.)

§ 143A-8. Internal organization of departments; allocation and reallocation of duties and functions; limitations.

The Governor shall cause the administrative organization of each department to be examined with a view to promoting economy and efficiency. The Governor may reorganize and organize the principal departments and assign and reassign the duties and functions among the divisions and other units, division heads, officers, and employees; except as otherwise expressly provided by statute. When such changes affect existing law they must be submitted in accordance with Article III, Sec. 5 of the Constitution. The head of a principal department shall have legal custody of all books, papers, documents and other records of the department. The head of a principal department shall be responsible for the preparation and presentation of the department budget request which shall include all funds requested and all receipts expected for all elements of the department. (1971, c. 864, s. 1.)

§ 143A-9. Appointment of officers and employees; salaries of department heads.

Any provisions of law to the contrary notwithstanding, and subject to the provisions of the Constitution of the State of North Carolina, the head of a principal department, except those departments headed by elected officials who are constitutional officers, shall be appointed by the Governor and serve at his pleasure.

The head of a principal department shall appoint the chief deputy or chief assistant and such chief deputy or chief assistant shall be subject to the North Carolina Human Resources Act. Except where appointment by the Governor is prescribed by existing statute, the head of the principal department shall appoint the administrative head of each transferred agency and, subject to the provisions of the North Carolina Human Resources Act, appoint all employees of each division, section or other unit under a principal department.

In establishing the position of secretary, and the supporting staff for the principal departments, the cost of such staff positions will be met insofar as possible by utilizing existing positions or funds available from vacant positions within agencies assigned to the principal departments. (1971, c. 864, s. 1; 1983, c. 717, s. 50; 2013-382, s. 9.1(c).)

§ 143A-10. Governor; continuation of powers and duties; staff.

221

All powers, duties and functions vested by law in the Governor or in the office of Governor are continued, except as otherwise provided by this Chapter.

The immediate staff of the Governor shall not be subject to the North Carolina Human Resources Act. (1971, c. 864, s. 1; 2006-203, s. 100; 2013-382, s. 9.1(c).)

§ 143A-11. Principal departments.

Except as otherwise provided by this Chapter, or the State Constitution, all executive and administrative powers, duties and functions, not including those of the General Assembly and the judiciary, previously vested by law in the several State agencies, are vested in the following principal offices or departments:

(1)   Office of the Governor.

(2)   Office of the Lieutenant Governor.

(3)   Department of the Secretary of State.

(4)   Department of State Auditor.

(5)   Department of State Treasurer.

(6)   Department of Public Instruction.

(7)   Department of Justice.

(8)   Department of Agriculture and Consumer Services.

(9)   Department of Labor.

(10)   Department of Insurance.

(11)   through (13) Repealed by Session Laws 1995, c. 509, s. 96.

(14)   Repealed by Session Laws 1973, c. 476, s. 6.

(15),   (16) Repealed by Session Laws 1995, c. 509, s. 96.

(17),   (18) Repealed by Session Laws 1973, c. 476, s. 6.

(19)   Repealed by Session Laws 1973, c. 620, s. 9. (1971, c. 864, s. 1; 1973, c. 476, s. 6; c. 620, s. 9; 1975, c. 716, s. 7; 1977, c. 771, s. 4; 1989, c. 727, s. 218(120); c. 751, s. 7(17); 1991 (Reg. Sess., 1992), c. 959, s. 36; 1993, c. 522, s. 12; 1995, c. 509, s. 96; 1997-261, s. 93.)

§ 143A-12. Office of the Governor; creation.

There is hereby created an office of the Governor. (1971, c. 864, s. 2.)

§ 143A-13. Office of the Lieutenant Governor; creation.

There is hereby created an office of the Lieutenant Governor. (1971, c. 864, s. 3.)

§ 143A-14. Creation of new departments by executive order.

All departments not now in existence which this Chapter directs to be created shall be made operative by executive order of the Governor; provided that all new departments shall be activated by executive order not later than July 1, 1972. (1971, c. 864, s. 21.)

§ 143A-15. Date of transfer of agencies into existing departments.

The transfer of all agencies into departments of State government which now exist shall take place not later than October 1, 1971. (1971, c. 864, s. 21.)

§ 143A-16. Transfer of funds by Governor.

To implement this Chapter, the Governor shall have authority to transfer all or a part of any appropriations or funds of an agency to the department to which such agency is transferred. (1971, c. 864, s. 21.)

§ 143A-17: Repealed by Session Laws 1993 (Reg. Sess., 1994), c. 769, s. 11.

§ 143A-18. Additional funds for reorganization.

When adequate funds to implement reorganization are not available from the budgets of the transferred agencies, the Governor and the Council of State may make other funds available for these purposes, not to exceed a total of five hundred thousand dollars ($500,000) per year for all departments created by this Chapter. (1971, c. 864, s. 21.)

Article 2.

Department of the Secretary of State.

§ 143A-19. Creation.

There is hereby created a Department of the Secretary of State. The head of the Department of the Secretary of State is the Secretary of State. (1971, c. 864, s. 4.)

§ 143A-20. Secretary of State; powers and duties.

The Secretary of State shall have such powers and duties as are conferred on him by this Chapter, delegated to him by the Governor, and conferred by the Constitution and laws of this State. (1971, c. 864, s. 4.)

§ 143A-21. Secretary of State; transfer of powers and duties to Department.

Except as otherwise provided in the Constitution or in this Chapter, all powers, duties and functions vested by law in the Secretary of State are transferred by a Type I transfer to the Department of the Secretary of State. (1971, c. 864, s. 4.)

§ 143A-22. Repealed by Session Laws 1973, c. 1409, s. 1.

§ 143A-23. Notaries public; powers, duties and functions; transfer.

All of the powers, duties and functions of the Governor under G.S. 10-1 of the General Statutes are transferred by a Type I transfer to the Department of the Secretary of State. (1971, c. 864, s. 4.)

Article 3.

Department of State Auditor.

§ 143A-24. Creation.

There is hereby created a Department of State Auditor. The head of the Department of the State Auditor is the State Auditor. (1971, c. 864, s. 5.)

§ 143A-25. State Auditor; powers and duties.

The State Auditor shall have such powers and duties as are conferred on him by this Chapter, delegated to him by the Governor, and conferred by the Constitution and laws of this State. (1971, c. 864, s. 5.)

§ 143A-26. State Auditor; transfer of powers and duties to Department.

Except as otherwise provided in the Constitution or by this Chapter, all powers, duties and functions of the State Auditor are transferred by a Type I transfer to the Department of the State Auditor. (1971, c. 864, s. 5.)

§ 143A-27. North Carolina Firemen's Pension Fund; transfer.

The North Carolina Firemen's Pension Fund, as contained in Article 86 of Chapter 58 of the General Statutes and the laws of this State, is hereby transferred by a Type II transfer to the Department of State Auditor. (1971, c. 864, s. 5.)

§ 143A-27.1. North Carolina Firemen's and Rescue Squad Workers' Pension Fund; transfer.

The "North Carolina Firemen's and Rescue Squad Workers' Pension Fund", as contained in Article 86 of Chapter 58 of the General Statutes is hereby transferred by a Type II transfer to the Department of State Auditor. (1981, c. 1029, s. 3.)

§ 143A-28. Repealed by Session Laws 1977, 2nd Sess., c. 1204, s. 2.

§ 143A-29. State Board of Pensions; transfer.

The State Board of Pensions, as contained in Article 2 of Chapter 112 of the General Statutes and the laws of this State, is hereby transferred by a Type II transfer to the Department of State Auditor. (1971, c. 864, s. 5.)

Article 4.

Department of State Treasurer.

§ 143A-30. Creation.

There is hereby created a Department of State Treasurer. The head of the Department of State Treasurer is the State Treasurer. (1971, c. 864, s. 6.)

§ 143A-31. State Treasurer; powers and duties.

The State Treasurer shall have such powers and duties as are conferred on him by this Chapter, delegated to him by the Governor, and conferred by the Constitution and laws of this State. (1971, c. 864, s. 6.)

§ 143A-32. State Treasurer; transfer of powers and duties to Department.

Except as otherwise provided in the Constitution or in this Chapter, all powers, duties and functions vested by law in the State Treasurer are transferred by a Type I transfer to the Department of State Treasurer. (1971, c. 864, s. 6.)

§ 143A-33. Local Government Commission; transfer.

The Local Government Commission, as contained in Article 1 of Chapter 159 of the General Statutes and the laws of this State, is hereby transferred by a Type II transfer to the Department of State Treasurer. (1971, c. 864, s. 6.)

§ 143A-34. Teachers' and State Employees' Retirement System; transfer.

The Teachers' and State Employees' Retirement System, and the board of trustees, as contained in Article 1 of Chapter 135 of the General Statutes and the laws of this State, is hereby transferred by a Type II transfer to the Department of State Treasurer. (1971, c. 864, s. 6.)

§ 143A-35. North Carolina Local Governmental Employees' Retirement System; transfer.

The North Carolina Local Governmental Employees' Retirement System, as contained in Article 3 of Chapter 128 of the General Statutes and the laws of this State, is hereby transferred by a Type II transfer to the Department of State Treasurer. (1971, c. 864, s. 6.)

§ 143A-36. Public Employees' Social Security Agency; powers, duties and functions; transfer.

All of the powers, duties and functions of the Public Employees' Social Security Agency as contained in Article 2 of Chapter 135 of the General Statutes and the laws of this State, are transferred by a Type I transfer to the Department of State Treasurer. (1971, c. 864, s. 6.)

§ 143A-37. Legislative Retirement Fund; transfer.

The Legislative Retirement Fund, as provided for in G.S. 120-4.1 of the General Statutes and the laws of this State, is hereby transferred by a Type II transfer to the Department of State Treasurer. (1971, c. 864, s. 6.)

§ 143A-38: Repealed by Session Laws 2007-491, s. 2, effective January 1, 2008.

§ 143A-38.1. The Law-Enforcement Officers' Benefit and Retirement Fund; transfer.

The Law-Enforcement Officers' Benefit and Retirement Fund, as contained in Article 12 of Chapter 143 of the General Statutes and the laws of this State, is hereby transferred by a Type II transfer to the Department of State Treasurer. (1977, 2nd Sess., c. 1204, s. 1.)

Article 5.

Department of Public Instruction.

§§ 143A-39 through 143A-42: Repealed by Session Laws 1993, c. 522, s. 14.

§ 143A-43: Repealed by Session Laws 1983, c. 768, s. 14.

§ 143A-44: Repealed by Session Laws 1993, c. 522, s. 14.

§ 143A-44.1. Creation.

There is hereby created a Department of Public Instruction. The head of the Department of Public Instruction is the State Board of Education. Any provision of G.S. 143A-9 to the contrary notwithstanding, the appointment of the State Board of Education shall be as prescribed in Article IX, Section (4)(1) of the Constitution. (1995, c. 72, s. 3; 2008-187, s. 24.)

§ 143A-44.2. State Board of Education; transfer of powers and duties to State Board.

The State Board of Education shall have all powers and duties conferred on the Board by this Article, delegated to the Board by the Governor, and conferred by the Constitution and laws of this State. (1995, c. 72, s. 3.)

§ 143A-44.3. Superintendent of Public Instruction; creation; transfer of powers and duties.

The office of the Superintendent of Public Instruction, as provided for by Article III, Section 7 of the Constitution, and the Department of Public Instruction are transferred to the Department of Public Instruction. The Superintendent of Public Instruction shall be the Secretary and Chief Administrative Officer of the State Board of Education, and shall have all powers and duties conferred by the Constitution, by the State Board of Education, Chapter 115C of the General Statutes, and the laws of this State. (1995, c. 72, s. 3.)

§ 143A-45. Interstate Compact for Education; rights, duties and privileges.

All of the rights, duties and privileges of this State obtained as a party to the Interstate Compact for Education as contained in Part 5 of Article 8 of Chapter 115C of the General Statutes and the laws of this State, shall be supervised and administered by the Superintendent of Public Instruction. (1971, c. 864, s. 7; 1983, c. 768, s. 16.)

§ 143A-46: Repealed by Session Laws 1983, c. 768, s. 14.

§ 143A-47. Interstate Agreement on Qualifications of Educational Personnel; rights, duties and privileges.

All of the rights, duties and privileges of this State obtained as a party to the Interstate Agreement on Qualifications of Educational Personnel as contained in Article 24 of Chapter 115C of the General Statutes and the laws of this State shall be supervised and administered by the Superintendent of Public Instruction. (1971, c. 864, s. 7; 1983, c. 768, s. 17.)

§ 143A-48. Textbook Commission; transfer.

The Textbook Commission, as created by G.S. 115C-87 and the laws of this State, is hereby transferred by a Type I transfer to the Department of Public Instruction. (1971, c. 864, s. 7; 1983, c. 768, s. 18; 1993, c. 522, s. 15.)

§ 143A-48.1. North Carolina Council on the Holocaust; creation; purpose; membership; expenses; assistance.

(a)   There is hereby created the North Carolina Council on the Holocaust. The purpose of the Council is to prevent future atrocities similar to the systematic program of genocide of six million Jews and others by the Nazis. This purpose shall be accomplished by developing a program of education and observance of the Holocaust.

(b)   The Council shall consist of 24 members, six appointed by the Governor, six appointed by the President Pro Tempore of the Senate, six appointed by the Speaker of the House of Representatives, and six appointed by the other 18 members. Members shall be appointed for two-year terms to begin July 1 of each odd-numbered year. The six at-large appointments shall be made by the Council at its first meeting after July 1 of each odd-numbered year. To be eligible for appointment as an at-large member, a person must either be a survivor of the Holocaust or a first-generation lineal descendant of such person. A majority of the members shall constitute a quorum for the transaction of business.

(c)   The members of the Council shall be compensated and reimbursed for their expenses in accordance with G.S. 138-5.

(d)   The Superintendent of Public Instruction may arrange for clerical or other assistance required by the Council. (1985, c. 757, s. 81(a); 1989, c. 47; 1995, c. 490, s. 23; 2002-126, s. 10.10D(a), (b).)

Article 6.

Department of Justice.

§ 143A-49. Creation.

There is hereby created a Department of Justice. The head of the Department of Justice is the Attorney General. (1971, c. 864, s. 8.)

§ 143A-49.1. Attorney General; powers and duties.

The Attorney General shall have such powers and duties as are conferred on him by this Chapter, delegated to him by the Governor, and conferred by the Constitution and laws of this State. (1971, c. 864, s. 8.)

§ 143A-50. Attorney General; transfer of powers and duties to Department.

Except as otherwise provided in the Constitution or in this Chapter, all powers, duties and functions vested by law in the Attorney General are transferred by a Type I transfer to the Department of Justice. (1971, c. 864, s. 8.)

§ 143A-51. State Bureau of Investigation; transfer.

The State Bureau of Investigation, as contained in Article 4 of Chapter 114 of the General Statutes and the laws of this State, is hereby transferred by a Type I transfer to the Department of Justice. (1971, c. 864, s. 8.)

§ 143A-52. Fire investigations; transfer.

The duties of the Commissioner of Insurance with respect to the investigation of all fires, including forest fires, as contained in Article 1 of Chapter 69 of the General Statutes and the laws of this State, are hereby transferred by a Type I transfer to the Department of Justice; provided, however, that the duties of the Commissioner of Insurance with respect to the inspection of buildings, the removal of dangerous materials therefrom, hospital insurance, insurance regulation, and the preparation of annual reports, as contained in Chapters 57 and 58 of the General Statutes and G.S. 69-4, shall continue to be among the duties of the Commissioner of Insurance. (1971, c. 864, s. 8; 1977, c. 596, s. 3.)

§ 143A-53: Repealed by Session Laws 2011-97, s. 10, effective June 1, 2011.

§ 143A-54. Company police; powers, duties and functions; transfer.

All of the powers, duties and functions of the Governor contained in Chapter 74A of the General Statutes and the laws of this State relating to the appointment and commission of special police are hereby transferred by a Type I transfer to the Department of Justice. (1971, c. 864, s. 8.)

§ 143A-55. Police information Network; transfer.

The Police Information Network, as created by G.S. 114-10.1 and the laws of this State, is hereby transferred by a Type I transfer to the Department of Justice. (1971, c. 864, s. 8.)

§ 143A-55.1. North Carolina Criminal Justice Training and Standards Council; transfer.

The North Carolina Criminal Justice Training and Standards Council, as created by Chapter 17A of the General Statutes and laws of this State, is hereby transferred by a Type II transfer to the Department of Justice. (1975, c. 372, s. 1.)

§ 143A-55.2. North Carolina Sheriffs' Education and Training Standards Commission; transfer.

The North Carolina Sheriffs' Education and Training Standards Commission, as created by Chapter 17E of the General Statutes and laws of this State, is hereby transferred by a Type II transfer as defined in G.S. 143A-6(b) to the Department of Justice. (1983, c. 558, s. 4.)

§§ 143A-55.3 through 143A-55.7: Not effectuated.

Article 7.

Department of Agriculture and Consumer Services.

§ 143A-56. Creation.

There is hereby created a Department of Agriculture and Consumer Services. The head of the Department is the Commissioner of Agriculture. (1971, c. 864, s. 9; 1997-261, s. 95.)

232

§ 143A-57. Commissioner of Agriculture; powers and duties.

The Commissioner of Agriculture shall have such powers and duties as are conferred on him by this Chapter, delegated to him by the Governor, and conferred by the Constitution and laws of this State. (1971, c. 864, s. 9.)

§ 143A-58. Commissioner of Agriculture; transfer of powers and duties to Department.

Except as otherwise provided in the Constitution or in this Chapter, all powers, duties and functions vested by law in the Commissioner of Agriculture are transferred by a Type I transfer to the Department of Agriculture and Consumer Services. (1971, c. 864, s. 9; 1997-261, s. 96.)

§ 143A-59. Board of Agriculture; transfer.

The Board of Agriculture, as contained in Article 1 of Chapter 106 of the General Statutes and the laws of this State, is hereby transferred by a Type II transfer to the Department of Agriculture and Consumer Services. (1971, c. 864, s. 9; 1997-261, s. 97.)

§ 143A-60. Structural Pest Control Division; transfer.

The Structural Pest Control Division of the Department of Agriculture, as contained in Article 4C of Chapter 106 of the General Statutes and the laws of this State, is hereby transferred by a Type II transfer to the Department of Agriculture and Consumer Services. (1971, c. 864, s. 9; 1997-261, s. 98.)

§ 143A-61. The North Carolina Agricultural Hall of Fame; transfer.

The North Carolina Agricultural Hall of Fame, as contained in Article 50B of Chapter 106 of the General Statutes and the laws of this State, is hereby transferred by a Type I transfer to the Department of Agriculture and Consumer Services. (1971, c. 864, s. 9; 1997-261, s. 99.)

143A-62. Gasoline and Oil Inspection Board; transfer.

The Gasoline and Oil Inspection Board, as contained in Article 3 of Chapter 119 of the General Statutes and the laws of this State, is hereby transferred by a Type II transfer to the Department of Agriculture and Consumer Services. (1971, c. 864, s. 9; 1997-261, s. 100.)

§ 143A-63. North Carolina Rural Rehabilitation Corporation; transfer.

The North Carolina Rural Rehabilitation Corporation, and board of directors, as contained in Chapter 137 of the General Statutes and the laws of this State, is transferred by a Type I transfer to the North Carolina Agricultural Finance Authority in the Department of Agriculture and Consumer Services. (1971, c. 864, s. 9; 1997-261, s. 101; 2001-424, s. 17.2(a).)

§ 143A-64. North Carolina Board of Crop Seed Improvement; transfer.

The North Carolina Board of Crop Seed Improvement, as contained in Article 30 of Chapter 106 of the General Statutes and the laws of this State, is hereby transferred by a Type II transfer to the Department of Agriculture and Consumer Services. (1971, c. 864, s. 9; 1997-261, s. 102.)

§ 143A-65. North Carolina Public Livestock Market Advisory Board; transfer.

The North Carolina Public Livestock Market Advisory Board, as contained in Article 35 of Chapter 106 of the General Statutes and the laws of this State, is hereby transferred by a Type I transfer to the Department of Agriculture and Consumer Services. (1971, c. 864, s. 9; 1997-261, s. 103.)

§ 143A-65.1. North Carolina Forest Service.

The Department of Agriculture and Consumer Services shall have charge of the work of forest maintenance, forest fire prevention, reforestation, and the protection of lands and water supplies by the preservation of forests; it shall also have the care of State forests and State recreational forests. (2011-145, s. 13.25(c); 2013-155, s. 23.)

§ 143A-66: Repealed by Session Laws 1993, c. 561, s. 116.

§ 143A-66.1. Forestry Council - creation; powers and duties.

There is hereby created the Forestry Council of the Department of Agriculture and Consumer Services. The Forestry Council shall have the following functions and duties:

(1)   To advise the Commissioner of Agriculture with respect to all matters concerning the protection, management, and preservation of State-owned, privately owned, and municipally owned forests in the State, including but not limited to:

a.   Profitable use of the State's forests consistent with the principles of sustained productivity.

b.   Best management practices, including those for protection of soil, water, wildlife, and wildlife habitat, to be used in managing the State's forests and their resources.

c.   Restoration of forest ecosystems and protection of rare and endangered species occurring in the State's private forests consistent with principles of private ownership of land.

(2)   To maintain oversight of a continuous monitoring and planning process, to provide a long-range, comprehensive plan for the use, management, and sustainability of North Carolina's forest resources, and to report regularly on progress made toward meeting the objectives of the plan.

(3)   To provide a forum for the identification, discussion, and development of recommendations for the resolution of conflicts in the management of North Carolina's forests.

(4)   To undertake any other studies, make any reports, and advise the Commissioner of Agriculture on any matter as the Commissioner may direct. (1973, c. 1262, s. 52; 1977, c. 771, s. 4; 1989, c. 727, s. 218(139); 1995 (Reg. Sess., 1996), c. 653, s. 1; 1997-443, s. 11A.119(a); 2011-145, s. 13.25(f), (g).)

§ 143A-66.2. Forestry Council - members; chairperson; selection; removal; compensation; quorum.

(a)   The Forestry Advisory Council of the Department of Agriculture and Consumer Services shall consist of 18 members appointed as follows:

(1)   Three persons who are registered foresters and who represent the primary forest products industry, one each from the Mountains, Piedmont and Coastal Plain.

(2)   One person who represents the secondary wood-using industry.

(3)   One person who represents the logging industry.

(4)   Four persons who are nonindustrial woodland owners actively involved in forest management, one of whom has agricultural interests, and at least one each from the Mountains, Piedmont, and Coastal Plain.

(5)   Three persons who are members of statewide environmental or wildlife conservation organizations.

(6)   One consulting forester.

(7)   Two persons who are forest scientists with knowledge of the functioning and management of forest ecosystems.

(8)   One person who represents a banking institution that manages forestland.

(9)   One person with expertise in urban forestry.

(10)   One person with active experience in city and regional planning.

(b)   The Governor shall appoint one person from categories (1) and (5), two persons from category (4), and the persons from categories (6), (7), (8), (9), and (10). The President Pro Tempore of the Senate shall appoint the person from category (2) and one person each from categories (1), (4), and (5). The Speaker of the House of Representatives shall appoint the person from category (3) and one person each from categories (1), (4), and (5). The Governor, the President Pro Tempore of the Senate, and the Speaker of the House of Representatives shall consult with one another to insure that each of the three geographic

236

regions of the State are represented in appointments made to fill categories (1) and (4).

(c)   The Governor shall designate one member of the Council to serve as chairperson at the pleasure of the Governor.

(d)   Members shall serve staggered terms of office of four years. The terms of office of members filling categories (1), (4), and (5) shall expire on 30 June of years that follow by one year those years that are evenly divisible by four. The terms of office of members filling categories (2), (3), (6), (7), (8), (9), and (10) shall expire on 30 June of years that follow by three years those years that are evenly divisible by four. Terms shall expire as provided by this subsection except that members of the Council shall serve until their successors are appointed and duly qualified as provided by G.S. 128-7. Any appointment to fill a vacancy on the Council created by the resignation, dismissal, death or disability of a member shall be for the balance of the unexpired term and shall be made by the appointing authority responsible for that category. Vacancies in appointments made by the General Assembly shall be filled in accordance with G.S. 120-122.

(e)   The Governor shall have the power to remove, in accordance with G.S. 143B-13, any member appointed by the Governor. The General Assembly shall have the power to remove, in accordance with G.S. 143B-13, any member appointed by the General Assembly.

(f)   Members of the Council shall receive per diem and necessary travel and subsistence expenses in accordance with the provisions of G.S. 138-5.

(g)   A majority of the Council shall constitute a quorum for the transaction of business.

(h)   All clerical and other services required by the Council, including the support required to carry out studies it is requested to make, shall be supplied by the Commissioner of Agriculture. (1973, c. 1262, s. 53; 1977, c. 771, s. 4; 1989, c. 727, s. 218(140); 1995 (Reg. Sess., 1996), c. 653, s. 2; 1997-443, s. 11A.119(a); 2011-145, s. 13.25(f), (h).)

§ 143A-66.3. Forestry Council - meetings.

The Forestry Council shall meet annually in October and at least three other times a year and may hold special meetings at any time and place within the State at the call of the chairperson or upon the written request of at least a majority of the members. At least one meeting during each two-year period shall be held in the Mountains, Piedmont, and the Coastal Plain. (1973, c. 1262, s. 54; 1995 (Reg. Sess., 1996), c. 653, s. 3; 2011-145, s. 13.25(f).)

Article 8.

Department of Labor.

§ 143A-67. Creation.

There is hereby created a Department of Labor. The head of the Department of Labor is the Commissioner of Labor. (1971, c. 864, s. 10.)

§ 143A-68. Commissioner of Labor; powers and duties.

The Commissioner of Labor shall have such powers and duties as are conferred on him by this Chapter, delegated to him by the Governor, and conferred by the Constitution and laws of this State. (1971, c. 864, s. 10.)

§ 143A-69. Commissioner of Labor; transfer of powers and duties to Department.

Except as otherwise provided in the Constitution or in this Chapter, all powers, duties and functions vested by law in the Commissioner of Labor are transferred by a Type I transfer to the Department of Labor. (1971, c. 864, s. 10.)

§ 143A-70. Board of Boiler Rules and Bureau of Boiler Inspection; transfer.

The Board of Boiler Rules and the Bureau of Boiler Inspection, as contained in Article 7 of Chapter 95 of the General Statutes and the laws of this State, are hereby transferred by a Type I transfer to the Department of Labor. (1971, c. 864, s. 10.)

§ 143A-71: Repealed by Session Laws 2013-72, s. 2(b), effective January 1, 2014.

§ 143A-72. Voluntary arbitration of labor disputes; appointment of arbitrator or panel; Commissioner of Labor; transfer.

All of the powers, duties and functions of the Commissioner of Labor under Article 4A of Chapter 95 of the General Statutes and the laws of this State, are transferred by a Type I transfer to the Department of Labor. (1971, c. 864, s. 10.)

Article 9.

Department of Insurance.

§ 143A-73. Creation.

There is hereby created a Department of Insurance. The head of the Department of Insurance is the Commissioner of Insurance. (1971, c. 864, s. 11.)

§ 143A-74. Commissioner of Insurance; powers and duties.

The Commissioner of Insurance shall have such powers and duties as are conferred on him by this Chapter, delegated to him by the Governor, and conferred by the Constitution and laws of this State. (1971, c. 864, s. 11.)

§ 143A-75. Commissioner of Insurance; transfer of powers and duties to Department.

Except as otherwise provided in the Constitution or in this Chapter, all powers, duties and functions vested in the Commissioner of Insurance are transferred by a Type I transfer to the Department of Insurance. (1971, c. 864, s. 11.)

§ 143A-76: Repealed by Session Laws 1985, c. 666, s. 11.

§ 143A-77: Repealed by Session Laws 1985, c. 666, s. 12.

§ 143A-78. Building Code Council; transfer.

The Building Code Council, as contained in Article 9 of Chapter 143 of the General Statutes and the laws of this State, is hereby transferred by a Type II transfer to the Department of Insurance. (1971, c. 864, s. 11.)

§ 143A-79. State Volunteer Fire Department; transfer.

The State Volunteer Fire Department, as contained in Article 3 of Chapter 69 of the General Statutes and the laws of this State, is hereby transferred by a Type I transfer to the Department of Insurance. (1971, c. 864, s. 11.)

§ 143A-79.1. Public Officers and Employees Liability Insurance Commission; transfer.

The Public Officers and Employees Liability Insurance Commission, as contained in Part 20 of Article 9 of General Statutes Chapter 143B, is transferred by a Type II transfer to the Department of Insurance. (1985, c. 666, s. 78.)

§ 143A-79.2. State Fire Commission; transfer.

The State Fire Commission, described in Part 4 of Article 11 of Chapter 143B of the General Statutes, is transferred from the Department of Crime Control and Public Safety to the Department of Insurance. This transfer shall include all elements of a Type I transfer as defined in G.S. 143A-6. (1985, c. 757, s. 167(a); 2011-145, s. 19.1(g); 2012-194, s. 39.)

Article 10.

Department of Administration.

§§ 143A-80 through 143A-96. Repealed by Session Laws 1975, c. 879, s. 46.

§ 143A-96.1. Transfer of Department of Veterans Affairs.

The Division of Veterans Affairs of the Department of Military and Veterans Affairs as described in Article 5 of Chapter 143B is hereby transferred by a Type I transfer, as defined in G.S. 143A-6, to the Department of Administration. The Secretary of Administration is hereby empowered and directed to employ within the Department of Administration an additional assistant secretary as Assistant Secretary for Veterans Affairs. (1977, c. 70, s. 26.)

Article 11.

Department of Transportation and Highway Safety.

§§ 143A-97 through 143A-108. Repealed by Session Laws 1975, c. 716, s. 5.

Article 12.

Department of Natural and Economic Resources.

§§ 143A-109 through 143A-129. Repealed by Session Laws 1973, c. 1262, s. 86.

Article 13.

Department of Human Resources.

§§ 143A-130 through 143A-162. Repealed by Session Laws 1973, c. 476, s. 183.

Article 14.

Department of Social Rehabilitation and Control.

§§ 143A-163 through 143A-170. Repealed by Session Laws 1973, c. 1262, s. 10.

Article 15.

Department of Commerce.

§§ 143A-171 through 143A-180. Repealed by Session Laws 1977, c. 198, s. 25.

§§ 143A-180.1 through 143A-180.2. Recodified as §§ 143B-448, 143B-449 by Session Laws 1977, c. 198, s. 26.

§ 143A-181. Recodified as § 143B-439 by Session Laws 1977, c. 198, s. 26.

§§ 143A-182 through 143A-185.1. Repealed by Session Laws 1977, c. 198, s. 25.

Article 16.

Department of Revenue.

§§ 143A-186 through 143A-190. Repealed by Session Laws 1973, c. 476, s. 193.

Article 17.

Department of Art, Culture and History.

§§ 143A-191 through 143A-230. Repealed by Session Laws 1973, c. 476, s. 16.

Article 18.

Department of Military and Veterans' Affairs.

§§ 143A-231 through 143A-238. Repealed by Session Laws 1973, c. 620, s. 9.

Article 19.

Transfers to Department of Crime Control and Public Safety.

§ 143A-239. North Carolina National Guard.

The North Carolina National Guard as provided for in Chapter 127A is hereby transferred by a Type I transfer, as defined in G.S. 143A-6, to the Department of Crime Control and Public Safety. (1977, c. 70, s. 1; 2009-281, s. 1; 2011-145, s. 19.1(g); 2012-194, s. 39.)

§ 143A-240. North Carolina Civil Preparedness Agency.

The State Civil Preparedness Agency as provided for in Chapter 166 is hereby transferred by a Type I transfer, as defined in G.S. 143A-6, to the Department of Crime Control and Public Safety. (1977, c. 70, s. 1; 2011-145, s. 19.1(g); 2012-194, s. 39.)

§ 143A-241. State Civil Air Patrol.

The State Civil Air Patrol as provided for in G.S. 167-2 is hereby transferred by a Type I transfer, as defined in G.S. 143A-6, to the Department of Crime Control and Public Safety. (1977, c. 70, s. 1; 2011-145, s. 19.1(g); 2012-194, s. 39.)

§ 143A-242. State Highway Patrol.

The State Highway Patrol as provided for in Article 4 of Chapter 20 is hereby transferred by a Type I transfer, as defined in G.S. 143A-6, to the Department of Crime Control and Public Safety. (1977, c. 70, s. 1; 2011-145, s. 19.1(g); 2012-194, s. 39.)

§ 143A-243. North Carolina Alcoholic Beverage Control Commission Enforcement Division.

The North Carolina Alcoholic Beverage Control Commission Enforcement Division as provided for in Part 2 of Article 2 of Chapter 18A is hereby transferred by a Type I transfer, as defined in G.S. 143A-6, to the Department of Crime Control and Public Safety. (1977, c. 70, s. 1; 1981, c. 412, s. 4; 2011-145, s. 19.1(g); 2012-194, s. 39.)

§ 143A-244. Governor's Crime Commission.

The Governor's Crime Commission as provided for in Part 23 of Article 7 of Chapter 143B and 1977 Session Laws, Chapter 11 is hereby transferred by a Type II transfer, as defined in G.S. 143A-6, to the Department of Crime Control and Public Safety. (1977, c. 70, s. 1; 2011-145, s. 19.1(g); 2012-194, s. 39.)

§ 143A-245. Crime Control Division.

The Crime Control Division, Department of Natural and Economic Resources, as provided for in Part 23 of Article 7 of Chapter 143B and 1977 Session Laws, Chapter 11 is hereby transferred by a Type I transfer, as defined in G.S. 143A-6, to the Department of Crime Control and Public Safety. (1977, c. 70, s. 1; 2011-145, s. 19.1(g); 2012-194, s. 39.)

Chapter 143B.

Executive Organization Act of 1973.

Article 1.

General Provisions.

Part 1. In General.

§ 143B-1. Short title.

This Chapter shall be known and may be cited as the "Executive Organization Act of 1973." (1973, c. 476, s. 1.)

§ 143B-2. Interim applicability of the Executive Organization Act of 1973.

The Executive Organization Act of 1973 shall be applicable only to the following named departments:

(1)   Department of Cultural Resources.

(2)   Department of Health and Human Services.

(3)   Department of Revenue.

(4)   Department of Public Safety.

(5)   Repealed by Session Laws 2012-83, s. 47, effective June 26, 2012.

(6)   Department of Environment and Natural Resources.

(7)   Department of Transportation.

(8)   Department of Administration.

(9)   Department of Commerce.

(10)   Repealed by Session Laws 2012-83, s. 47, effective June 26, 2012. (1973, c. 476, s. 2; c. 620, s. 9; c. 1262, ss. 10, 86; 1975, c. 716, s. 5; c. 879, s. 46; 1977, c. 70, s. 22; c. 198, s. 21; c. 771, s. 4; 1989, c. 727, s. 218(121); c. 751, s. 7(18); 1991 (Reg. Sess., 1992), c. 959, s. 37; 1997-443, ss. 11A.118(a), 11A.119(a); 2000-137, s. 4(ll); 2011-145, s. 19.1(g), (h), (l); 2012-83, s. 47.)

§ 143B-3. Definitions.

As used in the Executive Organization Act of 1973, except where the context clearly requires otherwise, the words and expressions defined in this section shall be held to have the meanings here given to them.

(1)   Agency: whenever the term "agency" is used it shall mean and include, as the context may require, an existing department, institution, commission, committee, board, division, bureau, officer or official.

245

(2)   Board: a collective body which assists the head of a principal department or his designee in the development of major programs including the tender of advice on departmental priorities.

(3)   Commission: a collective body which adopts rules and regulations in a quasi-legislative manner and which acts in a quasi-judicial capacity in rendering findings or decisions involving differing interests.

(4)   Committee: a collective body which either advises the head of a principal department or his designee or advises a commission in detailed technical areas.

(5)   Council: a collective body which advises the head of a principal department or his designee as representative of citizen advice in specific areas of interests.

(6)   Division: the principal subunit of a principal State department.

(7)   Head of department: head of one of the principal State departments.

(8)   Higher education: State senior institutions of higher learning.

(9)   Principal State department: one of the departments created by the General Assembly in compliance with Article III, Sec. 11, of the Constitution of North Carolina. (1973, c. 476, s. 3.)

§ 143B-4. Policy-making authority and administrative powers of Governor; delegation.

The Governor, in accordance with Article III of the Constitution of North Carolina, shall be the Chief Executive Officer of the State. The Governor shall be responsible for formulating and administering the policies of the executive branch of the State government. Where a conflict arises in connection with the administration of the policies of the executive branch of the State government with respect to the reorganization of State government, the conflict shall be resolved by the Governor, and the decision of the Governor shall be final. (1973, c. 476, s. 4.)

§ 143B-5. Governor; continuation of powers and duties.

All powers, duties, and functions vested by law in the Governor or in the Office of Governor are continued except as otherwise provided by the Executive Organization Act of 1973.

The immediate staff of the Governor shall not be subject to the North Carolina Human Resources Act. (1973, c. 476, s. 5; 2013-382, s. 9.1(c).)

§ 143B-6. Principal departments.

In addition to the principal departments enumerated in the Executive Organization Act of 1971, all executive and administrative powers, duties, and functions not including those of the General Assembly and its agencies, the General Court of Justice and the administrative agencies created pursuant to Article IV of the Constitution of North Carolina, and higher education previously vested by law in the several State agencies, are vested in the following principal departments:

(1)   Department of Cultural Resources.

(2)   Department of Health and Human Services.

(3)   Department of Revenue.

(4)   Department of Public Safety.

(5)   Repealed by Session Laws 2012-83, s. 48, effective June 26, 2012.

(6)   Department of Environment and Natural Resources.

(7)   Department of Transportation.

(8)   Department of Administration.

(9)   Department of Commerce.

(10)   Community Colleges System Office.

(11)   Repealed by Session Laws 2012-83, s. 48, effective June 26, 2012. (1973, c. 476, s. 6; c. 620, s. 9; c. 1262, ss. 10, 86; 1975, c. 716, s. 5; c. 879, s. 46; 1977, c. 70, s. 23; c. 198, s. 22; c. 771, s. 4; 1979, 2nd Sess., c. 1130, s. 3; 1989, c. 727, s. 218(122); c. 751, s. 7(19); 1991 (Reg. Sess., 1992), c. 959, s. 38; 1997-443, ss. 11A.118(a), 11A.119(a); 1999-84, s. 23; 2000-137, s. 4(mm); 2011-145, s. 19.1(g), (h), (l); 2012-83, s. 48.)

§ 143B-7. Continuation of functions.

Each principal State department shall be considered a continuation of the former agencies to whose power it has succeeded for the purpose of succession to all rights, powers, duties, and obligations of the former agency. Where a former agency is referred to by law, contract, or other document, that reference shall apply to the principal State department now exercising the functions of the former agency. (1973, c. 476, s. 7.)

§ 143B-8. Unassigned functions.

All functions, duties, and responsibilities established by law that are not specifically assigned to any principal State department may be assigned by the Governor to that department which, in accordance with the organization of State government, can most appropriately and effectively perform those functions, duties, and responsibilities. This provision shall not apply to professional and occupational licensing boards or to higher education. (1973, c. 476, s. 8.)

§ 143B-9. Appointment of officers and employees.

The head of each principal State department, except those departments headed by popularly elected officers, shall be appointed by the Governor and serve at his pleasure.

The salary of the head of each of the principal State departments shall be set by the Governor, and the salary of elected officials shall be as provided by law.

The head of a principal State department shall appoint a chief deputy or chief assistant, and such chief deputy or chief assistant shall not be subject to the North Carolina Human Resources Act. The salary of such chief deputy or chief assistant shall be set by the Governor. Unless otherwise provided for in the

Executive Organization Act of 1973, and subject to the provisions of the Personnel Act, the head of each principal State department shall designate the administrative head of each transferred agency and all employees of each division, section, or other unit of the principal State department. (1973, c. 476, s. 9; 1977, c. 802, s. 42.20; 1983, c. 717, s. 51; 2012-142, s. 25.02(c); 2013-382, s. 9.1(c).)

§ 143B-10. Powers and duties of heads of principal departments.

(a)   Assignment of Functions. - Except as otherwise provided by this Chapter, the head of each principal State department may assign or reassign any function vested in him or in his department to any subordinate officer or employee of his department.

(b)   Reorganization by Department Heads. - With the approval of the Governor, each head of a principal State department may establish or abolish within his department any division. Each head of a principal State department may establish or abolish within his department any other administrative unit to achieve economy and efficiency and in accordance with sound administrative principles, practices, and procedures except as otherwise provided by law. When any such act of the head of the principal State department affects existing law the provisions of Article III, Sec. 5(10) of the Constitution of North Carolina shall be followed.

Each Department Head shall report all reorganizations under this subsection to the President of the Senate, the Speaker of the House of Representatives, the Chairmen of the Appropriations Committees in the Senate and the House of Representatives, and the Fiscal Research Division of the Legislative Services Office, within 30 days after the reorganization if the General Assembly is in session, otherwise to the Joint Legislative Committee on Governmental Operations and the Fiscal Research Division of the Legislative Services Office, within 30 days after the reorganization. The report shall include the rationale for the reorganization and any increased efficiency in operations expected from the reorganization.

(c)   Department Staffs. - The head of each principal State department may establish necessary subordinate positions within his department, make appointments to those positions, and remove persons appointed to those positions, all within the limitations of appropriations and subject to the North Carolina Human Resources Act. All employees within a principal State

249

department shall be under the supervision, direction, and control of the head of that department. The head of each principal State department may establish or abolish positions, transfer officers and employees between positions, and change the duties, titles, and compensation of existing offices and positions as he deems necessary for the efficient functioning of the department, subject to the North Carolina Human Resources Act and the limitations of available appropriations. For the purposes of the foregoing provisions, a member of a board, commission, council, committee, or other citizen group shall not be considered an "employee within a principal department."

(d)   Appointment of Committees or Councils. - The head of each principal department may create and appoint committees or councils to consult with and advise the department. The General Assembly declares its policy that insofar as feasible, such committees or councils shall consist of no more than 12 members, with not more than one from each congressional district. If any department head desires to vary this policy, he must make a request in writing to the Governor, stating the reasons for the request. The Governor may approve the request, but may only do so in writing. Copies of the request and approval shall be transmitted to the Joint Legislative Commission on Governmental Operations. The members of any committee or council created by the head of a principal department shall serve at the pleasure of the head of the principal department and may be paid per diem and necessary travel and subsistence expenses within the limits of appropriations and in accordance with the provisions of G.S. 138-5, when approved in advance by the Director of the Budget. Per diem, travel, and subsistence payments to members of the committees or councils created in connection with federal programs shall be paid from federal funds unless otherwise provided by law.

An annual report listing these committees or councils, the total membership on each, the cost in the last 12 months and the source of funding, and the title of the person who made the appointments shall be made to the Joint Legislative Commission on Governmental Operations by March 31 of each year.

(e)   Departmental Management Functions. - All management functions of a principal State department shall be performed by or under the direction and supervision of the head of that principal State department. Management functions shall include planning, organizing, staffing, directing, coordinating, reporting, and budgeting.

(f)   Custody of Records. - The head of a principal State department shall have legal custody of all public records as defined in G.S. 132-1.

(g)   Budget Preparation. - The head of a principal State department shall be responsible for the preparation of and the presentation of the department budget request which shall include all funds requested and all receipts expected for all elements of the department.

(h)   Plans and Reports. - Each principal State department shall submit to the Governor an annual plan of work for the next fiscal year prior to the beginning of that fiscal year. Each principal State department shall submit to the Governor an annual report covering programs and activities for each fiscal year. These plans of work and annual reports shall be made available to the General Assembly. These documents will serve as the base for the development of budgets for each principal State department of State government to be submitted to the Governor.

(i)   Reports to Governor; Public Hearings. - Each head of a principal State department shall develop and report to the Governor legislative, budgetary, and administrative programs to accomplish comprehensive, long-range coordinated planning and policy formulation in the work of his department. To this end, the head of the department may hold public hearings, consult with and use the services of other State agencies, employ staff and consultants, and appoint advisory and technical committees to assist in the work.

(j)   Departmental Rules and Policies. - The head of each principal State department and the Director of the Office of State Human Resources may adopt:

(1)   Rules consistent with law for the custody, use, and preservation of any public records, as defined in G.S. 132-1, which pertain to department business;

(2)   Rules, approved by the Governor, to govern the management of the department, which shall include the functions of planning, organizing, staffing, directing, coordinating, reporting, budgeting, and budget preparation which affect private rights or procedures available to the public;

(3)   Policies, consistent with law and with rules established by the Governor and with rules of the State Human Resources Commission, which reflect internal management procedures within the department. These may include policies governing the conduct of employees of the department, the distribution and performance of business and internal management procedures which do not affect private rights or procedures available to the public and which are listed in (e) of this section. Policies establishing qualifications for employment

shall be adopted and filed pursuant to Chapter 150B of the General Statutes; all other policies under this subdivision shall not be adopted or filed pursuant to Chapter 150B of the General Statutes.

Rules adopted under (1) and (2) of this subsection shall be subject to the provisions of Chapter 150B of the General Statutes.

This subsection shall not be construed as a legislative grant of authority to an agency to make and promulgate rules concerning any policies and procedures other than as set forth herein. (1973, c. 476, s. 10; c. 1416, ss. 1, 2; 1977, 2nd Sess., c. 1219, s. 46; 1983, c. 76, ss. 1, 2; c. 641, s. 8; c. 717, s. 78; 1985 (Reg. Sess., 1986), c. 955, ss. 97, 98; 1987, c. 738, s. 147; c. 827, s. 1; 1991 (Reg. Sess., 1992), c. 1038, s. 15; 2006-203, s. 101; 2013-382, s. 9.1(c).)

§ 143B-11. Subunit nomenclature.

(a)   The principal subunit of a department is a division. Each division shall be headed by a director.

(b)   The principal subunit of a division is a section. Each section shall be headed by a chief.

(c)   If further subdivision is necessary, sections may be divided into subunits which shall be known as branches and which shall be headed by heads, and branches may be divided into subunits which shall be known as units and which shall be headed by supervisors. (1973, c. 476, s. 11.)

§ 143B-12. Internal organization of departments; allocation and reallocation of duties and functions; limitations.

(a)   The Governor shall cause the administrative organization of each department to be examined periodically with a view to promoting economy, efficiency, and effectiveness. The Governor may assign and reassign the duties and functions of the executive branch among the principal State departments except as otherwise expressly provided by statute. When the changes affect existing law, they must be submitted to the General Assembly in accordance with Article III, Sec. 5(10) of the Constitution of North Carolina.

(b)   The Governor shall report all transfers of departmental functions under this section to the President of the Senate, the Speaker of the House of Representatives, the Chairmen of the Appropriations Committees in the Senate and the House of Representatives, and the Fiscal Research Division of the Legislative Services Office, within 30 days after the transfer if the General Assembly is in session, otherwise to the Joint Legislative Committee on Governmental Operations and the Fiscal Research Division of the Legislative Services Office, within 30 days after the transfer. The report shall include the rationale for the transfer and the increased efficiency in operations expected from the transfer. (1973, c. 476, s. 12; 1985, c. 479, s. 164.)

§ 143B-13. Appointment, qualifications, terms, and removal of members of commissions.

(a)   Each member of a commission created by or under the authority of the Executive Organization Act of 1973 shall be a resident of the State of North Carolina, unless otherwise specifically authorized by law.

Unless more restrictive qualifications are provided in the Executive Organization Act of 1973, the Governor shall appoint each member on the basis of interest in public affairs, good judgment, knowledge, and ability in the field for which appointed, and with a view to providing diversity of interest and points of view in the membership.

The balance of unexpired terms of existing commission members shall be served in accordance with their most recent appointment.

A vacancy occurring during a term of office is filled in the same manner as the original appointment is made and for the balance of the unexpired term, unless otherwise provided by law or by the Constitution of North Carolina.

(b)   A commission membership becomes vacant on the happening of any of the following events before the expiration of the term: (i) the death of the incumbent, (ii) his incompetence as determined by final judgment or final order of a court of competent jurisdiction, (iii) his resignation, (iv) his removal from office, (v) his ceasing to be a resident of the State, (vi) his ceasing to discharge the duties of his office over a period of three consecutive months except when prevented by sickness, (vii) his conviction of a felony or of any offense involving a violation of his official duties, (viii) his refusal or neglect to take an oath within the time prescribed, (ix) the decision of a court of competent jurisdiction declaring void his appointment, and (x) his commitment as a substance abuser under Part 8 of Article 5 of Chapter 122C of the General Statutes; but in that event, the office shall not be considered vacant until the order of commitment has become final.

(c)   No member of the State commission may use his position to influence any election or the political activity of any person, and any such member who violates this subsection may be removed from such office by the Governor, if such member was appointed by the Governor, or by the appointing authority, if such member was not appointed by the Governor. Nothing herein shall prohibit such member from publishing the fact of his membership in his own campaign for public office.

(d)   In addition to the foregoing, any member of a commission may be removed from office by the Governor for misfeasance, malfeasance, and nonfeasance.

(e)   Any appointment by the Governor to a commission, board, council or committee made subsequent to January 5, 1973, and prior to July 1, 1973, for a term that would extend for a period inconsistent with the staggered term provisions of the Executive Organization Act of 1973, may be reduced by the Governor to conform to those staggered term provisions.

(f)   Whenever a statute requires that the Governor appoint at least one person from each congressional district to a board or commission, and due to congressional redistricting, two or more members of the board or commission shall reside in the same congressional district, then such members shall continue to serve as members of the board or commission for a period equal to the remainder of their unexpired terms, provided that upon the expiration of said term or terms the Governor shall fill such vacancy or vacancies in such a manner as to insure that as expeditiously as possible there is one member of the board or commission who is a resident of each congressional district in the State.

(f1)   Whenever a statute requires that the Governor or any board, commission, council, person, or agency (whether or not that board, commission, council, or agency was established under this Chapter) appoint one or more persons from each congressional district to a board, commission, or council, and due to congressional redistricting, a person no longer resides in the district the member has been appointed to represent, such member or members shall, if otherwise qualified, continue to serve as members of the board or commission

254

for the remainder of their unexpired terms, and shall be considered to meet the residency requirement.

(f2)   Whenever a statute requires that the Governor or any board, commission, council, person, or agency (whether or not that board, commission, council, or agency was established under this Chapter) appoint one or more persons from each congressional district to a board, commission, or council, and the statute fails to provide for a procedure to fill the extra position due to the addition of an additional congressional district, then the appointing authority shall appoint a person for a term commencing on January 3rd of the year in which the addition of the additional congressional district becomes effective. Unless the statute provides for persons to serve at the pleasure of the appointing authority, the appointing authority shall set the length of the initial term of office. (1973, c. 476, s. 13; 1975, c. 879, s. 47; 1981, c. 520, s. 1; 1981 (Reg. Sess., 1982), c. 1191, s. 5; 1985, c. 589, ss. 45, 46; 1991 (Reg. Sess., 1992), c. 1038, s. 16.)

§ 143B-14. Administrative services to commissions.

(a)   The head of the principal State department to which a commission has been assigned is responsible for the provision of all administrative services to the commission.

(b)   Except as otherwise provided by law, the powers, duties, and functions of a commission are not subject to the approval, review, or control of the head of the department or of the Governor.

(c)   The Governor may assign to an appropriate commission created by the Executive Organization Act of 1973 duties of a quasi-legislative and quasi-judicial nature existing in the executive branch of State government which have not been assigned by this Chapter to any other commission. All such assignment of duties by the Governor to a commission shall be made in accordance with Article III, Sec. 5(10) of the Constitution of North Carolina.

(d)   All management functions of a commission shall be performed by the head of the principal State department. Management functions shall include planning, organizing, staffing, directing, coordinating, reporting, and budgeting. (1973, c. 476, s. 14; c. 1416, s. 3; 1979, 2nd Sess., c. 1137, s. 41.2; 1981, c. 688, s. 20; 1983, c. 927, s. 11; 1987, c. 827, s. 221; 1991, c. 418, s. 9.)

255

§ 143B-15. Compensation of members of commissions.

The salary of members of full-time commissions shall be set by the General Assembly upon recommendation of the Governor to be submitted as a part of his budget requests. (1973, c. 476, s. 15.)

§ 143B-16. Appointment and removal of members of boards, councils and committees.

Unless more restrictive qualifications are provided in this Chapter, the Governor shall appoint each member of a board, council, or committee on the basis of his interest in public affairs, good judgment, knowledge and ability in the field for which appointed, and with a view to providing diversity of interest and points of view in the membership. Unless other conditions are provided in the Executive Organization Act of 1973, any member of a board, council, or committee may be removed from office by the Governor for misfeasance, malfeasance, or nonfeasance.

No member of a board, council, or committee may use his position to influence any election or the political activity of any person, and any such member who violates this paragraph may be removed from such office by the Governor, if such member was appointed by the Governor, or by the appointing authority, if such member was not appointed by the Governor. Nothing herein shall prohibit such member from publishing the fact of his membership in his own campaign for public office. (1973, c. 476, s. 16; 1981, c. 520, s. 2.)

§ 143B-17. Commission investigations and orders.

Unless otherwise provided for in the Executive Organization Act of 1973, any commission created by the Executive Organization Act of 1973 may order an investigation into areas of concern over which it has rule-making authority, and the head of the department required to give staff support to such commission shall render such reports and information as the commission may require. In default of the production of information by the head of the principal department or any employee or agent thereof, the commission may seek the aid of the Wake County Superior Court to require the production of information as hereinafter provided.

In proceedings before any commission or any hearing officer or member of the commission so authorized by the commission, if any person refuses to respond to a subpoena, or refuses to take the oath or affirmation as a witness or thereafter refuses to be examined or refuses to obey any lawful order of a commission contained in its decision rendered after hearing, the chairman of the commission may apply to the Superior Court of Wake County or to the superior court of the county where the proceedings are being held for an order directing that person to take the requisite action. Should any person willfully fail to comply with an order so issued, the court shall punish him as for contempt. (1973, c. 476, s. 17.)

§ 143B-18: Repealed by Session Laws 1991, c. 418, s. 10.

§ 143B-19. Pending actions and proceedings.

No action or proceeding pending at the time the Executive Organization Act of 1973 takes effect and brought by or against any State agency whose functions, powers, and duties are transferred by the Executive Organization Act of 1973 to a principal State department shall be affected by any provision of the Executive Organization Act of 1973, but the same may be prosecuted or defended in the name of the head of the principal State department. In all such actions and proceedings, the principal State department to which the functions, powers, and duties of a State agency have been transferred shall be substituted as a party upon appropriate application to the courts. (1973, c. 476, s. 19.)

§ 143B-20: Repealed by Session Laws 1991, c. 418, s. 10.

§ 143B-21. Affirmation of prior acts of abolished agencies.

The abolition of certain agencies by the Executive Organization Act of 1973 should not be construed as invalidating any lawful prior act of such agency. (1973, c. 476, s. 21.)

§ 143B-22. Terms occurring in laws, contracts and other documents.

257

Any reference or designation in any statute, contract, or other document pertaining to functions, powers, obligations, and duties of a State agency assigned by the Executive Organization Act of 1973 to a principal State department shall be deemed to refer to the principal State department or the head of the principal State department, as may be appropriate. (1973, c. 476, s. 22.)

§ 143B-23. Completion of unfinished business.

Any business or other matter undertaken or commenced by any State agency or the commissioners or directors thereof, pertaining to or connected with the functions, powers, obligations, and duties hereby transferred to a principal State department, and pending on July 1, 1973, may be conducted and completed by the principal State department in the same manner and under the same terms and conditions and with the same effect as if conducted and completed by the State agency or commissioners and directors thereof. (1973, c. 476, s. 23.)

§ 143B-24. Cooperative agreements; prohibition regarding Health Benefit Exchanges.

(a)   Except as otherwise provided by law, each principal State department may, with the approval of the Department of Administration, enter into cooperative agreements with the federal government, any state government, any agency of the State government, any local government of the State, jointly with any two or more, or severally, in carrying out its functions.

(b)   The General Assembly reserves the authority to define the State's level of interaction, if any, with the federally facilitated Health Benefit Exchange that will operate in the State. No department, agency, or institution of this State shall enter into any contracts or commit any resources for the provision of any services related to the federally facilitated Health Benefit Exchange under a "Partnership" Exchange model, except as authorized by the General Assembly. No department, agency, or institution of this State shall take any actions not authorized by the General Assembly toward the formation of a State-run Health Benefit Exchange. It is not the intent of this section to prohibit State-federal interaction that does not pursue a State-run Exchange or "Partnership" Exchange model. (1973, c. 476, s. 24; 2013-5, s. 1(c).)

§ 143B-25. Agencies not enumerated.

Any agency not enumerated in the Executive Organization Act of 1973 but established or created by the General Assembly shall continue to exercise all its powers, duties, and functions subject to the provisions of Chapter 143A of the General Statutes of the State of North Carolina. (1973, c. 476, s. 25.)

§ 143B-26. Constitutional references.

All references to the Constitution of North Carolina in the Executive Organization Act of 1973 refer to the Constitution of North Carolina as effective July 1, 1973. (1973, c. 476, s. 26.)

§ 143B-27. Repealed by Session Laws 1983, c. 717, s. 79.

§ 143B-28. Goals of continuing reorganization.

Structural reorganization of State government should be a continuing process, accomplished through careful executive and legislative appraisal of the placement of proposed new programs and coordination of existing programs in response to changing emphases in public needs and should be consistent with the following goals:

(1)   The organization of State government should assure its responsiveness to popular control. It is the goal of reorganization to improve the administrative capability of the executive to carry out these policies.

(2)   The organization of State government should aid communication between citizens and government. It is the goal of reorganization through coordination of related programs in function-oriented departments to improve public understanding of government programs and policies and to improve the relationships between citizens and administrative agencies.

(3)   The organization of State government should assure efficient and effective administration of the policies established by the General Assembly. It is the goal of reorganization to promote efficiency and effectiveness by improving the management and coordination of State services and by eliminating ineffective, overstaffed, obsolete or overlapping activities. (1973, c. 476, s. 28.)

§ 143B-29. Reserved for future codification.

Part 2. Governor's Administrative Rules Review Commission.

§§ 143B-29.1 through 143B-29.5: Repealed by Session Laws 1985, c. 746, s. 7.

Part 3. Rules Review Commission.

§ 143B-30: Repealed by Session Laws 1991, c. 418, s. 5.

§ 143B-30.1. Rules Review Commission created.

(a)   The Rules Review Commission is created. The Commission shall consist of 10 members to be appointed by the General Assembly, five upon the recommendation of the President Pro Tempore of the Senate, and five upon the recommendation of the Speaker of the House of Representatives. These appointments shall be made in accordance with G.S. 120-121, and vacancies in these appointments shall be filled in accordance with G.S. 120-122. Except as provided in subsection (b) of this section, all appointees shall serve two-year terms.

(b)   In 1990, two of the appointments made by the General Assembly upon the recommendation of the President of the Senate shall expire June 30, 1991, and two shall expire June 30, 1992. In 1990, two of the appointments made by the General Assembly upon the recommendation of the Speaker of the House of Representatives shall expire June 30, 1992, and two shall expire June 30, 1993. Subsequent terms shall be for two years.

(c)   Any appointment to fill a vacancy on the Commission created by the resignation, dismissal, ineligibility, death, or disability of any member shall be for the balance of the unexpired term. The chairman shall be elected by the Commission, and he shall designate the times and places at which the Commission shall meet. The Commission shall meet at least once a month. A quorum of the Commission shall consist of six members of the Commission.

(d)   Members of the Commission who are not officers or employees of the State shall receive compensation of two hundred dollars ($200.00) for each day or part of a day of service plus reimbursement for travel and subsistence expenses at the rates specified in G.S. 138-5. Members of the Commission who are officers or employees of the State shall receive reimbursement for travel and subsistence at the rate set out in G.S. 138-6.

(e)   The Chief Administrative Law Judge, Office of Administrative Hearings, shall assign the staff and designate the Director of the Commission in accordance with G.S. 7A-760.

(f)   The Commission shall prescribe procedures and forms to be used in submitting rules to the Commission for review. The Commission may have computer access to the North Carolina Administrative Code to enable the Commission and its staff to view and copy rules in the Code. (1985 (Reg. Sess., 1986), c. 1028, s. 32; 1987 (Reg. Sess., 1988), c. 1111, s. 2; 1989, c. 35, s. 2; 1989 (Reg. Sess., 1990), c. 1038, s. 18; 1991, c. 418, s. 11; 1991 (Reg. Sess., 1992), c. 1030, s. 43; 1995, c. 490, s. 43; 1997-495, s. 90(a), (b); 2004-124, s. 22A.1(b); 2006-66, s. 18.2(f); 2006-221, s. 20; 2009-451, s. 21A.2; 2009-575, s. 19.)

§ 143B-30.2. Purpose of Commission.

The Rules Review Commission reviews administrative rules in accordance with Chapter 150B of the General Statutes. (1985 (Reg. Sess., 1986), c. 1028, s. 32; 1987, c. 285, ss. 1-5; 1991, c. 418, s. 12.)

§ 143B-30.3: Repealed by Session Laws 1991, c. 418, s. 5.

§ 143B-30.4. Evidence.

Evidence of the Commission's failure to object to and delay the filing of a rule or its part shall be inadmissible in all civil or criminal trials or other proceedings before courts, administrative agencies, or other tribunals. (1985 (Reg. Sess., 1986), c. 1028, s. 32.)

§ 143B-31: Reserved for future codification purposes.

§ 143B-32: Reserved for future codification purposes.

§ 143B-33: Reserved for future codification purposes.

§ 143B-34: Reserved for future codification purposes.

§ 143B-35: Reserved for future codification purposes.

§ 143B-36: Reserved for future codification purposes.

§ 143B-37: Reserved for future codification purposes.

§ 143B-38: Reserved for future codification purposes.

§ 143B-39: Reserved for future codification purposes.

§ 143B-40: Reserved for future codification purposes.

§ 143B-41: Reserved for future codification purposes.

§ 143B-42: Reserved for future codification purposes.

§ 143B-43: Reserved for future codification purposes.

§ 143B-44: Reserved for future codification purposes.

§ 143B-45: Reserved for future codification purposes.

§ 143B-46: Reserved for future codification purposes.

§ 143B-47: Reserved for future codification purposes.

§ 143B-48: Reserved for future codification purposes.

Article 2.

Department of Cultural Resources.

Part 1. General Provisions.

§ 143B-49. Department of Cultural Resources - creation, powers and duties.

There is hereby created a department to be known as the "Department of Cultural Resources," with the organization, duties, functions, and powers defined in the Executive Organization Act of 1973. (1973, c. 476, s. 29.)

§ 143B-50. Duties of the Department.

It shall be the duty of the Department to provide the necessary management, development of policy and establishment and enforcement of standards for the furtherance of resources, services and programs involving the arts and the historical and cultural aspects of the lives of the citizens of North Carolina. (1973, c. 476, s. 30.)

§ 143B-51. Functions of the Department.

(a)   The functions of the Department of Cultural Resources shall comprise, except as otherwise expressly provided by the Executive Organization Act of 1973 or by the Constitution of North Carolina, all executive functions of the State in relation to the development and preservation of libraries, historical records, sites and property, and of an appreciation of art and music and further including those prescribed powers, duties, and functions enumerated in Article 17 of Chapter 143A of the General Statutes of this State.

(b)   All such functions, powers, duties, and obligations heretofore vested in any agency enumerated in Article 17 of Chapter 143A of the General Statutes are hereby transferred to and vested in the Department of Cultural Resources except as otherwise provided by the Executive Organization Act of 1973. They shall include, by way of extension and not of limitation, the functions of:

(1)   The Secretary and Department of Art, Culture and History;

(2)   The State Department of Archives and History;

(3)   The North Carolina Advisory Council on Historic Preservation;

(4)   The North Carolina State Library;

(5)   The Interstate Library Compact;

(6)   The North Carolina Museum of Art;

(7)   Repealed by Session Laws 2012-120, s. 1(c), effective October 1, 2012.

(8)   The North Carolina Symphony Society, Inc.;

(9)   The State Art Museum Building Commission;

(10)   The Library Certification Board;

(11)   The Tryon Palace Commission;

(12)   The North Carolina Arts Council;

(13)   The U.S.S. North Carolina Battleship Commission;

(14)   The Memorials Commission;

(15)   The Commission to Promote Plans for the Celebration of the Four Hundredth Anniversary of the Landing of Sir Walter Raleigh's Colony on Roanoke Island;

(16)   The Executive Mansion Fine Arts Commission;

(17)   The North Carolina American Revolution Bicentennial Commission;

(18)   The North Carolina Awards Commission;

(19)   The Tobacco Museum Board;

(20)   The Roanoke Island Historical Association, Inc.;

(21)   The Sir Walter Raleigh Memorial Commission;

(22)   The Governor Richard Caswell Memorial Commission;

(23)   The Historic Swansboro Commission;

264

(24)   The Edenton Historical Commission;

(25)   The Historic Bath Commission;

(26)   The Historic Hillsborough Commission;

(27)   The John Motley Morehead Memorial Commission;

(28)   The Historic Murfreesboro Commission;

(29)   The Charles B. Aycock Memorial Commission;

(30)   The Frying Pan Lightship Marine Museum Commission;

(31)   The Guilford County Bicentennial Commission;

(32)   The Daniel Boone Memorial Commission;

(33)   The Bennett Place Memorial Commission;

(34)   The Durham-Orange Historical Commission;

(35)   The Pitt County Historical Commission;

(36)   The Transylvania County Historical Commission;

(37)   The Lenoir County Historical and Patriotic Commission;

(38)   The Raleigh Historic Sites Commission; and

(39)   The Stonewall Jackson Memorial Fund. (1973, c. 476, s. 31; 2012-120, s. 1(c).)

§ 143B-52. Head of the Department.

The Secretary of Cultural Resources shall be the head of the Department. (1973, c. 476, s. 32.)

§ 143B-53. Organization of the Department.

The Department of Cultural Resources shall be organized initially to include the Art Commission, the Art Museum Building Commission, the North Carolina Historical Commission, the Tryon Palace Commission, the U.S.S. North Carolina Battleship Commission, the Sir Walter Raleigh Commission, the Executive Mansion Fine Arts Committee, the American Revolution Bicentennial Committee, the North Carolina Awards Committee, the America's Four Hundredth Anniversary Committee, the North Carolina Arts Council, the Public Librarian Certification Commission, the State Library Commission, the North Carolina Symphony Society, Inc., and the Division of the State Library, the Division of Archives and History, the Division of the Arts, and such other divisions as may be established under the provisions of the Executive Organization Act of 1973. (1973, c. 476, s. 33; 1981, c. 918, s. 1; 2006-66, s. 22.22(e); 2006-221, s. 23; 2012-120, s. 1(d).)

§ 143B-53.1. Appropriation, allotment, and expenditure of funds for historic and archeological property.

The Department of Cultural Resources may not expend any State funds for the acquisition, preservation, restoration, or operation of historic or archeological real and personal property, and the Director of the Budget may not allot any appropriations to the Department of Cultural Resources for a particular historic site until (i) the property or properties shall have been approved for such purpose by the Department of Cultural Resources according to criteria adopted by the North Carolina Historical Commission, (ii) the report and recommendation of the North Carolina Historical Commission has been received and considered by the Department of Cultural Resources, and (iii) the Department of Cultural Resources has found that there is a feasible and practical method of providing funds for the acquisition, restoration and/or operation of such property. (1963, c. 210, s. 3; 1973, c. 476, s. 48; 1985 (Reg. Sess; 1986), c. 1014, s. 171(e); 2006-203, s. 7.)

§ 143B-53.2. Salaries, promotions, and leave of employees of the North Carolina Department of Cultural Resources.

(a)   and (b) Repealed by Session Laws 2007-484, s. 9(b), effective August 30, 2007.

(c)   The exemptions to Chapter 126 of the General Statutes authorized by G.S. 126-5(c11) for the employees of the Department of Cultural Resources listed in that subsection shall be used to develop organizational classification and compensation innovations that will result in the enhanced efficiency of operations. The Office of State Human Resources shall assist the Secretary of the Department of Cultural Resources in the development and implementation of an organizational structure and human resources programs that make the most appropriate use of the exemptions, including (i) a system of job categories or descriptions tailored to the agency's needs; (ii) policies regarding paid time off for agency personnel and the voluntary sharing of such time off; and (iii) a system of uniform performance assessments for agency personnel tailored to the agency's needs. The Secretary of the Department of Cultural Resources may, under the supervision of the Office of State Human Resources, develop and implement organizational classification and compensation innovations having the potential to benefit all State agencies. (2006-204, s. 3; 2007-484, s. 9(b); 2013-382, s. 9.1(c).)

Part 2. Art Commission.

§§ 143B-54 through 143B-57. Repealed by Session Laws 1979, 2nd Session, c. 1306, s. 5.

Part 3. Art Museum Building Commission.

§ 143B-58 through 143B-61.1: Repealed by Session Laws 2000-140, s. 78.

Part 4. North Carolina Historical Commission.

§ 143B-62. North Carolina Historical Commission - creation, powers and duties.

There is hereby created the North Carolina Historical Commission of the Department of Cultural Resources to give advice and assistance to the Secretary of Cultural Resources and to promulgate rules and regulations to be followed in the acquisition, disposition, preservation, and use of records, artifacts, real and personal property, and other materials and properties of historical, archaeological, architectural, or other cultural value, and in the extension of State aid to other agencies, counties, municipalities, organizations, and individuals in the interest of historic preservation.

(1)   The Historical Commission shall have the following powers and duties:

a.   To advise the Secretary of Cultural Resources on the scholarly editing, writing, and publication of historical materials to be issued under the name of the Department.

b.   To evaluate and approve proposed nominations of historic, archaeological, architectural, or cultural properties for entry on the National Register of Historic Places.

c.   To evaluate and approve the State plan for historic preservation as provided for in Chapter 121.

d.   To evaluate and approve historic, archaeological, architectural, or cultural properties proposed to be acquired and administered by the State.

e.   To evaluate and prepare a report on its findings and recommendations concerning any property not owned by the State for which State aid or appropriations are requested from the Department of Cultural Resources, and to submit its findings and recommendations in accordance with Chapter 121.

f.   To serve as an advisory and coordinative mechanism in and by which State undertakings of every kind that are potentially harmful to the cause of historic preservation within the State may be discussed, and where possible, resolved, particularly by evaluating and making recommendations concerning any State undertaking which may affect a property that has been entered on the National Register of Historic Places as provided for in Chapter 121 of the General Statutes of North Carolina.

g.   To exercise any other powers granted to the Commission by provisions of Chapter 121 of the General Statutes of North Carolina.

h.   To give its professional advice and assistance to the Secretary of Cultural Resources on any matter which the Secretary may refer to it in the performance of the Department's duties and responsibilities provided for in Chapter 121 of the General Statutes of North Carolina.

i.   To serve as a search committee to seek out, interview, and recommend to the Secretary of Cultural Resources one or more experienced and professionally trained historian(s) for either the position of Deputy Secretary of

Archives and History when a vacancy occurs, and to assist and cooperate with the Secretary in periodic reviews of the performance of the Deputy Secretary.

j.   To assist and advise the Secretary of Cultural Resources and the Deputy Secretary of Archives and History in the development and implementation of plans and priorities for the State's historical programs.

(2)   The Historical Commission shall have the power and duty to establish standards and provide rules and regulations as follows:

a.   For the acquisition and use of historical materials suitable for acceptance in the North Carolina Office of Archives and History.

b.   For the disposition of public records under provisions of Chapter 121 of the General Statutes of North Carolina.

c.   For the certification of records in the North Carolina State Archives as provided in Chapter 121 of the General Statutes of North Carolina.

d.   For the use by the public of historic, architectural, archaeological, or cultural properties as provided in Chapter 121 of the General Statutes of North Carolina.

e.   For the acquisition of historic, archaeological, architectural, or cultural properties by the State.

f.   For the extension of State aid or appropriations through the Department of Cultural Resources to counties, municipalities, organizations, or individuals for the purpose of historic preservation or restoration.

f1.   For the extension of State aid or appropriations through the Department of Cultural Resources to nonstate-owned nonprofit history museums.

g.   For qualification for grants-in-aid or other assistance from the federal government for historic preservation or restoration as provided in Chapter 121 of the General Statutes of North Carolina. This section shall be construed liberally in order that the State and its citizens may benefit from such grants-in-aid.

(3)   The Commission shall adopt rules and regulations consistent with the provisions of this section. All current rules and regulations heretofore adopted by the Executive Board of the State Department of Archives and History, the

Historic Sites Advisory Committee, the North Carolina Advisory Council on Historical Preservation, the Executive Mansion Fine Arts Commission, and the Memorials Commission shall remain in full force and effect unless and until repealed or superseded by action of the Historical Commission. All rules and regulations adopted by the Commission shall be enforced by the Department of Cultural Resources. (1973, c. 476, s. 44; 1977, c. 513, s. 2; 1979, c. 861, s. 6; 1985 (Reg. Sess., 1986), c. 1014, s. 171(f); 1997-411, ss. 1-3; 2002-159, s. 35(k).)

§ 143B-63. Historical Commission - members; selection; quorum; compensation.

The Historical Commission of the Department of Cultural Resources shall consist of 11 members appointed by the Governor.

The members of the North Carolina Historical Commission shall include the members of the existing North Carolina Historical Commission who shall serve for a period equal to the remainder of their current terms on the Commission, plus four additional appointees of the Governor, two of whose appointments shall expire March 31, 1979, and two of whose appointments shall expire March 31, 1981. At the end of the respective terms of office of the members, their successors shall be appointed for terms of six years and until their successors are appointed and qualify. Of the members, at least five shall have professional training or experience in the fields of archives, history, historic preservation, historic architecture, archaeology, or museum administration, including at least three currently involved in the teaching of history at the college or university level or in administering archives or historical collections or programs. Any appointment to fill a vacancy on the Commission created by resignation, dismissal, death, or disability of a member shall be for the balance of the unexpired term.

The Governor shall have the power to remove any member of the Commission from office for misfeasance, malfeasance or nonfeasance according to the provisions of G.S. 143B-13 of the Executive Organization Act of 1973.

The members of the Commission shall receive per diem and necessary travel and subsistence expenses in accordance with the provisions of G.S. 138-5.

270

A majority of the Commission shall constitute a quorum for the transaction of business.

All clerical and other services required by the Commission shall be supplied by the Secretary of Cultural Resources. (1973, c. 476, s. 45; 1977, c. 513, s. 1.)

§ 143B-64. Historical Commission - officers.

The Historical Commission shall have a chairman and a vice-chairman. The chairman shall be designated by the Governor from among the members of the Commission to serve as chairman at the pleasure of the Governor. The vice-chairman shall be elected by and from the members of the Commission and shall serve for a term of two years or until the expiration of his regularly appointed term. (1973, c. 476, s. 46.)

§ 143B-65. Historical Commission - regular and special meetings.

The Historical Commission shall meet at least twice per year and may hold special meetings at any time and place within the State at the call of the chairman or upon the written request of at least four members. (1973, c. 476, s. 42.)

Part 5. Archaeological Advisory Committee.

§ 143B-66. Repealed by Session Laws 1985 (Reg. Sess., 1986), c. 1028, s. 10.

Part 6. Public Librarian Certification Commission.

§ 143B-67. Public Librarian Certification Commission - creation, powers and duties.

There is hereby created the Public Librarian Certification Commission of the Department of Cultural Resources with the power and duty to adopt rules and regulations to be followed in the certification of public librarians. The Commission is authorized to establish and require written examinations for certified public librarian applicants.

The Commission shall adopt such rules and regulations consistent with the provisions of this Chapter. All rules and regulations consistent with the provisions of this Chapter heretofore adopted by the Library Certification Board shall remain in full force and effect unless and until repealed or superseded by action of the Public Librarian Certification Commission. All rules and regulations adopted by the Commission shall be enforced by the Department of Cultural Resources. (1973, c. 476, s. 49; 1981 (Reg. Sess., 1982), c. 1359, s. 4.)

§ 143B-68. Public Librarian Certification Commission - members; selection; quorum; compensation.

The Public Librarian Certification Commission of the Department of Cultural Resources shall consist of five members as follows: (i) the chairman of the North Carolina Association of Library Trustees, (ii) the chairman of the public libraries section of the North Carolina Library Association, (iii) an individual named by the Governor upon the nomination of the North Carolina Library Association, (iv) the dean of a State or regionally accredited graduate school of librarianship in North Carolina appointed by the Governor and (v) one member at large appointed by the Governor.

The members shall serve four-year terms or while holding the appropriate chairmanships. Any appointment to fill a vacancy created by the resignation, dismissal, death or disability of a member shall be for the balance of the unexpired term.

The Governor shall have the power to remove any member of the Commission from office for misfeasance, malfeasance, and nonfeasance according to the provisions of G.S. 143B-13 of the Executive Organization Act of 1973.

The members of the Commission shall receive per diem, and necessary travel expenses in accordance with the provisions of G.S. 138-5.

A majority of the Commission shall constitute a quorum for the transaction of business.

All clerical and other services required by the Commission shall be supplied by the Secretary of the Department through the regular staff of the Department. (1973, c. 476, s. 50.)

§ 143B-69. Public Librarian Certification Commission - officers.

The Public Librarian Certification Commission shall have a chairman and a vice-chairman. The chairman shall be designated by the Governor from among the members of the Commission to serve as chairman at his pleasure. The vice-chairman shall be elected by and from the members of the Commission and shall serve for a term of two years or until the expiration of his regularly appointed term. (1973, c. 476, s. 51.)

§ 143B-70. Public Librarian Certification Commission - regular and special meetings.

The Public Librarian Certification Commission shall meet at least once in each quarter and may hold special meetings at any time and place within the State at the call of the chairman or upon the written request of at least three members. (1973, c. 476, s. 52.)

Part 7. Tryon Palace Commission.

§ 143B-71. Tryon Palace Commission - creation, powers and duties.

There is hereby created the Tryon Palace Commission of the Department of Cultural Resources with the power and duty to adopt, amend and rescind rules and regulations concerning the restoration and maintenance of the Tryon Palace complex, and other powers and duties as provided in Article 2 of Chapter 121 of the General Statutes of North Carolina, including the authority to charge reasonable admission and related activity fees. The Commission is exempt from the requirements of Chapter 150B of the General Statutes when adopting, amending, or repealing rules for admission fees or related activity fees at Tryon Palace Historic Sites and Gardens. The Commission shall submit a report to the Joint Legislative Commission on Governmental Operations on the amount and purpose of a fee change within 30 days following its effective date. (1973, c. 476, s. 54; 2013-297, s. 2(b); 2013-360, s. 19.2(b).)

§ 143B-72. Tryon Palace Commission - members; selection; quorum; compensation.

273

The Tryon Palace Commission of the Department of Cultural Resources shall consist of the following members: 25 voting members appointed by the Governor, nonvoting members emeriti appointed by the Governor, and five voting ex officio members as provided in this section.

The Governor shall appoint 25 voting members. The terms of the initial members shall be staggered as follows: Nine of the members shall be appointed to serve four-year terms, eight of the members shall be appointed to serve three-year terms, and eight of the members shall be appointed to serve two-year terms. At the end of the respective terms of office of the initial appointed members of the Commission, the appointments of their successors, with the exception of ex officio members and members emeriti, shall be for terms of four years and until their successors are appointed and qualify. Any appointment to fill a vacancy on the Commission shall be for the balance of the unexpired term. The Governor shall designate the chair of the Tryon Palace Commission. The other officers of the Tryon Palace Commission shall be elected by the members of the Tryon Palace Commission.

The Governor may also appoint any person who has previously served on the Tryon Palace Commission with distinction to the Commission as a member emeritus. A person appointed as a member emeritus shall be deemed a lifetime member of the Commission and shall serve as a nonvoting member.

In addition to the members who are appointed by the Governor, the Attorney General, the Secretary of Cultural Resources or the Secretary's designee, the mayor of the City of New Bern, the Dean of the College of Arts and Sciences at East Carolina University, and the chairman of the Board of County Commissioners of Craven County shall serve as voting ex officio members of said Commission. The provisions of the Executive Organization Act of 1973 pertaining to the residence of members of commissions shall not apply to the Tryon Palace Commission.

A majority of the voting members of the Commission shall constitute a quorum for the transaction of business.

The members of the Commission shall serve without pay and without expense allowance. (1973, c. 476, s. 55; 1977, c. 771, s. 4; 1979, c. 151, s. 1; 1993, c. 109, s. 1.)

Part 8. U.S.S. North Carolina Battleship Commission.

§ 143B-73. U.S.S. North Carolina Battleship Commission - creation, powers, and duties.

There is hereby created the U.S.S. North Carolina Battleship Commission of the Department of Cultural Resources with the power and duty to adopt, amend, and rescind rules and regulations under and not inconsistent with the laws of this State necessary in carrying out the provisions and purposes of this Part.

(1)   The U.S.S. North Carolina Battleship Commission is authorized and empowered to adopt such rules and regulations not inconsistent with the management responsibilities of the Secretary of the Department provided by Chapter 143A of the General Statutes and laws of this State and this Chapter that may be necessary and desirable for the operation and maintenance of the U.S.S. North Carolina as a permanent memorial and exhibit commemorating the heroic participation of the men and women of North Carolina in the prosecution and victory of the Second World War and for the faithful performance and fulfillment of its duties and obligations.

(2)   The U.S.S. North Carolina Battleship Commission shall have the power and duty to establish standards and adopt rules and regulations: (i) establishing and providing for a proper charge for admission to the ship; and (ii) for the maintenance and operation of the ship as a permanent memorial and exhibit.

(3)   The Commission shall adopt rules and regulations consistent with the provisions of this Chapter. The Commission is exempt from the requirements of Chapter 150B of the General Statutes when adopting, amending, or repealing rules for admission fees or related activity fees at the U.S.S. North Carolina Battleship. The Commission shall submit a report to the Joint Legislative Commission on Governmental Operations on the amount and purpose of a fee change within 30 days following its effective date. (1973, c. 476, s. 57; 1977, c. 741, s. 3; 2013-360, s. 19.2(c).)

§ 143B-73.1. U.S.S. North Carolina Battleship Commission - duties.

The Commission shall have the further duty and authority to select an appropriate site for the permanent berthing of the Battleship U.S.S. North Carolina, taking into consideration factors including, but not limited to, the accessibility, location in relation to roads and highways, scenic attraction, protection from hazards of weather, fire and sea, cost of site and berthing, cooperation of local governmental authorities in securing, equipping, and maintaining appropriate areas surrounding the site, and others which may affect the suitability of such site for establishment of the ship as a permanent memorial and exhibit; to accept gifts, grants, and donations for the purposes of this Article; to transport to, and berth the ship at the site; to ready the ship for visitation by the public; to establish and provide for a proper charge for admission to the ship, and for safekeeping of funds; to maintain and operate the ship as a permanent memorial and exhibit; to acquire property, both real and personal, with the approval of the Governor and the Council of State, and to accept donations of property, both real and personal, from any source; to establish, supervise, manage and maintain in New Hanover County with the approval and assistance of the Department of Cultural Resources exhibits, dramas, cultural activities, museums, and records pertaining to the marine and naval history of the State of North Carolina and the United States of America; to identify, preserve and protect properties having historical, marine and naval significance to New Hanover County, the State, its communities and counties and the nation; to establish and provide for a proper charge for admission to all properties maintained and operated by the Commission in New Hanover County; to otherwise provide in carrying out its duties for the establishment of appropriate activities to encourage interest in the marine and naval history of North Carolina; to perpetuate the memory of North Carolinians who gave their lives in the course of World War II and in the events in which the battleship was a participant, and to allocate funds for the fulfillment of the duties and authority herein provided as may be necessary and appropriate for the purpose of this Article. (1961, c. 158; 1977, c. 741, ss. 1, 8.)

§ 143B-74. U.S.S. North Carolina Battleship Commission - members; selection; quorum; compensation.

The U.S.S. North Carolina Battleship Commission of the Department of Cultural Resources shall consist of 18 members including the Secretary of Cultural Resources and the Secretary of Commerce who shall serve as voting ex officio members. The members of the Commission appointed for terms to end in 1991 shall serve for an additional two-year period. At the end of the respective terms of office of the members of the Commission serving in 1991, their successors shall be appointed for terms of four years and until their successors are appointed and qualify. Any appointment to fill a vacancy on the Commission created by the resignation, dismissal, death, or disability of a member shall be for the balance of the unexpired term. The provisions of the Executive

Organization Act of 1973 pertaining to the residence of members of commissions shall not apply to the U.S.S. North Carolina Battleship Commission.

The Governor shall have the power to remove any member of the Commission from office for misfeasance, malfeasance, or nonfeasance in accordance with the provisions of G.S. 143B-13 of the Executive Organization Act of 1973.

The members of the Commission shall receive per diem and necessary travel and subsistence expenses in accordance with the provisions of G.S. 138-5.

A majority of the Commission shall constitute a quorum for the transaction of business. The Governor shall designate from among the members of the Commission a chairman, vice-chairman and treasurer. The Secretary of Cultural Resources or his designee shall serve as Secretary of the Commission. The Commission shall meet at least twice annually upon the call of the chairman, the Secretary of Cultural Resources, or any seven members of the Commission. (1973, c. 476, s. 58; 1977, c. 741, s. 4; 1991, c. 73, s. 1; 1991 (Reg. Sess., 1992), c. 959, s. 39.)

§ 143B-74.1. U.S.S. North Carolina Battleship Commission - funds.

The Commission shall establish and maintain a "Battleship Fund" composed of the monies which may come into its hands from admission or inspection fees, gifts, donations, grants, or devises, which funds will be used by the Commission to pay all costs of maintaining and operating the ship for the purposes herein set forth. The Commission shall maintain books of accounting records concerning revenue derived and all expenses incurred in maintaining and operating the ship as a public memorial. The operations of the Commission shall be subject to the oversight of the State Auditor pursuant to Article 5A of Chapter 147 of the General Statutes. The Commission shall reimburse the State Auditor the cost of any audit. The Commission shall establish a reserve fund in an amount to be determined by the Secretary of Cultural Resources to be maintained and used for contingencies and emergencies beyond those occurring in the course of routine maintenance and operation, and may authorize the deposit of this reserve fund in a depository to be selected by the Treasurer of North Carolina. (1961, c. 158; 1977, c. 741, ss. 2, 8; 1983, c. 913, s. 40; 2010-31, s. 21.1; 2011-284, s. 97.)

§ 143B-74.2. U.S.S. North Carolina Battleship Commission - employees.

The Department of Cultural Resources is authorized to hire laborers, artisans, caretakers, stenographic and administrative employees, and other personnel, in accordance with the provisions of the North Carolina Human Resources Act, as may be necessary in carrying out the purposes and provisions of this Article, and to maintain the ship in a clean, neat, and attractive condition satisfactory for exhibition to the public. The Commission shall appoint and fix the salary of an Executive Director and Assistant Director to serve at its pleasure. Employees shall be residents of the State of North Carolina except as may, in emergency conditions, be necessary for the procurement of specially trained or specially skilled employees. Any materials used for any purpose in maintaining and operating the ship for the purposes of this Article shall be, insofar as practicable, North Carolina materials. (1961, c. 158; 1975, c. 879, s. 46; 1977, c. 741, ss. 6, 8; 2006-204, s. 1; 2013-382, s. 9.1(c).)

§ 143B-74.3. U.S.S. North Carolina Battleship Commission - employees not to have interest.

It shall be unlawful for any member of the Commission to charge, receive, or obtain, directly or indirectly, any fee, commission, retainer or brokerage other than established salaries to be fixed by the Commission, and no member of the Commission shall have any interest in any land, materials, commissions or contracts sold to or made with the Commission, or with any member thereof. Violation of any provisions of this section shall be a Class 2 misdemeanor. (1961, c. 158; 1977, c. 741, ss. 7, 8; 1993, c. 539, s. 1037; 1994, Ex. Sess., c. 24, s. 14(c).)

Part 9. Sir Walter Raleigh Commission.

§§ 143B-75 through 143B-78. Repealed by Session Laws 1979, c. 504, s. 1.

Part 10. Executive Mansion Fine Arts Committee.

§ 143B-79. Executive Mansion Fine Arts Committee - creation, powers and duties.

There is hereby created the Executive Mansion Fine Arts Committee. The Executive Mansion Fine Arts Committee shall have the following functions and duties:

(1)   To advise the Secretary of Cultural Resources on the preservation and maintenance of the Executive Mansion located at 200 North Blount Street, Raleigh, North Carolina;

(2)   To encourage gifts and objects of art, furniture and articles of historical value for furnishing the Executive Mansion, and advise the Secretary of Cultural Resources on major changes in the furnishings of the Mansion;

(3)   To make recommendations to the Secretary of Cultural Resources concerning major renovations necessary to preserve and maintain the structure;

(4)   To aid the Secretary of Cultural Resources in keeping a complete list of all gifts and articles received together with their history and value;

(5)   No gifts or articles shall be accepted for the Executive Mansion without the approval of the Committee; and

(6)   The Committee shall advise the Secretary of Cultural Resources upon any matter the Secretary may refer to it.

(7)   The Committee may dispose of property held in the Executive Mansion after consultation with a review committee comprised of one person from the Executive Mansion Fine Arts Committee, appointed by its chairman; one person from the Department of Administration appointed by the Secretary of Administration; and two qualified professionals from the Department of Cultural Resources, Division of Archives and History, appointed by the Secretary of Cultural Resources. Upon request of the Executive Mansion Fine Arts Committee, the review committee will view proposed items for disposition and make a recommendation to the North Carolina Historical Commission who will make a final decision. The Historical Commission must consider whether the disposition is in the best interest of the State of North Carolina. If any property is sold, the net proceeds of each sale shall be deposited in the State Treasury to the credit of the Executive Mansion, Special Fund, and shall be used only for the purchase, conservation, restoration or repair of other property for use in the Executive Mansion. (1973, c. 476, s. 65; 1983, c. 632, s. 1; 1987, c. 251; 2013-360, s. 19.8(a).)

§ 143B-80. Executive Mansion Fine Arts Committee - members; selection; quorum; compensation.

The Executive Mansion Fine Arts Committee shall consist of 16 members appointed by the Governor. The initial members of the Committee shall be the appointed members of the present Executive Mansion Fine Arts Commission who shall serve for a period equal to the remainder of their current terms on the Executive Mansion Fine Arts Commission, four of whose appointments expire June 30, 1973, four of whose appointments expire June 30, 1974, four of whose appointments expire June 30, 1975, and four of whose appointments expire June 30, 1976. At the end of the respective terms of office of the initial members, the appointments of their successors shall be for terms of four years and until their successors are appointed and qualify. Any appointment to fill a vacancy on the Committee created by the resignation, dismissal, death, or disability of a member shall be for the balance of the unexpired term.

The Governor shall have the power to remove any member of the Committee from office in accordance with the provisions of G.S. 143B-16 of the Executive Organization Act of 1973.

The Governor shall designate a member of the Committee to serve as chairman at his pleasure.

Members of the Committee shall receive per diem and necessary travel and subsistence expenses in accordance with the provisions of G.S. 138-5.

A majority of the Committee shall constitute a quorum for the transaction of business.

All clerical and other services required by the Committee shall be supplied by the Secretary of Cultural Resources. (1973, c. 476, s. 66.)

§ 143B-80.1. Regular and special meetings.

The Executive Mansion Fine Arts Committee shall meet at least twice per year and may hold special meetings at any time and place within the State at the call of the chairman or upon the written request of at least five members.

Whenever a member shall fail, except for ill health or other valid reason, to be present for two successive regular meetings of the Board, his place as a member shall be deemed vacant. (1983, c. 632, s. 2.)

§ 143B-80.2. Reserved for future codification purposes.

§ 143B-80.3. Reserved for future codification purposes.

§ 143B-80.4. Reserved for future codification purposes.

Part 10A. State Capitol Preservation Act.

§§ 143B-80.5 through 143B-80.14: Repealed by Session Laws 1995, c. 507, s. 12(a).

Part 11. American Revolution Bicentennial Committee.

§§ 143B-81 through 143B-82: Repealed by Session Laws 1979, c. 504, s. 2.

Part 12. North Carolina Awards Committee.

§ 143B-83. North Carolina Awards Committee - creation, powers and duties.

There is hereby created the North Carolina Awards Committee with the duty to advise the Secretary of Cultural Resources on the formulation and administration of the program governing North Carolina awards and on the selection of a committee in each award area to choose the recipients.

The Committee shall advise the Secretary of the Department upon any matter the Secretary may refer to it. (1973, c. 476, s. 71; 1979, c. 504, s. 2; 1983 (Reg. Sess., 1984), c. 995, s. 22.)

§ 143B-84. North Carolina Awards Committee - members; selection; quorum; compensation.

The North Carolina Awards Committee shall consist of five members appointed by the Governor to serve at the Governor's pleasure.

The Governor shall designate a member of the Committee as chairman to serve in such capacity at the pleasure of the Governor.

Members of the Committee shall serve without compensation or travel or per diem.

A majority of the Committee shall constitute a quorum for the transaction of business.

The Secretary of Cultural Resources is hereby authorized to request contingency and emergency funds for the administration of the North Carolina Awards Committee, for the period between July 1, 1973, and ratification of the next general appropriations bill for the Department.

All clerical and other services required by the Committee shall be supplied by the Secretary of Cultural Resources. (1973, c. 476, s. 72.)

Part 13. America's Four Hundredth Anniversary Committee.

§ 143B-85. America's Four Hundredth Anniversary Committee - creation, powers and duties.

There is hereby created the America's Four Hundredth Anniversary Committee of the Department of Cultural Resources. The Committee shall have the following functions and duties:

(1)   To advise the Secretary of the Department on the planning, conducting, and directing appropriate observances of, and on providing necessary physical facilities and other requirements for, the commemoration of the landing of Sir Walter Raleigh's colony on Roanoke Island; and

(2)   To advise the Secretary of the Department upon any matter the Secretary might refer to it. (1973, c. 476, s. 74.)

§ 143B-86. America's Four Hundredth Anniversary Committee - members; selection; quorum; compensation.

The America's Four Hundredth Anniversary Committee shall consist of 14 members as follows: 10 members at large appointed by the Governor and four ex officio members as follows: the mayor of the Town of Manteo, the Secretary of Environment and Natural Resources, the chairman of the Roanoke Island Historical Association, and the chairman of the Dare County Board of Commissioners, or their designees. Of the initial members of the America's Four Hundredth Anniversary Committee appointed by the Governor five shall be appointed for terms expiring June 30, 1975, and five for terms expiring June 30, 1977. At the end of their respective terms of office, the appointments shall be for a term of four years and until their successors are appointed and qualify. Any appointment to fill a vacancy on the Committee created by the resignation, dismissal, death, or disability of a member shall be for the balance of the unexpired term.

The Governor shall have the power to remove any member of the Committee from office in accordance with the provisions of G.S. 143B-16 of the Executive Organization Act of 1973.

The Governor shall designate a member of the Committee to serve as chairman at his pleasure.

Members of the Committee shall receive per diem and necessary travel and subsistence expenses in accordance with the provisions of G.S. 138-5.

A majority of the Committee shall constitute a quorum for the transaction of business. (1973, c. 476, s. 75; 1977, c. 771, s. 4; 1989, c. 727, s. 218(123); 1997-443, s. 11A.119(a).)

Part 14. North Carolina Arts Council.

§ 143B-87. North Carolina Arts Council - creation, powers and duties.

There is hereby created the North Carolina Arts Council with the following duties and functions:

(1)   To advise the Secretary of Cultural Resources on the study, collection, maintenance and dissemination of factual data and pertinent information relative to the arts;

(2)   To advise the Secretary concerning assistance to local organizations and the community at large in the area of the arts;

(3)   To advise the Secretary on the exchange of information, promotion of programs and stimulation of joint endeavor between public and nonpublic organizations;

(4)   To identify research needs in the arts area and to encourage such research;

(5)   To advise the Secretary in regard to bringing the highest obtainable quality in the arts to the State and promoting the maximum opportunity for the people to experience and enjoy those arts;

(6)   To advise the Secretary of the Department upon any matter the Secretary may refer to it; and

(7)   To advise the Secretary concerning the promotion of theater arts in the State. (1973, c. 476, s. 77; 1985 (Reg. Sess., 1986), c. 1028, s. 14.)

§ 143B-87.1: Reserved for future codification purposes.

§ 143B-87.2. A+ Schools Special Fund.

(a)   Fund. - The A+ Schools Special Fund is created as a special interest-bearing revenue fund in the Department of Cultural Resources, North Carolina Arts Council. The Fund shall consist of all receipts derived from private donations, grant funds, and earned revenue. The revenue in the Fund may be used only for contracted services, conference and meeting expenses, travel, staff salaries, and other administrative costs related to the A+ Schools program. The staff of the North Carolina Arts Council and the Department shall determine how the funds will be used for the purposes of the A+ Schools program.

(b)   Application. - This section applies to the A+ Schools program, which was transferred to the North Carolina Arts Council by Section 9.8 of S.L. 2010-31.

(c)   Reports. - The Department shall submit a report to the Joint Legislative Commission on Governmental Operations, the House of Representatives

Appropriations Subcommittee on General Government, the Senate Appropriations Committee on General Government and Information Technology, and the Fiscal Research Division by September 30 of each year that includes the source and amount of all funds credited to the Fund and the purpose and amount of all expenditures from the Fund during the prior fiscal year. (2013-297, s. 3.)

§ 143B-88. North Carolina Arts Council - members; selection; quorum; compensation.

The North Carolina Arts Council shall consist of 24 members appointed by the Governor. The initial members of the Council shall be the appointed members of the present Arts Council who shall serve for a period equal to the remainder of their current terms on the Arts Council, eight of whose terms expire June 30, 1973, eight of whose terms expire June 30, 1974, and eight of whose terms expire June 30, 1975. At the end of the respective terms of office of the initial members, the appointments of their successors shall be for terms of three years and until their successors are appointed and qualify. Any appointment to fill a vacancy on the Council created by the resignation, dismissal, death, or disability of a member shall be for the balance of the unexpired term.

The Governor shall have the power to remove any member of the Council from office in accordance with the provisions of G.S. 143B-16 of the Executive Organization Act of 1973.

The Governor shall designate a member of the Council as chairman to serve at his pleasure.

Members of the Council shall receive per diem and necessary travel and subsistence expenses in accordance with the provisions of G.S. 138-5.

A majority of the Council shall constitute a quorum for the transaction of business.

All clerical and other services required by the Council shall be supplied by the Secretary of Cultural Resources. (1973, c. 476, s. 78.)

Part 15. North Carolina State Art Society, Incorporated.

§ 143B-89: Repealed by Session Laws 2012-120, s. 1(c), effective October 1, 2012.

Part 16. State Library Commission.

§ 143B-90. State Library Commission - creation, powers and duties.

There is hereby created the State Library Commission of the Department of Cultural Resources. The State Library Commission has the following functions and duties:

(1)   To advise the Secretary of Cultural Resources on matters relating to the operation and services of the State Library;

(2)   Repealed by Session Laws 1991, c. 757, s. 2.

(2a)   To work for the financial support of statewide and local public library services;

(3)   To advise the Secretary upon any matter the Secretary might refer to it;

(4)   Repealed by Session Laws 1991, c. 757, s. 2.

(4a)   To work for the financial support of statewide interlibrary services;

(5)   Repealed by Session Laws 1991, c. 757, s. 2.

(5a)   To aid and advise the Secretary of Cultural Resources in the development of information services for the promotion of cultural, educational, and economic well-being of the State.

(6)   through (8) Repealed by Session Laws 1991, c. 757, s. 2.

(8a)   To aid and advise the Secretary of Cultural Resources on the recruitment and appointment of the State Librarian. (1973, c. 476, s. 82; 1981, c. 918, s. 2; 1991, c. 757, s. 2.)

§ 143B-91. State Library Commission - members; selection; quorum; compensation.

(a)   The State Library Commission shall consist of 15 members. All members shall have an interest in the development of library and information services in North Carolina. Eight members shall be appointed by the Governor. One member shall be appointed by the President Pro Tempore of the Senate. One member shall be appointed by the Speaker of the North Carolina House of Representatives. Three members shall be appointed by the North Carolina Public Library Directors Association. Two members shall be the President and the President-elect of the North Carolina Library Association or two appointees as determined by the North Carolina Library Association's Board of Directors. The State Librarian shall be an ex officio member and act as secretary to the Commission.

All appointments shall be for four-year terms with eight of the commissioners taking office on the first four-year cycle and seven commissioners taking office on the second four-year cycle. Any appointment to fill a vacancy in one of the positions appointed by the Governor, President Pro Tempore or Speaker of the House of Representatives shall be for the remainder of the unexpired term. Appointees shall not serve more than two successive four-year terms.

The Governor shall choose a chairperson from among the gubernatorial appointees. The chairperson shall serve not more than two successive two-year terms as chair.

Members of the Commission shall receive per diem and necessary travel and subsistence expenses as provided in G.S. 138-5.

A majority of the Commission shall constitute a quorum for the transaction of business.

All clerical and other services required by the Commission shall be supplied by the Secretary of Cultural Resources.

The Commission shall meet at least twice a year.

(b)   There shall be standing committees established to advise the Secretary of Cultural Resources, the Commission, and the State Librarian. These committees shall be: Public Library Development; Interlibrary Cooperation; State Government Information Services; State Library Development; and any other

287

committee deemed appropriate. Each committee shall be composed of a committee chairperson and at least six persons appointed annually by the Secretary of Cultural Resources with the approval of the Commission. At least one of the members of each committee shall be a member of the Commission. Each committee shall report to the Commission at least once a year. (1973, c. 476, s. 83; 1981, c. 918, s. 3; 1991, c. 757, s. 3; 1995, c. 490, s. 53.)

Part 17. Roanoke Island Historical Association.

§ 143B-92. Roanoke Island Historical Association - creation, powers and duties.

There is hereby recreated the Roanoke Island Historical Association with the powers and duties delineated in Article 19 of Chapter 143 of the General Statutes of North Carolina. (1973, c. 476, s. 85.)

§ 143B-93. Roanoke Island Historical Association - status.

The Roanoke Island Historical Association is hereby declared not to be a State agency within the meaning of the Executive Organization Act of 1973 and shall be exempt from all provisions of the Executive Organization Act of 1973 except G.S. 143B-92 and G.S. 143B-93. (1973, c. 476, s. 86.)

Part 18. North Carolina Symphony Society.

§ 143B-94. North Carolina Symphony Society, Inc.

The North Carolina Symphony Society, Incorporated, shall continue to be under the patronage of the State as provided in Article 2 of Chapter 140 of the General Statutes of North Carolina. The governing body of the North Carolina Symphony Society, Incorporated, shall be a board of trustees consisting of not less than 16 members of which the Governor of the State and the Superintendent of Public Instruction shall be ex officio members and four other members shall be named by the Governor. The remaining trustees shall be chosen by members of the North Carolina Symphony Society, Incorporated, in such manner and for such terms as that body shall determine. The initial members named by the Governor shall be appointed from the members of the existing board of trustees of the

North Carolina State Symphony Society, Incorporated, for the balance of their existing terms. Subsequent appointments shall be made for terms of four years each. (1973, c. 476, s. 88.)

Part 19. Edenton Historical Commission.

§ 143B-95. Edenton Historical Commission - creation, purposes and powers.

There is hereby recreated the Edenton Historical Commission. The purposes of the Commission are to effect and encourage preservation, restoration, and appropriate presentation of the Town of Edenton and Chowan County, as a historic, educational, and aesthetic place, to the benefit of the citizens of the place and the State and of visitors. To accomplish its purposes, the Commission has the following powers and responsibilities:

(1)   To acquire, hold, and dispose of title to or interests in historic properties in the Town of Edenton and County of Chowan and to repair, restore, and otherwise improve the properties, and to maintain them;

(2)   To acquire, hold, and dispose of title to or interests in other land there, upon which historic structures have been or shall be relocated, and to improve the land and maintain it;

(3)   To acquire, hold, and dispose of suitable furnishings for the historic properties, and to provide and maintain suitable gardens for them;

(4)   To develop and maintain one or more collections of historic objects and things pertinent to the history of the town and county, to acquire, hold, and dispose of the items, and to preserve and display them;

(5)   To develop and conduct appropriate programs, under the name "Historic Edenton" or otherwise, for the convenient presentation and interpretation of the properties and collections to citizens and visitors, as places and things of historic, educational, and aesthetic value;

(6)   To conduct programs for the fostering of research, for the encouragement of preservation, and for the increase of knowledge available to the local citizens and the visitors in matters pertaining to the history of the town and county;

(7)   To cooperate with the Secretary and Department of Cultural Resources and with appropriate associations, governments, governmental agencies, persons, and other entities, and to assist and advise them, toward the furtherance of the Commission's purposes;

(8)   To solicit gifts and grants toward the furtherance of these purposes and the exercise of these powers;

(9)   To conduct other programs and do other things appropriate and reasonably necessary to the accomplishment of the purposes and the exercise of the powers; and

(10)   To adopt and enforce any bylaws and rules that the Commission deems beneficial and proper. (1973, c. 476, s. 90; 1979, c. 733, s. 1.)

§ 143B-96. Edenton Historical Commission - status.

The Edenton Historical Commission is hereby declared not to be a State agency within the meaning of the Executive Organization Act of 1973 and shall be exempt from all provisions of the Executive Organization Act of 1973 except G.S. 143B-95 through G.S. 143B-98. (1973, c. 476, s. 91.)

§ 143B-97. Edenton Historical Commission - reports.

The Edenton Historical Commission shall submit an annual report of its activities, holdings, and finances, including an audit of its accounts by a certified public accountant, to the Secretary of Cultural Resources. In the event such annual report is not received by the Secretary, or if such report does not indicate the need for the continuation of the Commission, the Secretary of Cultural Resources is authorized to recommend to the next General Assembly the abolition of the Commission. (1973, c. 476, s. 92.)

§ 143B-98. Edenton Historical Commission - members; selection; compensation; quorum.

The Edenton Historical Commission shall consist of 33 members, 22 appointed by the Governor to serve at his pleasure, four appointed by the President Pro Tempore of the Senate, four appointed by the Speaker of the House of Representatives, and, ex officio, the Mayor of the Town of Edenton, the

Chairman of the Board of Commissioners of Chowan County, and the Secretary of Cultural Resources or his designee.

All the present members of the Commission may continue to serve, at the pleasure of the Governor, until the end of his present term of office. The Commission shall elect its own officers, and the members of the Commission shall serve without pay and without expense allowance from State funds. The Commission shall determine its requirements for a quorum. (1973, c. 476, s. 93; 1979, c. 733, s. 2; 2005-421, s. 3.1(a).)

Part 20. Historic Bath Commission.

§ 143B-99. Historic Bath Commission - creation, powers and duties.

There is hereby created the Historic Bath Commission. The Historic Bath Commission shall have the following powers:

(1)   To acquire and dispose of title to or interests in historic properties in and near the Town of Bath in Beaufort County, and to repair, restore, or otherwise improve such properties, and to maintain them;

(2)   To offer such historic properties to the State of North Carolina, subject to the acceptance of such properties by the State;

(3)   To cooperate with, assist, and advise the Secretary of Cultural Resources upon any matter pertaining to the administration of Bath State Historic Site, which the Secretary of the Department may refer to it; and

(4)   To carry out other programs reasonably related to these purposes. (1973, c. 476, s. 95.)

§ 143B-100. Historic Bath Commission - status.

The Historic Bath Commission is hereby declared not to be a State agency within the meaning of the Executive Organization Act of 1973 and shall be exempt from all provisions of the Executive Organization Act of 1973 except G.S. 143B-99 through G.S. 143B-102. (1973, c. 476, s. 96.)

§ 143B-101. Historic Bath Commission - reports.

The Historic Bath Commission shall submit an annual report of its activities, holdings, and finances, including an audit of its accounts by a certified public accountant, to the Secretary of Cultural Resources. In the event such annual report is not received by the Secretary, or if such report does not indicate the need for the continuation of the Commission, the Secretary of Cultural Resources is authorized to recommend the abolition of the Commission to the next General Assembly. (1973, c. 476, s. 97.)

§ 143B-102. Historic Bath Commission - members; selection; quorum; compensation.

The Historic Bath Commission shall consist of 25 members appointed by the Governor plus, ex officio, the mayor of the Town of Bath, the Chairman of the Board of Commissioners of Beaufort County, and the Secretary of Cultural Resources or designee. The initial members of the Commission shall be the members of the present Historic Bath Commission who shall serve for a period equal to the remainder of their current terms on the Historic Bath Commission. At the end of the respective terms of office of the initial members of the Commission, the appointments of their successors, with the exception of the ex officio members, shall be for terms of five years and until their successors are appointed and qualify. Any appointments to fill a vacancy on the Commission created by the resignation, dismissal, death or disability of a member shall be for the balance of the unexpired term. The Commission shall elect its own officers. Members of the Commission shall serve without pay and without expense allowance from State funds. The Commission shall determine its requirements for a quorum. (1973, c. 476, s. 98.)

Part 21. Historic Hillsborough Commission.

§ 143B-103. Historic Hillsborough Commission - creation, powers and duties.

There is hereby recreated the Historic Hillsborough Commission. The Historic Hillsborough Commission shall have the following powers:

(1)   In cooperation with the Hillsborough Historical Society, the elected officials of Hillsborough and Orange County, and appropriate public agencies, to use every legal aid and method to preserve and restore the Town of

Hillsborough, and its immediately adjacent area, as a living, functioning, educational, and historical exhibit of North Carolina's early life and times;

(2)   To acquire and to dispose of property, real and personal; to repair, restore, or otherwise improve such properties; to have prepared a history of the town and area; and to write, compile, publish, or sponsor such historical works as may pertain to the town and area; and

(3)   To carry on other programs reasonably related to these purposes. (1973, c. 476, s. 100.)

§ 143B-104. Historic Hillsborough Commission - status.

The Historic Hillsborough Commission is hereby declared not to be a State agency within the meaning of the Executive Organization Act of 1973 and shall be exempt from all provisions of the Executive Organization Act of 1973 except G.S. 143B-103 through G.S. 143B-106. (1973, c. 476, s. 101.)

§ 143B-105. Historic Hillsborough Commission - reports.

The Historic Hillsborough Commission shall submit an annual report of its activities, holdings, and finances, including an audit of its accounts by a certified public accountant, to the Secretary of Cultural Resources. In the event such annual report is not received by the Secretary, or if such report does not indicate the need for the continuation of the Commission, the Secretary of Cultural Resources is authorized to recommend to the next General Assembly the abolition of the Commission. (1973, c. 476, s. 102.)

§ 143B-106. Historic Hillsborough Commission - members; selection; quorum; compensation.

The Historic Hillsborough Commission shall consist of not fewer than 25 members appointed by the Governor plus, ex officio, the mayor of the Town of Hillsborough, the Chairman of the Board of Commissioners of Orange County, the Orange County Register of Deeds, the Orange County Clerk of Superior Court, and the Secretary of Cultural Resources or designee. The initial appointed members of the Commission shall be the members of the present Historic Hillsborough Commission who shall serve for a period equal to the remainder of their current terms on the Historic Hillsborough Commission. At the end of the respective terms of office of the present members, the appointments of members, excepting the ex officio members, shall be for terms of six years and until their successors are appointed and qualify. Any appointment to fill a vacancy on the Commission created by the resignation, dismissal, death or disability of a member shall be for the balance of the unexpired term. The Commission shall elect its own officers. Members of the Commission shall serve without pay and without expense allowance from State funds. The Commission shall determine its requirements for a quorum. (1973, c. 476, s. 103.)

Part 22. Historic Murfreesboro Commission.

§ 143B-107. Historic Murfreesboro Commission - creation, powers and duties.

There is hereby recreated the Historic Murfreesboro Commission. The Historic Murfreesboro Commission shall have the following powers:

(1)   To acquire and dispose of title to or interests in historic properties in and near the Town of Murfreesboro, and to repair, restore, or otherwise improve and maintain such properties;

(2)   To conduct research and planning to carry out a program for the preservation of historic sites, buildings, or objects in and near the Town of Murfreesboro;

(3)   To carry out other programs reasonably related to these purposes. (1973, c. 476, s. 105.)

§ 143B-108. Historic Murfreesboro Commission - status.

The Historic Murfreesboro Commission is hereby declared not to be a State agency within the meaning of the Executive Organization Act of 1973 and shall be exempt from all provisions of the Executive Organization Act of 1973 except G.S. 143B-107 through G.S. 143B-110. (1973, c. 476, s. 106.)

Vision Books Order Form

Fax Orders: 1-980-299-5965

Phone Orders: 1-704-898-0770

E-mail Orders: www.visionbooks.org

Mail Orders: Vision Books, LLC
         P.O. Box 42406
         Charlotte, NC 28215

Shipp To:
Name_____
Address_____
City_____State_____Zip_____
Phone_____Fax_____
Email_____@_____

Bill To: We can bill a third party on your behalf.
Name_____
Address_____
City_____State_____Zip_____
Phone___(   )_____Fax_____
Email_____@_____

Pamphlet Number ($15.00 Each)	Qty	Total Cost
_____	_____	_____
_____	_____	_____
_____	_____	_____
_____	_____	_____
_____	_____	_____
_____	_____	_____
_____	_____	_____
_____	_____	_____
Full Volume Set 1-92	92 Pamphlets	1,380.00

Free Shipping & Handling on Full Volume Orders
Add $1.00 Shipping & Handling Per Pamphlet $_____

Total Cost $_____

Thank you for your support. Management!

DID YOU ENJOY THIS BOOK?

Vision Books, LLC would like to hear from you! If you or someone you know has been fasely imprisoned, we would like to hear your story. If the 'North Carolina Criminal Law and Procedure' has had an effect in your life or if you have suggestions, we would like to hear from you. Send your letters to:

Vision Books, LLC
Attn: Staff Writers
P.O. Box 42406
Charlotte, NC 28215
Email: staff@visionbooks.org

Order Additional Copies:

Fax Orders: 1-980-299-5965

Phone Orders: 1-704-898-0770

E-mail Orders: www.visionbooks.org

Mail Orders: Vision Books, LLC
                       P.O. Box 42406
                       Charlotte, NC 28215

www.ingramcontent.com/pod-product-compliance
Lightning Source LLC
Chambersburg PA
CBHW051631170526
45167CB00001B/145